REEL
Knockouts

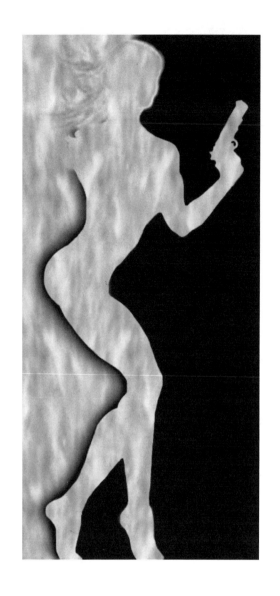

REEL Knockouts

Violent Women in the Movies

Edited by
Martha McCaughey
and Neal King

University of Texas Press, Austin

First edition, 2001

Requests for permission to reproduce material from
this work should be sent to Permissions, University
of Texas Press, Box 7819, Austin, TX 78713-7819.

⊗ The paper used in this book meets the minimum
requirements of ANSI/NISO Z39.48-1992 (R1997)
(Permanence of Paper).

Library of Congress Cataloging-in-Publication Data
Reel knockouts : violent women in the movies /
edited by Martha McCaughey and Neal King.—
1st ed.

     p.   cm.
  Includes index.
  ISBN 0-292-75250-4 (cloth : alk. paper)—
  ISBN 0-292-75251-2 (pbk. : alk. paper)
    1. Women in motion pictures.   2. Violence in
  motion pictures.   I. McCaughey, Martha, 1966 –
  II. King, Neal.

PN1995.9.W6 R454   2001
791.43'652042 — dc21   00-047977

Contents

Illustrations

Acknowledgments

We are grateful to colleagues who have encouraged our interest in mean women for years. We have benefited from the editorial comments of Ben Carton on the volume, not to mention his help formatting the final manuscript, as well as from conversations with Toni Calasanti. Rosemary Ellis also deserves thanks for her help preparing the final manuscript. Ian Carton, Mike Hudson, and Michael Rohd offered helpful feedback on our introduction. Finally, thanks goes to our contributors and to editor Jim Burr and the staff at the University of Texas Press.

REEL
Knockouts

What's a Mean Woman like You Doing in a Movie like This?

Neal King and Martha McCaughey

Officer Rita Rizolli stops a pimp from beating a prostitute. They scuffle; he calls her a bitch, circles around her, and fires his weapon. Rita dodges, admires his agility ("Nice move, asshole"), and shoots him when he tries to fire again. As he bleeds his last she quips, "and don't call me 'bitch.'"

In the middle of a robbery designed to bankroll their move from their dead-end lives, Cleo, Tisean, and Stony face down the local police with weapons drawn. An unwise bank guard shoots one, and the other two women blow him away with a hail of gunfire. Stony, the only survivor of the ensuing battles, drives off with the cash.

Mad at her philandering boyfriend, Mallory starts to make out with a man in an auto garage. At her command he goes down on her, but too soon commences intercourse. She whips a handgun from her purse and blows his brains out. "That was the worst fucking head I ever got in my life. Next time don't be so fucking eager!" She stalks off in disgust.

Why Mean Women?

Violent women draw strong responses, on-screen and off, whether they're agents of the law like *Fatal Beauty*'s Rizolli, novice bank robbers like the heroes of *Set It Off*, or mass murderers like Mallory of *Natural Born Killers*. Violent women appear in a variety of genres, from classic horror and film noir to 1970s

1

blaxploitation and 1990s road movies. Our contributors wrestle with the meanings of women's violence in films from Hollywood to Hong Kong, top-grossing to straight-to-video, cop-action movies to porn flicks.

Sometimes violent female characters are malicious villains; other times they save the world from destruction or just uphold the law. In almost all cases, however, somebody will imply that such action, because done by a woman, falls below standards of human decency. This is why we call them all "mean women." Depictions of women's violence seem more horrific to many people, perhaps because we find far fewer of them than we find scenes of male violence. Moreover, cultural standards still equate womanhood with kindness and nonviolence, manhood with strength and aggression. Controversies abound over the potential for imitative violence (e.g., *Natural Born Killers, Thelma and Louise*), the use of women as agents of sexist or racist oppression (*Aliens, The Silence of the Lambs*), and the deviant status of sexually assertive women (*Basic Instinct, Eve of Destruction, Fatal Attraction*). The contributions gathered here analyze violent women's respective places in the history of cinema, in the lives of viewers, and in the feminist response to male violence against women. They focus less on victimhood than on the subversion of that hallmark of femininity.

This volume offers the first book-length treatment of violent women in the movies, though other analysts have tackled some of the issues addressed here. Indeed, a rich and diverse literature examines such movies as *The Silence of the Lambs, Blue Steel, Basic Instinct, Thelma and Louise,* and *Terminator 2,* as well as such genres as detective films and slasher movies. This volume adds to this literature, answering a decade-long debate about the role of these violent heroines in feminist progress.

Most feminists oppose violence, define it as patriarchal and oppressive, yet often enjoy scenes in which female characters defend themselves, save the day, seek revenge, and get away with it in the end. Many feminists insist that we can and should do better than patriarchs; hence, they celebrate images that define women's heroic power in "female" terms—giving birth, forming community, and remaining nonviolent even in the face of violence.[1] Are the heroes in this book "phallic women," and if so do they reproduce male domination? Do they contribute to resistance or replication?

We argue that it's not the business of analysts to decide which images will suit sexist reaction and which feminist revolution, which express dominance and which resistance. Rebellion never runs free of oppression, and we should stop trying to get more mileage out of the oft-repeated argument that women in the movies bear marks of their patriarchal, heterocentrist, and white-supremacist origins. The places and patterns into which women fit in the popular imagination deserve attention, but we need to stop asserting that nothing is what it seems, that all of women's attempts at resistance in movies lead to failure.

Some might prefer that we celebrate movie violence only for women on the "right" side of the law, as in cop movies such as *Blue Steel, Lethal Weapon 3,* and *Fatal Beauty.* Others fear sellout and prefer their violent women to act outside the (racist, colonialist, patriarchal) law. Still others worry about racism even among the lawless women and so prefer vengeful force against men or the systems that abuse women first, as in *Foxy Brown, Thelma and Louise,* and *Set It Off.* After all, we can feel their anger and maybe duck the "recuperation" or co-optation that racism represents. Some dislike the sexual charge attending much of women's violent action. Others celebrate such images in most any context. Still others remain skeptical of those they see as "masculinist," "objectified," or otherwise "patriarchal." We find that most of our university students cheer when we screen such images.[2]

We assembled this book on violent women in the movies not because we fear these women are too sexy, too co-opted by state authority, or too deranged, nor because we worry that women will imitate the violence. We do not think that becoming maternal or being objectified ruins the toughness of heroines. Many feminist scholars have worried precisely about these matters, and sometimes the contributors to this volume do too. But arguments in this book move beyond these in important ways.

The essays in this volume look at films not simply in terms of whether they properly represent women or feminist principles, but also as texts with social contexts and possible uses in the reconstruction of masculinity and femininity. We can use these images, whether they're lies or not. This is how *Reel Knockouts* discusses them. These analyses of violent women in the movies will enable feminists to question assumptions about gender, violence, pleasure, and fantasy. They will allow film theorists to question models of female passivity and narrative closure. They also will help cultural historians and social scientists question assumptions about the development of political community among oppressed peoples.

Where do these women come from? Which genres welcomed them and why? What expectations shape them and in what ways? Which traditional images of femininity accompany their violence, and which disappear when women prepare to fight? Whom do they battle and why? What solidarity with others do they build? The contributions in this book shed light on the connections between female violence and feminism, racial identity, sexual identity, and generic patterns. Some of the authors here take more of an interest in pointing out the downsides of cinematic approaches; others spend more time looking at the positive uses of violent women.

We have chosen the chapters in this volume not because we agree with every interpretive point that each makes, but because they represent the best and most important trends in the study of violent women in film: assessment of political utility (Arons, Dole, Springer); analysis of generic roots (Arons, Brown, Grindstaff, Walters); application of psychoanalytic theory (Brown, Miller); and consideration of the meanings of "real" and "fantasy" (Brown, Halberstam, Knobloch, Miller) as well as "violent" (Arons, Halberstam, Miller). Contributors address popular reception (Dole, Halberstam, Knobloch, Miller, Vares), old stereotypes in new movies (Arons, Brown, Springer), and definition of violent womanhood through the formal elements of cinema (Grindstaff, Halberstam, Knobloch, Miller).

Why Mean Women Now?

Violent women in the movies arise in different eras depending on race and class. Low-brow movies on the 1960s drive-in circuits featured plenty of white-trash mamas wielding baseball bats, broken bottles, and shotguns. In the early 1970s, blaxploitation movies made a star of prison-movie queen Pam Grier as a woman who would take no more abuse from whitey, while no-budget rape-revenge movies began to square off middle-class white women against hillbilly abusers. Such white women don't pick up guns in remarkable numbers, however, until the 1980s—by which point slashers such as *Halloween* had introduced us to the teenage "Final Girl" who could defeat the madman who skewered her friends. Science fiction/fantasy movies introduced big-budget female heroes in *Aliens* and *The Terminator*. In the 1990s, the doors opened wider.

No doubt many cultural changes have spawned mean women in movies. Late-twentieth-century trends include the health and fitness movement that made one's body a symbol of one's overall fitness as a citizen (witness the influence of Arnold Schwarzenegger); the student antirape movement that—

through its new sexual assault policies, peer education programs, and press coverage—sparked a nationwide conversation about gender, violence, and power;[3] and on a broader economic scale, the movement of middle-class white women back into the paid labor force. Barbara Ehrenreich observes the recent "decline of patriarchy," in which many women became economically independent of men (though often raising children in poverty) and many men gave up the pretense of providing for and protecting women.[4] In this new world, women move away from the moral (and nonviolent) purity of the Victorian "Cult of True Womanhood" and onto men's turf—police work, military service, and a growing self-defense movement.[5] Such a culture puts violent women (as heroes or villains) in its movies.

The feminist movement that represented the interests of professional women—less harassment and more pay at work, greater opportunities in politics, fewer compulsory ties to husbands, an end to stereotypes of women as unable to hold jobs, freedom from or assistance with housework, freedom to move in public without fear of random attack by men—also made those professional women seem tougher in our popular culture: larger, with bigger muscles, meaner, mouthier, and more likely to pick up weapons when attacked.

We, the editors, were enthused consumers of popular culture in 1991, a banner year for violent women in film, when the releases of movies such as *La Femme Nikita, The Silence of the Lambs, Terminator 2,* and *Thelma and Louise* drew mass media and scholarly attention.[6] As academics and anti–sexual assault activists, we found uses for these images in our work. We wondered why colleagues accepted only the display of male aggressors and female victims as a consciousness-raising tool, and moved instead to celebrate women who knocked the stuffing out of men who bothered them. In our classroom strategies as well as in our own lives, it seemed not only easy but also productive to identify with, enjoy, and share images of women who could express their rage, defend their bodies, and usurp some of manhood's most vital turf.[7] Although we share the feminist analysis of violence against women and of compulsory heterosexuality that underlies most sexual assault prevention work, we have tried different ways to attend to men's violence against women, specifically by deconstructing "violence" and the related ideas about "sex difference."

But we realize that violent women present quagmires for feminists. Fellow activists and journal reviewers have criticized our employment of images of violent women in our anti–sexual assault work as "Reaganesque" forces in a sort of a sex-war arms race—images that will escalate violence rather than stop it. Feminist activists, many of whom define any violence as masculinist and wrong, sometimes tell us that screening images of women's violence doesn't accomplish the consciousness-raising we think it does, but rather becomes "part of the problem." We criticize any visual culture that sexualizes male domination and have worked for years both in and out of the classroom to challenge structural inequalities. However, we reject arguments for women's pacifism in light of both the relative license to do violence given men and the obvious political uses of it for women. Our own approach sees the pervasive abuse of women by men as an activity maintained in part by traditional images of women unable to fight and of men immune to injury. Visions of sexually attractive women skilled with weaponry, licensed to kill, beating up men might rather take the wind out of the sails of the culture in which sex difference seems unalterable. Such images might challenge smug oppressors. For these reasons, we like the threat that women's movie violence presents to the all-important divide between women and men.

We wonder what effect such images could have on men who assault women partly because they're so confident that they'll win the fights.[8] We also wonder what effect they could have on women who so often regard themselves as helpless victims and men as unstoppable predators. Of course, like most fans, we still have problems with the movies and want better ones. We assume that popular movies arise in part from male fantasies. We assembled this book not to demonstrate what should need no further proof—that violent women in the movies were born in a male-dominant society and reflect the interests of people living in it—but rather to recommend that we dig deeper into these films to see what tarnished prizes lie there.

Volume Layout

This book begins by giving violent female characters a generic history. The essays in part one, "Genre Films," turn to film cycles in which violent women have routinely appeared: martial arts films, film noir/erotic thrillers, cop movies, and prison movies. Wendy Arons begins with Hong Kong martial arts movies, and shows how the popular cycles treat Asian women as sexual and violent at the same time, featuring characters who take for granted women's fighting skills, even as those women must perform their heroism amidst a gallery of less flattering archetypes: venal Dragon Ladies, dimwitted girlfriends, psychotic lesbians. The Hong Kong action genre has welcomed women as skilled fighters, while Hollywood has kept them mostly on the sidelines.

In "If Looks Could Kill: Power, Revenge, and Stripper Movies," Jeffrey A. Brown analyzes women's violence in erotic thrillers and finds women in positions recognizable from the martial arts movies: bisexual victims of stalkers, women who kill menacing johns and stand up for themselves—even as they operate in a genre often dismissed by feminists as oppressive for its objectification of perfected female bodies. These heroes puncture male fantasies of control over attractive women, as strippers slash and burn those who would subjugate them.

In "The Gun and the Badge: Hollywood and the Female Lawman," Carol M. Dole contributes to the extensive literature on female cop heroes a chronology of methods by which Hollywood filmmakers have tried to build the perfect woman with a gun. Cop movies have tolerated little violence from women (compared to the damage that their men do), preferring women as lovers and victims for men to protect. She argues that female cops do violence in the context of imagery of physical weakness, maternal instincts, the castration of men, and the sexuality of women. Female cops stand out from the much larger crowd of male cops as less violent, more rational, and more conflicted about treading male turf.

In "Caged Heat," Suzanna Danuta Walters reviews the women-in-prison genre, which features some of Pam Grier's earliest performances. Walters argues that this exploitative genre presents some of the campiest, gutsiest, and most brutal women anywhere, many of whom are African American. The revenge of tortured inmates does not always depend on their innocence (as in, say, *The Shawshank Redemption*), though it does depend on the vision of men as heartless scum who deserve to die in entertaining ways. Some of these marginal movie cycles run free of typical Hollywood constraints and so can offer the toughest women in the direst straits, finding some sisterhood in their rebellion against the Man.

Finally, in "Sharon Stone's (An)Aesthetic," Susan Knobloch examines the "feminist fatales" in what amounts to a sort of minigenre of Sharon Stone movies. The actor's restrained persona engages audience expectations of performative sincerity but then twists them in subversive ways as she gears up for murder. Knobloch finds that critics admire Stone's acting and find her more "real" when she plays a victim, whereas Stone's performances as violent and female-bonding heroes draw scorn from the arbiters of popular taste.

In all of these genres, loosely defined, women struggle with constraints on the use of lethal force. They prove to be tough indeed—far tougher than most of the men around them. The essays in the second section of the book, "New Bonds and New Communities," analyze movies singly or in pairs and survey uses of violent women in the larger feminist enterprise. For instance, how does women's brutality foster solidarity amongst the characters or their audiences?

Laura Grindstaff begins with a focus on the family through an analysis of *Dolores Claiborne*. Though rooted in gothic women's stories and melodramas, the movie turns away from the martyred mothers of classic Hollywood and builds a threatening family violence into its architecture, resulting in a sisterhood of purposeful bitches who respond murderously to male perfidy and aggression. These women do not connect easily: they exploit and mistrust each other across lines of class and age; but they find solidarity in the violence with which they defend themselves against misery and abuse.

Kimberly Springer examines the relation between vandalism, armed robbery, and rebellion against race-, class-, and sex-based constraints in *Waiting to Exhale* and *Set It Off*. Springer suggests that these movies depict black women's violence as coming both from a reasonable anger at a racist situation and from a devilish "Sapphire" within. The movies celebrate black sisterhood even as they pose uppity women as harpies and make sure that poor black women who dream of escape from dead-end lives die before the credits roll. Springer confronts the painful choices that we fans must make as we try to enjoy the few black female heroes in Hollywood movies while rebuking the film industry for recycling racist stereotypes.

In "The Gun-in-the-Handbag, a Critical Controversy, and a Primal Scene," Barbara L. Miller presents a film cycle in which meek white housewives come across handguns and make use of them, becoming figures of violent disorder to the shock of their families and friends. Miller reviews a decade of reaction to *Thelma and Louise,* showing that the movie remains a touchstone for women's belligerence. She employs psychoanalytic and postmodern theory to illuminate the formal elements of this small group of films, showing how the outlaw scripts subvert classical Hollywood characterization and form postmodern characters whose primal scenes involve more violence than sex, and whose stories lead them toward solidarity with women, but not men.

In "Action Heroines and Female Viewers: What Women Have to Say," Tiina Vares shows how women's political affiliations shape their reactions to *Thelma and Louise*. She argues that, depending on those ties and beliefs, female viewers use different definitions of "violence," find various ways to integrate subversive images into their daily lives, and hold distinct ideals about which actions are really rebellious.

Finally, in "Imagined Violence/Queer Violence" Judith Halberstam considers the politics of female rage and the uses of terrorist culture, arguing that women's screen violence fits a larger trend toward aggression against straight white men by those they oppress: gays, blacks, women. From gangster rap to AIDS documentaries, these assaultive media intend to frighten. They can bond those who wield them in righteous solidarity and perhaps scare those who prey upon others into some second thoughts. Halberstam recommends that we not cede symbolic violence to the straight white men who have proved so willing to assault others for real, but rather adopt it to feminist, antiracist, and queer uses.

Themes of the Volume

Kidnapped and raped by rednecks working for the local mobster, the title character of *Foxy Brown* must fight her way from mortal peril. She slaughters the bad guys with coat hangers to the eyes, a jug of gasoline over their heads, and a match. One of the dripping thugs can smell what's coming: "This is gasoline!"

"You know it, motherfucker!" says Foxy as she lights him up. As the men scream and thrash, Foxy makes her escape, heading off to do more damage, including a memorable castration, to the local men who have abused her.

Some viewers have looked kindly upon violent women in movies. Blaxploitation included the provocative work of such actors as Pam Grier and Tamara Dobson, who starred as civilians and law enforcers battling evil "whitey." Blaxploitation emerged through a window of opportunity opened in the early 1970s for filmmakers to produce and distribute low-budget crime dramas for black audiences. A rarity in a production system unfriendly to black heroes, blaxploitation added an important chapter to the history of violent women in film.

Analysts of the genre have often enjoyed the women's violence within it, though with some important caveats. In his celebration, Darius James writes that Pam Grier "was a genre unto herself. She had no equal . . . no Caucasian equivalent. . . . Not only did the revenge motifs of Pam's films quell the racial hostilities of inner-city audiences hungry to see the whyte man get his ass kicked, she also presented the perfect model of the woman beyond male control."[9] True enough, but perhaps Grier had no equal because she was black and saddled with stereotypes of animal aggression and matriarchal pathology. Springer's essay in this volume considers the painful choice between celebrating the presence of tough black women on-screen and criticizing the racist presentation of violence as a black trait.

Mike Phillips argues that images of black female violence "could cut both ways."[10] On the one hand, when time came for Foxy Brown to castrate her white male nemesis, "[b]laxploitation fans loved this"; on the other, "the [assertive, black, ghetto] style offered the white world a whole new set of caricatures which validated old prejudices."[11] Donald Bogle also observes that actors such as "Dobson and Grier represented Woman as Protector, Nurturer, Communal Mother Surrogate. . . . They were also often perceived as being exotic sex objects . . . yet with a twist . . . at times using [men] as playful, comic toys."[12] We find no simple reading of women's violence in a complicated world.

Traces of blaxploitation survive today, in the form of homage. Witness the revival of blaxploitation heroes in *Original Gangstas,* in which single mom Laurie

FIGURE 1. Pam Grier, longtime mean woman in movies, relives blaxploitation days as self-defense instructor Laurie in *Original Gangstas.* With her defensive stance and angry expression she typifies Hollywood's mean women.

(Grier again) and friends tangle with a local gang that has taken over their neighborhood. Laurie teaches a self-defense class and later battles armed hoods. She pummels one in an alley and then grabs a handgun. The young thug asks in condescension: "How do you know that motherfucker ain't going to blow up in your face?"

"Well, let's find out," says Laurie, as she blows him away with crackling gunfire. After a pause, she gloats over the corpse, "Women's intuition." Sexy and lethal, pro-black and marketed to crossover audiences, blaxploitation heroines created dilemmas that have since become familiar in mainstream (white) Hollywood. For instance, what shall we make of a woman who appears both physically empowered and sexually attractive? What shall we make of a black nationalist whose abuse and revenge amuses millions of white viewers?

Many critics understand antiracist work and spectacles made of blacks for whites as mutually exclusive. What shall we make of the black female castratrix— surely a white male fantasy? One could argue that the masochistic sexual fantasies of men make poor choices for symbols of female resistance. Suppose, for instance, that Foxy Brown's castration of her white male adversary fits a masochistic male fantasy. Does this deprive the image of any feminist or antiracist punch? We can easily argue that most images in Western culture are white male fantasies, and that many of those are useful to feminists and others whatever their political pedigrees. The essays in this book grapple with just such complicated framings of and responses to women's on-screen violence.

Certainly violent women in movies draw mixed responses. Cheering audiences compete with scornful critics and disinterested viewers for the final word on women's violence. Academic controversies over mean women tend to focus on matters of co-optation and realism. With the final section of this introduction we turn to the literature on violent women in the movies to review reasons for rejecting them as tools in feminist struggle. Readers unconcerned with academic debates might want to skip this discussion and begin the essays.

Why Not Mean Women?

Carol J. Clover has famously observed that violent women abound in horror movies, for example in the reviled slasher movies and a genre that she dubbed "rape revenge."[13] These women rose from the depths of victimhood to chew their oppressors to pieces. Could groups of young men watch these videos, over

FIGURE 2. Ellen Ripley becomes the invincible hero of *Aliens*. With child on one arm and artillery on the other, she is a typical Hollywood mean woman.

and over again, in grudging affirmation of feminist strength? Could women take pride in the images or need we be ashamed of them? In this final section, we summarize the four main objections to women's on-screen violence among feminist scholars and others: that the violent female characters are too unrealistic, too sexy, too emotional, and too co-opted. We examine these charges in turn.

Too Unrealistic

Ellen Ripley orders the men to stay behind and wait for her; descends into the flaming, steaming, dripping alien nest; throws a young girl over one shoulder and a massive rifle over another; and confronts the monsters who slaughtered most of her company of would-be protector Marines. After a dozen men die trying, Ripley stands tall and defeats her gigantic enemy.

Many violent-woman movies, such as the *Alien* series with its invincible hero Ripley, strike people as uselessly unrealistic. The women seem too strong, their stamina inhuman, pathetic imitations of the silly male fantasies. Women often laugh at the delusions of men, especially their dreams of themselves as unstoppable locomotives of destruction. Why on earth would women want to join that phallic crowd?

Sometimes, fantasies of female omnipotence scare people with the notion that women might imitate that violence. Others sometimes respond and defend such violent fantasies as safely unrealistic and thus impotent. For instance, when critics complained of the potential of *Thelma and Louise* to serve as a how-to manual for homicidal rebellion, the film's producers reassured them that they had intended the movie as an unrealistic tale, and that real women get along with men pretty well. Women do not really act the way Thelma and Louise do, the defensive argument went; the movie was just fantasy.[14] (See Barbara L. Miller's essay in this volume for more on this reception.) However, Lynda Hart argues (rightly, we believe) for an interpretation that does not impute displacement and dishonesty to the violent woman or her movie—an interpretation that allows for the possibility that women might actually do violence to men for the sake of other women. Yvonne Tasker offers a related and important caution that analysts of violent women in movies too often dismiss them as charades of no consequence.[15]

Indeed, many people resist violent women in the movies because they're too fantastic and not "real" enough to seem like part of genuine feminist struggle. For instance, the early-1990s set of violent women mentioned above sparked conversation in Hollywood about the parts that female actors where being offered:

Susan Sarandon, actor (*Thelma and Louise*): What we see in the media is closer to a man's idea of what women are. Women want to see things that are more surprising and truthful—not so sugarcoated.[16]

Natasha Richardson, actor (*Patty Hearst, The Handmaid's Tale*): I would like to see more "real women" portrayed in movies—vulnerable, strong, sexy, intelligent and full of the contradictions common to most women.[17]

Sandra Bullock, actor (*Demolition Man, Speed*): Women want a variety of fantasies. It's nice to lose yourself in another woman's life, but it has to be a real woman, not a man's creation.[18]

Martha Coolidge, director (*Rambling Rose, Introducing Dorothy Dandridge*): I think women want to see women portrayed in a more realistic way, that's all. That

doesn't mean you can't have bad guys as women, but I kind of resent that the big breakthrough was, "Hey, let's make the really bad guys women." That fulfills another male fantasy: Woman as Monster.[19]

Mariel Hemingway, actor (*Personal Best, Star 80*): This is a business run by guys who have fantasies about women and who want women to be a certain way. My way of dealing with it is to not be a part of it.[20]

Annette Bening, actor (*The Grifters, The Siege*): What we need are more human roles.[21]

Women in the movie business wish for violent female characters who do not look very much like violent men, and describe their wish in terms of "real" womanhood.

In her commentary on *The Silence of the Lambs*, Jodie Foster offered similar thoughts about her feminist heroism:

I think there's something very important about having a woman hero who's a true woman hero, in the most archetypal sense of the word, and yet doesn't have to clothe herself in men's clothing. She's not six-foot-two; she doesn't kill the dragon by being mightier. She actually does it because of her instinct, because of her brain, and because somehow she's seen something, a detail that other people have missed. And that's a real side of female heroism that should be applauded and should be respected. . . . Clarice is a real female hero, not a bad imitation of a male hero.[22]

Foster explained, in another interview, "Male fantasy is interesting terrain. . . . Nobody is saying 'Don't make movies about male fantasy,' or 'Don't make movies about women who are complex and evil.' The thing to stress is that you want to create characters that are *real*."[23] In this volume, Susan Knobloch looks at a violent actor, Sharon Stone, often accused of unrealistic performance.

The feminist study of popular culture often sticks at these issues of realism and progressive impact. In her review of 1970s feminist scholarship on sexism in the media, Suzanna Danuta Walters explains that those early studies described the persistence of sexist imagery and the relegation of women to home-and-family roles.[24] Such work trains our attention on women's injury, oppression, or vilification as monsters. Feminist activists called our attention to the representation in the media of women's bodies as objectified and violated by the putatively more aggressive bodies of men. In the name of realism, feminists have neglected images of women as potentially active, violent, or vengeful.

Feminist scholars of film have rejected the simplest models of such socialist-feminist realism, rightly noting that one person's realism might amount to another's fantasy and that disputes over veracity lead nowhere because "realistic" images might not help activists anyhow.[25] After all, stories of impoverishment and abandonment, abuse and endless workdays, however realistic, can't provide all of the imagery that a movement needs. Nor could depictions of women exploiting each other across lines of class or race prove very inspiring, however realistic they might be. Laura Grindstaff's essay in this volume considers tough women fighting across lines of age and social class. Images of women fighting for new rights might not always seem realistic, but they are worth circulating anyway.

Beyond asking whether images were true, analysts have asked what activists or their oppressors could do with them. Scholars have advanced more complex models in the interim, most famously Stuart Hall's reworking of Raymond Williams's distinction between the "dominant" and the "emergent."[26] This model allows analysts to specify audiences who might read pop culture in particular ways that served the (proto-) political purposes of their communities. With this framework, analysts could distinguish between the "resistant" (i.e., feminist, antiracist) aspects of a movie or its audience, and the "dominant" parts to be reviled.

Unfortunately, this shift from realism to various audience activities retains the most serious problem of the putatively rejected "positive-image" framework. Both frameworks lend themselves better to moralistic denunciation than to building knowledge of complicated genres. For example, we can see Ripley's resourcefulness and ability to fight as "resistant" because we like that part of the film, and then interpret her handling of weapons or her bossing of black men as "dominant" because we were embarrassed by liberal guilt or outraged by the apparent racial subordination (see discussion of racism in *Aliens* below). In another context, Eve Kosofsky Sedgwick pokes fun at this theoretical model ("kinda subversive, kinda hegemonic") as "the good dog/bad dog rhetoric of puppy obedience school"[27] and dismisses it for its "intense moralism" and "wholesale reification of the status quo."[28] The "dominance/resistance" framework pats some images or interpretations on the head as useful to "us" and slaps others as collaborating with oppressors, leaving aside the pesky matters of what anyone means by "us," how we know what "we" do with the images, and what any "dominant" group might do with them, mean by them, gain from them, and so on.

Like critics of dominant/resistant images and interpretations, we intend this volume to offer readers ways to use images—inaccurate, irreverent, or otherwise offensive as they might be. We have assembled this volume in the spirit of celebration more than diminution, not because we have divided the good dogs (feminist visions) from the bad dogs (male fantasies), but because we know that movies belong to both breeds at every moment for every audience, and we'd rather take space discovering patterns in film narrative and reception than bark at them. The skewering assessments of violent women in the rich film literature tend to leave one wondering what such heroes must do to escape derision as hollow, limited, male fantasies.

There must be more to analysis than condemnation, the perpetual unmasking of violent women as frauds whose "resistance" to some reified patriarchy must always be undercut by recuperation into a "dominant" order. We'd like to move beyond the objection that violent women are often unrealistic, sexy, nurturing, emotional, or working for the government. Thus, this volume explores uses of violent fantasies, and so moves beyond critiques of them as sexist and otherwise oppressive. Male fantasies abound in our male-dominated culture, and surely these violent women are among them.[29] How could they not be, after all? They didn't drop from the sky pure of our culture's taint. Can't we find use for them despite their being unreal male fantasies?

Too Sexy

Catherine makes passionate love to a man tied by his wrists to his bedposts. Just as they appear to climax together, she draws an ice pick from the satin sheets and stabs her lover over and over as he screams, thrashes, and bleeds.

Analysts observe that many violent women on-screen look like runway models: young, thin, large breasted, and bare skinned. Many feel that this pulls them from the realm of feminist activism and back into the uselessness of male fantasy. But must they be victims? Does Catherine Tramell—the sexy, rich, supersmart, fearless, enterprising woman in *Basic Instinct*—really not prevail, just because similar female characters die in this and other movies?[30] Maybe violent women fail even when they succeed. But where, other than to the satisfaction of moralizing ("bad puppy") resentment, could such an argument lead? Judith Halberstam's essay in this volume argues that down Catherine's path of imagined violence lies a genuine victory.

Analysts also complain of women being drawn into the fetishism of male sexuality and thus never amounting to powerful images for women. For instance, Linda Mizejewski worries that the cop movie *Blue Steel* blunts its subversive force for women and sinks into a conventional male-fantasy world by reducing "the gun significations into the simpler terms of female desire, penis envy, and male fetish."[31] That is, violent woman Megan "buys into the biological identification of gun as female phallus." Perhaps women who kill become phallic, and thus sexy, and thereby useless to feminism.

Other scholars decry the sexual vulnerability of female heroes (whose attractiveness or sexual assertiveness draws predatory male attention), as though survival of such attacks made them seem weak, and as though male heroes didn't face the same problems in a number of genres.[32] Of course, male heroes of cop movies can also be sexy and sexually vulnerable. Recall those extended S/M scenes in cop movies in which ultrabutch men leer at, trade homoerotic "I'm-going-to-fuck-your-ass" lines with, and then beat the stuffing out of half-naked heroes; or enjoy sex with women while murderers stalk them down their halls toward their imperiled bedrooms.[33] Does a woman's sexiness really make her less of a threat while she's beating a man senseless or shooting him dead? Jeffrey A. Brown's essay in this volume offers a rebuttal of the presumption that a female character's sexiness diminishes her toughness or the film's feminist potential. Wendy Arons's essay shows that female stars of martial arts movies are both sexy and empowered. Perhaps such images reconfigure what feminists have for years critiqued, namely the equation of sexiness and female subordination.

Too Emotional

Clarice feels her way through a room plunged into total darkness. A madman stalks her with his pistol raised for the kill. Breathing hard and obviously terrified, Clarice holds her own gun with shaking hands. Only when she hears the clack of his pistol cocking does she fire into the dark and blow him away.

Some fear that Hollywood films like *The Silence of the Lambs* undercut tough women by imbuing them with strong emotions, such as fear, maternal protec-

FIGURE 3. FBI Agent Clarice Starling moves from fear to violence in a heartbeat in *The Silence of the Lambs.*

tiveness, or ambivalence about killing. In her book surveying popular culture, *Tough Girls,* Sherrie Inness argues that signs of weakness among violent women in movies sap their subversive potential: "This emphasis implies that all tough women are not as tough as they appear and therefore pose no significant threat to male hegemony."[34] Carol M. Dole's essay in this volume provides examples of the facts that violent women can be small, devote themselves as much to childcare as to combat, lose their weapons as soon as they use them, and still disturb old ideas about women's incompetence or passivity. But are we so suspicious that Hollywood must be putting something over on us that we'll have to reject such violent women as not "really" tough? Films like *Lethal Weapon* reveal that emotional expressiveness and sexual attractiveness are common among heroes rather than distinguishing traits of female characters per se. Mel Gibson has certainly made a career of playing men so volatile they seem ready to pop their screws.[35] What may seem feminine at first glance often turns out to mark toughness and heroism in general.

Officer Megan Turner finds that her father has beaten her mother and for a moment looks stunned. "You hit her again, you son of a bitch."

The patriarch screams, "You don't have nothin' to say about it!"

Megan slams her father up against the wall, telling him that he's under arrest, manacles him, forces him into her car, and makes him admit what he's done.

In *Blue Steel*, Megan blows two men away: an armed robber in a grocery store and a serial killer on the street. In both cases she's in uniform acting as a police officer. Several critics have noticed that the few female heroes of the large cop-action genre tend to uphold the law more carefully than men do, perhaps serving repressive, antifeminist purposes by doing so.[36] Such women might be patsies, in other words, playing into a patriarchal system that hates all women.[37]

Camilla Griggers argues that violent women such as Ellen Ripley of *Alien* fame use their violence on behalf of a militarized patriarchy that employs white women to supervise the men of color who work the lower rungs of such institutions.[38] Does Ripley (however unwittingly) serve a military-industrial complex and, if so, spoil our pleasure at watching her?[39] Does she represent a conservative feminism that tells white women, specifically, that they can have a place in a white, male power structure only if they dominate others?

Answers to these questions are laden with untested and untestable assumptions about what various producers intended, how audiences responded, what characters wanted. Tiina Vares's essay provides an all-too-rare exemplar of audience study. This book cannot possibly decide whether the movies studied are hegemonic (bad) or subversive (good). We take it for granted that they're all both all the time in ways that undercut the moralistic distinctions. We like morals, of course, and wouldn't produce books like these if we didn't think that they, and the movies they study, could do some good. But we'd rather grant from the outset that one's victorious fantasy will send another away unsatisfied in a manner unlikely to be captured by intensive interpretation.[40]

Some of the films with violent women will be co-opted: racist, homophobic, procapitalist, nationalist. Others will be feminist, queer, or antiracist. We hope that all of these violent women frighten people who snicker at women's protests. Whatever their roots in male fantasies, their places in dominant orders, or their distance from real lives, may these images at least subvert the notion that women will suffer abuse patiently. Like many of the most notable moments in the history of popular film, the blaxploitation genre disappeared before long—a passing oddity in the menu of white-producer tastes. And women have a long way to go before they reach parity with male cops on-screen.

Perhaps many of the violent women studied herein share similar fates; it's not possible to know. What will become of the suburban housewives with handguns, or the gender-bending cops working white male turf? Can Hollywood stand another Sharon Stone or Kathy Bates? In "Caged Heat" Suzanne Danuta Walters recommends that we watch the lowest genres—the independently produced, grind-house, or straight-to-video fare such as women-in-prison movies—for the subconscious of our popular culture. The current crop of high-profile violent women may indeed find themselves driven back to those haunts before long. Whatever the case, we'll take these women seriously now, not as ideals of a utopian age or role models for kids, but as pop-cultural players shaped by fights over race, class, and family values in a vital game of sexual politics. They disrupt dreams of women's gracious acceptance of all that men hand them, and right now that's good enough for us. This volume studies violent women in the movies not merely as patriarchal pawns or broken promises but also as possible tools in the liberation of women from racial, class, gender, and other political constraints that oppress women and deny them equal chances and equal rights.

Notes

1. See, for example, Robin Morgan, *The Demon Lover: On the Sexuality of Terrorism* (New York: W. W. Norton, 1989).

2. Male students have told us that images of women's violence make them "not want to mess with the wrong female," and female students say that such images help them think that women can fight back if attacked. See Martha McCaughey and Neal King, "Rape Education Videos: Presenting Mean Women Instead of Dangerous Men," *Teaching Sociology* 23, no. 4 (1995): 380, 382. Paxton Quigley, renowned firearms instructor for women, suggests that Thelma and Louise prompted many women to take her self-defensive shooting class. See Martha McCaughey, *Real Knockouts: The Physical Feminism of Women's Self-Defense* (New York: New York University Press, 1997), 100.

3. See Jodi Gold and Susan Villari, eds., *Just Sex: Students Rewrite the Rules on Sex, Violence, Activism, and Equality* (Lanham, Md.: Rowan and Littlefield, 2000).

4. Barbara Ehrenreich, "The Decline of Patriarchy," in *Constructing Masculinity*, ed. Maurice Berger, Brian Wallis, and Simon Watson (New York: Routledge, 1995), 284–90.

5. See McCaughey, *Real Knockouts*.

6. See, for example, Richard Grenier, "Killer Bimbos," *Commentary*, September 1991, 50–52;

Kathi Maio, "Women Who Murder for the Man," *Ms.*, November/December 1991, 82–84; Laura Shapiro, "Women Who Kill Too Much," *Newsweek*, 17 June 1991, 63.

7. McCaughey and King, "Rape Education Videos," 374–88. An anecdote from each of us should give readers an idea where this book came from. *Martha:* A feminist activist against violence, I shuddered during the few violent scenes in films that I didn't avoid. My usual anger at the violence changed dramatically when I watched *Terminator 2* in 1991. Sarah Connor's competence with weapons and hand-to-hand combat exhilarated me. I remember driving my car home differently from the theater that day, flexing my arms as I clutched the steering wheel. That's when I realized that men must feel this way after seeing movies—all the time. My anger changed to envy; I could understand the power of seeing one's sex made heroic on-screen and wanted to feel that way more often. I realized that my own lectures on sexual assault failed to give women any feelings of strength and that this new strategy promised much for teachers and activists. *Neal:* A longtime action movie fan, I avoided genres in which men abuse women (rape-revenge, Western, war, slasher, etc.), and preferred the mobster and cop-action movies in which men molest each other instead. However, a scene in the mob movie *True Romance* seemed to offer another way to view women and screen violence. A hood beats the daylights out of the heroine Alabama and thus breaks the chivalric rule that reserves sadomasochism for characters played by Clint Eastwood, Bruce Willis, and Mel Gibson. Alabama takes the abuse with a macho defiance and scorn, survives terrible wounds, and goads the thug to keep it coming. In heroic fashion, she then comes back to blind, beat, burn, stab, and shotgun the man to pieces. The scene shocked me, not only with its brutality and her bellow of rage, but even more with Alabama's challenge to the dismissal of women from heroic turf. This woman would not go home when the real action began.

8. For analyses of the way fantasies of male physical power and female physical vulnerability affect gender violence, see Sharon Marcus, "Fighting Bodies, Fighting Words: A Theory and Politics of Rape Prevention," in *Feminists Theorize the Political,* ed. Judith Butler and Joan W. Scott (New York: Routledge, 1992); and McCaughey, *Real Knockouts.*

9. Darius James, *That's Blaxploitation! Roots of the Baadasssss 'Tude (Rated X by an All-Whyte Jury)* (New York: St. Martin's Press, 1995), 46.

10. Mike Phillips, "Chic and Beyond," *Sight and Sound* 6, no. 8 (1996): 26.

11. Ibid.

12. Donald Bogle, *Toms, Coons, Mulattoes, Mammies, and Bucks: An Interpretive History of Blacks in American Films* (New York: Continuum, 1991): 251–52.

13. "The women's movement has given many things to popular culture. . . . [O]ne of its main donations . . . is the image of an angry woman—a woman so angry that she can be imagined as a credible perpetrator . . . of the kind of violence on which . . . the status of full protagonist rests." Carol J. Clover, *Men, Women, and Chain Saws: Gender in the Modern Horror Film* (Princeton: Princeton University Press, 1992), 17.

14. Lynda Hart, *Fatal Women: Lesbian Sexuality and the Mark of Aggression* (Princeton: Princeton University Press, 1994), 74.

15. Tasker writes, "It is perhaps the centrality of images of women with guns . . . that has caused the most concern among feminist critics. The phallic woman . . . is seen as a male ruse, and a film like *Thelma and Louise* as 'little more than a masculine revenge fantasy' whose 'effect is perversely to reinforce the message that women cannot win.' . . . [D]isruptive narrative or representational elements exist, within such a critical view, as little more than precursors to their ultimate hegemonic

incorporation. Hence, these images are taken to represent a double betrayal, holding out a promise that can never be fulfilled ('This film is a con')." Yvonne Tasker, *Spectacular Bodies: Gender, Genre, and the Action Cinema* (New York: Routledge, 1993), 139.

16. Quoted in "The Women's Picture," ed. Laura Morice, *Us Magazine,* October 1994, 69.

17. Ibid., 73.

18. Ibid., 73

19. Ibid., 74.

20. Ibid., 79.

21. Ibid., 80.

22. Filmmaker's commentary, in *The Silence of the Lambs* (Voyager, laser disc and DVD, 1991).

23. Quoted in *Premiere: Women in Hollywood Special Issue* (1993), 63.

24. See Suzanna Danuta Walters, *Material Girls: Making Sense of Feminist Cultural Theory* (Berkeley: University of California Press, 1995), 29–49.

25. For instance, Diane Waldman wrote in 1978 that the simplest models of "positive image" critique could "lump together films that clearly represent different class interests, different types of role models." "There's More to a Positive Image than Meets the Eye," in *Issues in Feminist Film Criticism,* ed. Patricia Erens (Bloomington: Indiana University Press, 1990), 16.

26. Raymond Williams recommends that we "speak of the 'dominant' and the 'effective,' and in these senses of the hegemonic." In contrast, "emergent" meanings are "new," substantially alternative, or oppositional. See *Marxism and Literature* (Oxford University Press, 1977), 121. Stuart Hall carries these ideas forward by defining "dominant-hegemonic" as the interpretation that takes the meaning "full and straight," and "decodes in terms of the reference code in which [the object] has been encoded." See "Encoding/Decoding," in *The Cultural Studies Reader,* ed. Simon During (New York: Routledge, 1993), 101. Hall elaborates by defining a "preferred" meaning as one both intended by the object's producers and structured by the means of production. See Stuart Hall, "Reflections upon the Encoding/Decoding Model: An Interview" in *Viewing, Reading, Listening: Audiences and Cultural Reception,* ed. Jon Cruz and Justin Lewis (Boulder, Colo.: Westview Press, 1994), 261–62. In contrast, "negotiated" and the more extreme "oppositional" interpretations are those that "make their own ground rules" (Hall, "Encoding/Decoding," 102) and "decode the message in a globally contrary way" (103). Both Hall ("Reflections," 266) and Williams (*Marxism and Literature,* 122–23) warn that in practice people will find these meanings and readings really difficult to distinguish. Hall actually cautions against recourse to audience study in articulation of a "preferred reading," on the grounds that audiences cannot be relied upon to "decode" texts in the preferred manner, and in fact are likely to "read against the grain" ("Reflections," 266). The unruly behavior of mass audiences leaves Hall with little use for his "encoding/decoding" scheme in his own research (272–73); and his advice that we abjure reception study and "read as much as [we] can, as neutrally as [we] can get" (266) doesn't help. Hence the framework leads us to moralistic contrasts ungrounded in audience research.

27. Eve Kosofsky Sedgwick, "Shame in the Cybernetic Fold," in *Shame and Its Sisters: A Silvan Tomkins Reader,* ed. Eve Kosofsky Sedgwick and Adam Frank (Durham: Duke University Press, 1995), 5.

28. Ibid., 25.

29. In her look at *The Texas Chainsaw Massacre 2,* Judith Halberstam argues that the comical movie subverted standard Hollywood hegemony in a manner worth our attention rather than dis-

missal as unrealistic. The author of the final massacre turns out to be the "perfect antidote to the hapless, aristocratic, lethargic Gothic heroine—a white trash bitch with a chain saw." Judith Halberstam, "Bodies That Splatter: Queers and Chain Saws," in *Skin Shows: Gothic Horror and the Technology of Monsters* (Durham: Duke University Press, 1995), 143. The hero, Stretch, survives rape and murder attempts, butchers her assailants, and stands screaming in triumph, thrashing her new weapon about her. There's nothing vaguely realistic about her character or her awful predicament, but is that a bad thing? Halberstam observes that by "suturing" us into our spectatorship, classical Hollywood movies tried to create "natural" experiences with compelling emotional force; they'd satisfy us because they felt so real. Halberstam argues that slashers such as *The Texas Chainsaw Massacre 2* easily avoid this sense of "nature" and go right for the self-conscious parody of real-life experience. They often climax with the images of defiantly unnatural women who respect neither boundaries nor conventions, and who happily use masculine tools (carving knives, spears, drills, chain saws) to get what they want.

30. Camilla Griggers shows that the decline of Victorian-style patriarchal family types has produced in popular culture a raft of women living without the protection of male kin. These women become prey for wandering men, and sometimes turn to violence to defend themselves. Griggers ties all of this to the notorious Aileen Wuornos case, and argues that the persecution of such women as well as the slaughter of femmes fatales in the neonoir genre mitigates any victory among the Catherine Tramells. See "Lesbians and the Serial Killing-Machine," in *Becoming Woman* (Minneapolis: University of Minnesota Press, 1997), 91–103.

31. Linda Mizejewski, "Picturing the Female Dick: *The Silence of the Lambs* and *Blue Steel*," *Journal of Film and Video 45*, no. 2 (summer/fall 1993): 16.

32. Christine Holmlund, "A Decade of Deadly Dolls: Hollywood and the Woman Killer," in *Moving Targets: Women, Murder, and Representation,* ed. Helen Birch (Berkeley: University of California Press, 1994), 127–51; Sherrie A. Inness, *Tough Girls: Women Warriors and Wonder Women in Popular Culture* (Philadelphia: University of Pennsylvania Press, 1999). Both Clover and Lehman note that slasher and rape-revenge horror movies feature the punishment of bad men by women in sexual ways. Clover, *Men, Women, and Chain Saws;* Peter Lehman, "Don't Blame This on a Woman," in *Screening the Male: Exploring Masculinities in Hollywood Cinema,* ed. Steven Neale and Ina Rae Hark (New York: Routledge, 1993).

33. See Neal King, "Sodomy and Guts," in *Heroes in Hard Times: Cop Action Movies in the U.S.* (Philadelphia: Temple University Press, 1999), 150–201.

34. Inness, *Tough Girls,* 81.

35. One might argue that the really annoying tough-woman stereotype is not the emotionally expressive hero but the humorless and officious newcomer to men's turf, the bitch who needs to lighten up and who will learn to do so from the easygoing dude played by George Clooney, Bruce Willis, Clint Eastwood, or Tom Cruise.

36. Tasker, *Spectacular Bodies,* 31; Christopher Sharrett, "The Horror Film in Neoconservative Culture," *Journal of Popular Film and Television* 21, no. 3 (1993): 104; Anna Powell, "Blood on the Borders: *Near Dark* and *Blue Steel*," *Screen 35,* no. 2 (summer 1994): 147.

37. A study of the entire cop-action genre suggests that female cops don't enforce the law with any more rigor than men bring to the job. Megan and Clarice get into trouble with their superiors in conventional manner, just as most of the other dozen or so female heroes in the cop-action genre do. See King, *Heroes in Hard Times.* Relevant cop-action movies include *Betrayed, Blue Steel, Copycat, Fargo, Fatal Beauty, Impulse, The Long Kiss Goodnight, Out of Sight, The Silence of the Lambs,*

A Stranger among Us, and *Vampire in Brooklyn.* Only the maternal hero of *Fargo* avoids serious conflict with her superior. The heroes of *Betrayed, The Long Kiss Goodnight,* and *Out of Sight* either quit their jobs as cops or actively aid criminals. A very close relation to the law this is not.

38. Griggers, *Becoming Woman,* 65. Her argument rests on a mistake (she identifies the rabble in *Alien³* as mostly black when they're mostly white), but registers the concern that such women represent liberal feminism at its worst—in its haste to join privileged white men at the top rather than tear their monoliths down.

39. Whereas Griggers employs Deleuze and Guattari's terms to demonstrate military-industrial victory over the changeling hero of *Aliens,* Hills uses that same theoretical framework to argue for Ripley's subversive victory. Ibid., 59; Elizabeth Hills, "From 'Figurative Males' to Action Heroines: Further Thoughts on Active Women in the Cinema," *Screen* 40, no. 1 (spring 1999): 38–65. For the continental theory that both employ, see also Gilles Deleuze and Félix Guattari, *A Thousand Plateaus: Capitalism and Schizophrenia,* trans. Brina Massumi (Minneapolis: University of Minnesota Press, 1987).

40. In his jaundiced survey of cultural studies film literature, David Bordwell documents the dead ends to which most interpretive exposés of hegemonic movies lead, and suggests that we offer testable propositions rather than chase hidden and recuperative meanings in the movies that we enjoy. See *Making Meaning: Inference and Rhetoric in the Interpretation of Cinema* (Cambridge: Harvard University Press, 1989).

Part I

Genre Films

"If Her Stunning Beauty Doesn't Bring You to Your Knees, Her Deadly Drop Kick Will"

Violent Women in the Hong Kong Kung Fu Film

Wendy Arons

● ● ● ● ● ● ● ● ●

The quote in the title of this chapter appears in the promotional blurb for the videotape of *Wing Chun* (1994), which stars one of Hong Kong's most popular actresses, Michelle Yeoh.[1] Like virtually all recent kung fu films featuring female martial artists, *Wing Chun* presents its audience with a satisfying image of a powerful woman. The eponymous heroine is a skilled, aggressive, and effective fighter, who dispatches crowds of thugs with grace, style, and humor, and defends not only herself but also her female friends from the advances of lecherous men. But like many of these recent films, *Wing Chun* also problematizes the (ir)reconcilability of "femininity" and fighting: the heroine's "masculine" martial arts skills are at odds with her yearning to be accepted in her community as a desirable woman. The promotional blurb reduces to a simple either/or equation the thorny constellation of issues that arises when women are the subjects of violence in the kung fu film, as these films continually invoke and undermine stereotypes about the compatibility of beauty and power, femininity and violence, and desire and desirability. For even as such films depict women as strong, independent, and capable fighters, they continue to embed such images of women within a context that defines femininity in terms of physical beauty and sexual attractiveness to men, and that draws on traditional misogynist stereotypes that reduce femininity to a figure of "fascinating and threatening alterity."[2]

Because the kung fu genre as a whole is rather conservative (the films are formulaic, and more like each other than they are different), it tends to represent violent women in patterned ways. Many of these films, like *Wing Chun*,

FIGURE 4. Wing Chun (Michelle Yeoh) in her final battle with the bandit king reconciles the yin of feminine beauty with the yang of skilled martial artistry.

question the compatibility of femininity and violence. Some do this by sending mixed messages about the "attractiveness" of the fighting woman, framing her as a plain but earnest sidekick in contrast to the male hero's beautiful but helpless love interest. This reduces the threat posed by the violent woman by displacing her erotic power onto a more traditionally "feminine" figure. Other films, in contrast, explicitly turn the fighting woman into a sex object and use martial artistry to exploit the female body. While in some cases this results in a positive integration of female sexuality and power, in others the violent woman conforms obediently to the misogynist image of the "Dragon Lady" or femme fatale. The fantasy-action subgenre subverts gender norms by positing a mythical world in which gender is fluid and women can accrue supernatural powers. These films often use the instability of gender allegorically to express a political uncertainty and anxiety surrounding Hong Kong's status in light of its reversion to China in 1997. And finally, the kung fu comedy genre frequently draws its humor from reversing stereotypical gender roles or playing with established norms of behavior between the sexes. For example, a standard comic moment involves a hero who comes to the rescue of a woman he thinks helpless, only to watch as she capably defends herself. Although such reversals celebrate women's power and self-sufficiency, the comedy derives from the film's positioning of the gender reversal as "unnatural," and as a result normative gender stereotypes are often paradoxically reinforced. The Hong Kong film industry revels in these contradictory depictions of women—as Bey Logan has observed: "[N]o film industry has done so much to define women as sex objects nor so much to define them as superbeings with far greater powers than their male counterparts."[3] Thus although women frequently appear as stunningly powerful fighters, this positive image is often neutralized by the conventional depiction of women in the genre in general.

My purpose here, however, is not to generalize broadly about the depiction of violent women in kung fu films but rather to look closely at a number of recent films that I feel highlight the issues raised in the preceding paragraphs. This article is not intended to be exhaustive: given the huge number of films produced in Hong Kong each year, such a task would border on the absurd. Rather, I have focused on films that were *(a)* good, *(b)* exemplary, and *(c)*—a practical consideration—readily available.[4]

Before I look more closely at specific films, however, I think it is necessary to address two issues that pertain to the whole genre: first, the problem of cross-cultural analysis and, second, the nature of violence in the kung fu film. As E. Ann Kaplan argues, cross-cultural analysis is "fraught with danger" because "we are forced to read works produced by the other through the constraints of our own frameworks/theories/ideologies."[5] As a U.S. feminist critic who has never even been to Hong Kong, I am fully aware of the gulf that separates my own frameworks from those of the film's creators and primary audience, and in this paper I make no attempt to bridge that gulf. This is not to say that I ignore cultural difference or dismiss the danger that such an analysis might be "a new form of cultural imperialism, when . . . institutionalized in various college courses on Asian cinema."[6] The Hong Kong kung fu genre, however, is a strange animal: although produced primarily for consumption in the Asian market, it is also marketed heavily—and generally quite successfully—in the West. Because these films are aimed (even if secondarily) at a Western audience, I feel it is appropriate and justifiable to focus here on issues that are raised by their Western consumption. In addition, this article has as its primary audience the Western critic who will bring similar concerns to her viewing of these films. Thus I content myself to write from what Chris Berry would undoubtedly label "an unabashedly Western feminist point of view."[7] That said, gender in the kung fu film continues to beg a cross-cultural analysis that makes visible "the Hong

Kong way of thinking," and I hope this essay takes a step toward opening up a dialogue with critics who might be interested in tackling such an analysis.[8]

The second general issue that needs to be addressed is the nature of violence in these films. Kung fu films are primarily vehicles for the virtuoso display of choreographed violence. Like musicals, they put forth formulaic plots that serve mainly to allow performers to show off their physical skills.[9] King Hu, one of the genre's early masters, connected the kung fu fight scene to the tradition of dance in the musical:

I've always taken the action part of my films as dancing rather than fighting. . . . A lot of people have misunderstood me, and have remarked that my action scenes are sometimes "authentic," sometimes not. In point of fact, they're always keyed to the notion of dance.[10]

The pleasures of both the kung fu and musical genres derive from watching skilled performers execute difficult moves with incredible precision and timing. As a result, although the violence in kung fu films is often graphic and disgusting (an early scene in *Swordsman II* shows the bones of a man's forearm pop through the skin at his elbow, for example), it is stylized and framed in a way that mutes its impact. The kung fu film rarely ambushes the viewer with its violence: fight scenes are virtually always anticipated by a moment of acknowledgment establishing the combatants so that viewers know when a fight is about to begin and can enjoy the spectacle. In addition, both hero/ines and villains have superhuman capacities and can give and take an enormous number of blows without showing pain. This, along with the sheer length and complexity of the fight choreography, tends to reinforce the impression that the violence is "unrealistic."[11] And because fight scenes tend to involve equally matched combatants (two superhumans or a single superhero versus a slew of mere mortals), the violence seems less sadistic and cruel than in other genres; kung fu films do not generally indulge in scenes of brutality inflicted on totally powerless victims (for obvious reasons: it takes at least two to make an entertaining fight).[12]

Thus, to speak of violent women in the kung fu film requires a definition of a "violent" woman that has less to do with aggressivity, sadism, or villainy and more to do with the skill and the will to defend life or honor, and usually only when provoked. For the most part, the women warriors of the kung fu genre are the film's heroes rather than villains (although there are many interesting exceptions), and their violent behavior is framed as self-defense rather than aggression. The genre dwells lightly (if at all) on the heroine's violence as socially transgressive; her male colleagues or attackers might register surprise at her ability to fight, but once she establishes her martial arts skills they treat her like one of the guys. This is due in part to China's long tradition of female martial artistry, both in historical legend and in performance. For example, the legend of the male martial artist Fong Sai Yuk reports that he was trained by his mother in kung fu; Yim Wing Chun, the historical figure on which the film *Wing Chun* is based, purportedly learned her kung fu from the Buddhist nun who developed the style.[13] The Peking Opera (which was an early source for the kung fu film) had a rich tradition of fighting female characters, in latter days often played by actresses who trained in the martial arts in order to display them in a performance context. The woman warrior in the kung fu film is thus by no means a new phenomenon, and from its very beginning the genre has featured women in heroic fighting roles (one of the earliest martial arts films was Ren Pengnian's *Li Feifei* [*The Heroine*] of 1925).[14] As a result, the appearance of a woman who can and will use violence is already an accepted convention in the genre. Yet it is a telling comment on the continued power of gender stereotypes that more often than not the kung fu film will exploit the revelation of a woman's martial artistry for comic effect.

In addition, where violent women do appear as villains their gender often marks them as more evil than their male accomplices: a good example is the film *Midnight Angel* (aka *Angel/Iron Angels* 1988), in which Yukari Oshima plays the sadistic leader of a drug ring who takes pleasure in torturing her victims.[15] In some films female villains bear the added stigma of sexual deviancy or lesbianism (see my discussion of *Naked Killer* below). In other words, the genre continues to resurrect the traditional figure of the cruel and sexy "Dragon Lady," whose violence is framed as deviant and always punished. The violent behavior of heroines, on the other hand, usually conforms to generic conventions for heroes, and is both socially acceptable (within the film's narrative) and visually pleasurable (for the spectator).

These generalizations about violence, heroism, and women's roles are meant to establish a basic understanding of generic conventions and expectations rather than set any hard-and-fast rules about violent women in the kung fu film. I turn now to a more specific analysis of the ways women are framed in the genre. I start with two films that feature women as their heroes; I then look at violent women in the fantasy-action subgenre; and finally I discuss the appearance of women as the comic/action sidekick in films featuring male heroes.

Violent Beauties: *Wing Chun* and *Naked Killer*

In this section I focus on two films that could not be more dissimilar: *Wing Chun* and *Naked Killer* (1992). Both films feature women who move in a world of female potency and male impotency, but the resemblances end there. Where *Wing Chun* presents a positive image of a heroine attempting to understand, negotiate, and finally mitigate the threat that her martial artistry poses to the male community (without giving up or renouncing her power), *Naked Killer* depicts female eroticism and violence as a menace to men that can only be resolved through the annihilation of the women. My discussion of these two films reveals the very different ways in which the genre can link femininity, female sexuality, and women's violence.

Wing Chun deserves extended discussion for the way it both frames and resolves the problem of reconciling the yin of the heroine's desire with the yang of her violent fighting skills. As I noted above, *Wing Chun* is a comedy loosely based on the historical legend of Yim Wing Chun, who as a young girl learned martial arts from a Buddhist nun in order to defend herself against marriage to a villainous suitor. In the film this particular event is in the past, and Wing Chun has established herself as the most effective kung fu fighter in her village. But her skill comes with a price: as a strong, independent, and decidedly masculinized woman, she poses a threat to men, and has had to resign herself to what she believes will be her fate—a life without love and marriage. This seems to be cemented when her childhood sweetheart and fiancé, Pok To, returns after a ten-year absence and, mistaking her beautiful friend Charmy for her, woos Charmy in her stead. The film's plot revolves around Wing Chun's heroism in saving Charmy from the hands of a band of thieves. Wing Chun eventually comes up against the bandits' leader, who makes her fight not for her friend's liberty, but once again for her own autonomy: if she loses, she will have to become his wife. A stunning fight scene ensues, Wing Chun wins almost effortlessly, and the film ends with her marriage to Pok To.

Much of the film's humor (and pleasure) turns on the reversal of expectations about gender. In the opening scene, a wealthy scholar arrives with a plan to marry Wing Chun so that she will protect him from the local bandits (he reasons that hiring her for protection would be too expensive, but if he married her he would only have to feed her!); as the bandits attack, Wing Chun stands behind the scholar and comically manipulates his body so that "he" fights off the villains. In the film's third fight scene Wing Chun's opponent brags that "when it comes to martial arts, men are always better than women" and tells Wing Chun that after he beats her, she should "go home and bear children." Wing Chun doesn't even break a sweat as she trounces him, scoring a decisive victory for women in what the film has already framed as a battle of the sexes. Much of *Wing Chun*'s action depends on the villains' continued expectations that a woman cannot defeat them and on their humiliation when she does. For example, in one scene Wing Chun disables a member of the gang by burning off his "pecker," a move interpreted as the ultimate insult by the gang's leader. Thus the film derives humor from setting up and then undermining conventional sexist expectations of a woman's behavior and ability, and it clearly positions the villains' assumptions about Wing Chun (and women in general) as the "wrong" point of view.

But this comedy of reversal only thinly masks the dark side of Wing Chun's appropriation of the "masculine" skill of fighting. Contrary to the promise of the promotional blurb, Wing Chun is presented as a woman who has traded her "stunning beauty" for her "deadly drop kick." Before learning kung fu, Wing Chun had been the village "Tofu Beauty," but at the start of the narrative she is already an embarrassment to her family because she is unmarriageable: she dresses and acts like a man, and her androgyny makes her the laughingstock of the community. When her friend Charmy puts on Wing Chun's old clothes and becomes the new "Tofu Beauty," Wing Chun shows palpable regret at the loss of her former, feminine self. At the same time, she is philosophically resigned to her fate: the price she had to pay for her autonomy (in refusing to marry a villain) and her fighting skill was her acceptance of the fact that she "would scare other men away as well."

Thus on one level, the film insists on the incompatibility of beauty with skilled martial artistry: until the penultimate scene of the film, Wing Chun is represented as an extremely plain woman. (Yeoh wears no makeup or jewelry and keeps her hair tied back in an unglamorous braid.) It is Charmy who brings men to their knees with her beauty. The film explicitly evokes the erotic power of female beauty: the sight of Charmy turns the male population of the village into fawning idiots and makes Pok To forget all thought of marrying Wing Chun. But this power is, of course, derivative and illusory: Charmy cannot defend herself against the bandits who kidnap her, and it is clear that Wing Chun has the privileged form of power in her kung fu. Yet Charmy can easily obtain with her beauty what Wing Chun believes she can never obtain with her kung fu: Pok To's affection. Consequently, the film opposes beauty (and its associations with "femininity," passive power, dependence, and above all, romantic fulfillment) and martial artistry (with its links to masculinity, active power, autonomy, and loneliness).

On another level, however, the film situates the incompatibility of beauty and martial artistry not in any biological facts but rather in social expectations about gender, and in particular in Wing Chun's own belief that she has irreversibly traversed a gender boundary by devoting herself to mastering her martial arts. Wing Chun refuses to reveal her identity to Pok To because she has internalized the notion that as a powerful woman, she cannot be desirable to men; she believes that what he wants is the "Tofu Beauty" he left behind. When Pok To finally realizes his mistake, however, he is overjoyed to have found "his" Wing Chun, and surprisingly unthreatened by the fact that her kung fu is superior to his (even though he had spent six years training in kung fu in order to be able to protect her!). As a result, the film negates its original dichotomy by confirming Wing Chun's desirability as a love object. But running alongside her yearning to be desired by Pok To is her own sense of her independence and autonomy. Kung fu has given Wing Chun the power to control her own destiny, and it is clear that she cannot go back to being the woman she was before. Wing Chun retreats to her teacher, who obliquely advises her that the time has come for her to synthesize her martial artistry with her femininity and tells her to go and marry. Wing Chun sends for Pok To (it is noteworthy that she asks him to marry her!), and after a night of romance she emerges, transformed into a beauty, to fight the villain one final time. Having enhanced her kung fu with her rediscovered femininity and newly awakened sexuality, Wing Chun easily defeats the villain, and is finally free to marry the man of her choice.

Many feminist critics might object that her marriage recements the heroine into the patriarchal order, or that the film reinforces negative stereotypes about women who don't marry (i.e., spinsterhood). However, in comparison to other films in the genre, *Wing Chun* is unusual in that it reconciles the heroine's appropriation of kung fu with her desire for her childhood sweetheart by allowing her to have both.[16] At the end of the film, she has won the villains' respect (they call her "mom") and regained Pok To: she has not had to compromise her power for love. The film's final moment renders this abundantly clear: as Wing Chun leaps acrobatically onto the horse that she'll ride to her wedding, Pok To whispers to her, "You're a lady, remember?" She smiles in agreement—but the viewer knows that she's much more than that.

Where *Wing Chun* ends with an affirmation of the violent woman and depicts her acceptance and integration into the social order, *Naked Killer* condemns the violent woman as chaotic, dangerous, and subversive. *Naked Killer* features Chingmy Yau as Kitty, a beautiful young woman conscripted into a network of professional female assassins after she kills the man who killed her father. These women assassinate men only, and they are both ingenious and brutal in their methods. The story of the film also involves Tinam, a policeman assigned to the murders who loves Kitty but does not know that she has joined the assassins; and two lesbian assassins, Princess and Baby, who are ordered to kill Kitty and her mentor, Sister Cindy. The film ends with the destruction of all involved: Princess and Baby kill Sister Cindy, Kitty kills Princess and Baby, and finally Kitty and Tinam commit suicide together.

In the world of *Naked Killer* the war between the sexes seems to have reached a new peak. The film's opening ironically establishes and then reverses the expected scene of male victimizer/female victim. A woman runs from an unidentified man, enters an apartment building, opens the door to an apartment, takes off her clothes, and climbs into the shower. Intercut with these scenes are shots of another man with a gun entering the apartment and stalking toward the bathroom. He opens the shower door; she turns with a gasp. He asks, "What are you doing in my house?"—to which she answers, "I love cleaning my body before doing my job." She then whips out a gun and brutally kills him, finishing the job by shooting off his penis. No narrative connection is ever made between the man who pursued her on the street and the man she kills, but this opening scene establishes a theme that is repeatedly invoked in the film: the everyday threat that male sexuality poses for women in general has, in turn, provoked (and justified) female violence against men.

Paradoxically, the film also suggests that female violence is the horrific consequence of male impotence. Tinam, the sympathetic policeman, has been rendered doubly impotent by the trauma of having accidentally killed his brother; he can neither shoot a gun nor achieve an erection. The female violence toward men erupts in the vacuum left by his impotence, and subsides only after he has regained his potency (in both ways) through Kitty, the only woman who can give him an erection. Tinam stands for the pervasive lack of masculine potency in the world of the film: the male police cannot stop the murders, and Princess and Baby hold sway over a small army of men who are completely cowed by their power (at one point one of the men dutifully admits "Yes, I eat shit" at Baby's command). In light of Chiao Hsiung-Ping's observation that many Hong Kong films of the eighties and nineties reflect "the fear of chaos that hovers over the critical juncture of 1997," [17] we can read male impotence in *Naked Killer* as an expression of Hong Kong's anxiety over its imminent reversion to mainland China. The film depicts a world in crisis that has been invaded and emasculated by a seductive and powerful force (the violent women) that it can neither resist nor control—a situation that encapsulates many of the fears dominating the "political unconscious" of Hong Kong in the years before its reversion to the mainland.[18] *Naked Killer* displaces these fears onto the femme fatale and thereby makes the violent woman a stand-in for the fascinating and threatening other that is China.[19]

This allegorical reading aside, the representation of the violent woman in *Naked Killer* is tightly linked to the question of the connections between violence, power, and desire. While all of the women resemble femmes fatales (to borrow Elizabeth Bronfen's definition: "the fascinating but sexually withholding, powerful but lethal woman . . ."),[20] a subtle hierarchy of violence aligns the viewer *with* Kitty and Sister Cindy and *against* the lesbian lovers, Princess and Baby. The rape-revenge theme operates exclusively to justify the violence of Kitty and Cindy, and is wholly absent for Princess and Baby. Kitty and Cindy only kill men in self-defense, and the men they kill have already been framed as "guilty": Kitty first kills the man who killed her father and several of his henchmen, and then later we see her kill a rapist in Cindy's basement. Cindy also defends herself against the henchman and then later kills two rapists in the basement. In addition, the assassinations these two later carry out are cleverly covered with a cinematic trick: the film cuts away to show the "actual" violence being perpetrated on a male mannequin. As a result, we do not perceive Kitty and Cindy as malicious: their violence appears as a justifiable response to the pervasive threat of victimization. At one point Kitty asks Cindy why she is a killer, and Cindy replies, "To make big money. After that, you can control things yourself. You know, [one] who is powerful can give orders." The movie thus equates

Kitty and Cindy's usurpation of power (in the form of killing for money) with revenge for women's powerlessness at the hands of society's male "wolves."

Furthermore, the film represents Kitty as a desirable heterosexual woman whose erotic power is uniquely benign: only she can restore Tinam's potency. Yet when Kitty acts on her love for Tinam, Cindy tells her she must give up being a professional assassin, because her integration into a heterosexual love relationship will render her ineffectual as a killer and block her access to the female killer's power. Unlike Wing Chun, Kitty must trade power for love—however, this is a trade that the film's logic does not allow. For although the film works overtime to turn the violent women into sex objects (in a manner clearly aimed at the heterosexual male viewer), it also establishes violent women and heterosexual sex as mutually incompatible, and as a result, Kitty can never be reintegrated into a restored social order: she chooses death rather than punishment at the hands of the reempowered patriarchy. Thus, unlike *Wing Chun,* which finds a positive resolution to the question of the (ir)reconcilability of female sexuality and violence, *Naked Killer* insists that the link between female eroticism and women's violence poses a danger that can only be contained and controlled by eliminating the violent woman.

The threat Kitty poses as a violent woman is extinguished through her relationship with Tinam: once she has enabled and then submitted to male heterosexual desire, she is realigned with the social order and against the monstrosity of female violence represented by the lesbian lovers. As I noted above, unlike Kitty and Cindy, Princess and Baby have no motivation for their killing other than sexual hatred and a desire to render men impotent. They appear as man-hating and (literally) castrating bitches, whose connection to violence has irrevocably masculinized them (Sister Cindy warns Kitty that Princess might "rape" her, and in fact Princess does arrange to have Cindy raped before she kills her). Perpetuating a solidly established cliché, the film demonizes lesbianism as the ultimate threat to stability and to the proper social order; as women who usurp the male prerogative not only to violence and power but also to sex with women, the lesbians represent female violence at its most negative and pathological. At the same time, the film does not waste the opportunity that lesbian eroticism provides for exploiting female sexuality and the female body for visual and erotic pleasure. This film falls as much into the soft porn category as it does into the kung fu genre: not only do all four of the women wear fetishizing and revealing costumes, but there are also two highly charged scenes of Princess and Baby having sex, and part of the film's plot revolves around Princess's desire for Kitty. But where Kitty's heterosexual eroticism is benign, the erotic love between Princess and Baby appears deviant and dangerous. The first time we see them together they are making love in a pool slowly filling with the blood of Baby's latest male victim. The film thus problematically links transgressive (i.e., nonheterosexual) female sexuality and the expression of autonomous female desire directly with—that is, on the same visual plane as—malicious and sadistic violence against men. In other words, *Naked Killer* exploits a demonization of lesbianism in order to depict a world in which autonomous female desire is equated with violence against men, and which can be righted only by annihilating all traces of transgression of the heterosexual, patriarchal norm. That Tinam must die along with the women at the end of the film further bears this out: the man who depends on a woman for his potency is clearly a weak link in the system.

"Fant-Asia": *Swordsman II, The East Is Red,* and *The Heroic Trio*

The fantasy-action subgenre sets itself apart from other kung fu films by its extreme stylization and its use of special effects to evoke a world of supernatural powers, magical weapons, and mysterious, mystical forces and energies. The majority of these films occur in mythical rather than geographically real space, and thus lend themselves more readily to allegorical interpretations than more "realistic" kung fu films. Many of these films are remarkable in the way they redefine gender expectations and embrace a definition of gender as fluid and unfixed. In this section I look at three films—*Swordsman II* (1992), its sequel *The East Is Red* (1993), which for the purposes of analysis I will treat as a series, and *The Heroic Trio* (1992). I think these films point to some interesting ways the violent woman is positioned in the fantasy-action subgenre.

Swordsman II and *The East Is Red* draw their tension and mystery from the rise to power of a central figure, Asia, whose ambiguous gender is the key to his/her power. Although the films locate the action in "Ming China," the plot unfolds within the symbolic space of the "Martial Arts World," which is defined at the beginning of *The East Is Red* as a world existing alongside of and parallel to the real, historical world. The Martial Arts World is "a symbolic space which is used to portray political struggle in the human world,"[21] and in which allegiance to martial arts forms is substituted for national identity in factional and political conflicts over power. The plot of the series centers on the struggle for possession of the Sacred Scroll, which promises access to the most powerful form of kung fu.

In *Swordsman II*, Asia, played by the actress Brigitte Lin Ching Hsia, has taken possession of the scroll and used it to become "invincible." Ironically, the secret encoded in the Sacred Scroll is that mastery of its skills involves castration: Asia must render himself sexually impotent in order to become physically and politically potent. Furthermore, his castration has the magical effect of transforming him into a woman. Thus the figurative political meaning of emasculation (as weakness or debilitation) is parodically undermined by his access to power through "infemination" (my coinage). "His" transformation into a woman gives "him" a supernatural ability to defeat the enemy. The film thereby makes a move to gender violence and power female, and represents the violent woman as a transformed man. But Asia is not completely a woman. The price s/he pays for power is a total loss of sexual identity: Asia is not only impotent as a man, but also as a woman. S/he is in love with the swordsman Ling, but is physically incapable of consummating that love, and in the end s/he is defeated by "her" all too human passion for Ling and doomed to forgo power and exist on the margins of the Martial Arts World as myth. The violent woman is, in the end, a noncreature who is both man and woman—and neither.[22]

Director Tsui Hark's man-woman Asia does not emerge as an unequivocally monstrous figure, but rather as a sad and conflicted reflection of an ambiguously amoral world.[23] The complete dismantling of the easy dichotomy between man/woman and power/powerlessness in the figure of Asia is mirrored in the series' chaotic and recurrent realignment of the forces of good and evil. The two films cynically insist on the meaninglessness and evil of the urge to power, and refuse to buy into the conventional split between good and evil. The disturbing ending of *Swordsman II*—in which, after defeating Asia, the ostensibly "good" Master Wu begins to purge his troops of "traitors"—points to a parodic and subversive critique of the flow of history as an endless repetition of the same corrupt drive for power. In this way, as Leo Ou-Fan Lee notes in relation to a different Hark film, the series may reflect the cynicism with which Hong Kong residents see their history and their future: Asia's ambiguous and fluid gender and the ultimate futility of her power in both the personal and political sphere can be read as a trope for the ambivalent political situation in geographic Asia.[24] Toward the end of *Swordsman II*, Asia leaps off a cliff to avoid having to kill Ling, the man s/he loves. While it may be true that "[l]ike those in the colony swept up by the Tiananmen Square effect, a manic condition that had people looking for any exit, Asia's suicide symbolizes her desire to get out no matter what the price,"[25] the fact that Asia is driven to this "escape" by seemingly contradictory desires (for both a traditionally "masculine" power to rule through force and a traditionally "feminine" power derived from sexual attractiveness), coupled with the fact that s/he doesn't actually die from the fall, suggests Hong Kong's conflicted attitude toward its future status in the region. The figure of Asia thus operates as a metaphor for Hong Kong's strangely bi-"gendered" status as both (masculinized) financial powerhouse and (feminized) object of desire for China, and Asia's survival to fight on in *The East Is Red* may offer a hopeful prognosis for the former colony's future.[26]

In contrast to the asexualized nature of the violent woman in *Swordsman II* and *The East Is Red*, *Heroic Trio* presents a comic book version of ultrasexy and ultrafeminine superheroines. *Heroic Trio* pits its three heroines (played by Anita Mui, Michelle Yeoh, and Maggie Cheung) against an ultrapowerful Eunuch who has been kidnapping babies in a nefarious plot to find the next Emperor of the Underworld. The women all possess supernatural powers: Mui plays a masked Wonder Woman who can walk across power lines; Yeoh is Invisible Girl; and Cheung, the gun-toting Thief Catcher, can ride her motorcycle through the air. The plot is rather formulaic and predictable. Yeoh's Invisible Girl lives in servitude to the evil Eunuch and helps him steal the babies: she has a change of heart when confronted by the two other women and joins them to defeat the villain. In its depiction of violent women as heroines the film cleaves tightly to the conventions of the kung fu genre, showing them as righteous and powerful defenders of right against wrong and good against evil. What makes this film interesting is the lengths to which it goes to mitigate and neutralize the threat of female power by framing the women as sex objects and by putting their vulnerability (as women) on display.

In an on-line article for *Boxoffice Magazine* entitled "Those Wild Women of Fant-Asia," Craig Reed observes that "[i]n Hong Kong's male-dominated society, where women are considered to be submissive, meal-preparing, childbearing sexual objects, Fant-Asia film ironically depicts the female as fearless, overbearing, and unpredictable" and comments that the violent women of this genre are "coyly" portrayed "with just enough vulnerability so that they don't threaten the very fabric of their chauvinistic Chinese society."[27] *Heroic Trio* bears out the truth of this observation in many ways. The three women wear supertight, low-cut bodysuits and minidresses that fetishize their bodies in a blatant overdetermination of their femininity. The focus on the women as sex objects is reflected not only in their costumes, but also in the way the film is marketed. The promotional trailer confidently proclaims them "the world's most beautiful crimefighters" and emphasizes the actresses' circulation as objects of desire outside the world of the film, announcing the stars as "Anita Mui, the Madonna of Asia; Michelle Yeoh, Asia's top action actress; and Maggie Cheung, former Miss Hong Kong." Clearly, the film producers recognize that the combination of beautiful, sexy women and thrilling action sells tickets, particularly to young male viewers who are the primary consumers of the genre. But the hypersexualization of the heroines serves a double and somewhat contradictory function. On the one hand, it mutes the impact of their display of violence by reminding the viewer of their (primary) status as sex objects. The threat posed by the active, violent woman is thus contained by her confinement as a passive object of spectators' desire. On the other hand, it also provides a gratifying and satisfying image of the powerful woman as erotic *and* heroic, in stark contrast to the convention of the "Dragon Lady"/femme fatale. Whereas in *Naked Killer* female eroticism is posited as the site of origin of a threatening, subversive, and chaotic eruption of female power, *Heroic Trio* oscillates between a patronizing objectification of the female body and a breathless celebration of its power, without settling at one pole or the other. But the focus on the body as a *female* body—as a body in ostentatious display of breasts, legs, and buttocks—does mitigate the threat the women pose to "the very fabric of . . . society" by reassuring the (male) viewer of his privileged position as the possessor of the objectifying gaze.

Furthermore, the film goes overboard to show the women as vulnerable and weak despite their superhuman abilities, and it specifically links their vulnerability to their gender. For example, both Wonder Woman and Thief Catcher are shown to have a "natural" maternal instinct toward the babies: Wonder Woman lets a few surreptitious tears fall when the baby she has tried to rescue dies in her arms, and Thief Catcher automatically reaches out to catch a doll she thinks is a baby. In addition, the three women are shown to be physically vulnerable in ways that code them as conventionally feminine: for example, after the Eunuch has knocked Thief Catcher and Wonder Woman to the ground in the final fight scene, Thief Catcher touches her beautiful face in panic and asks, "Is it okay?"

Moreover, in contrast to the classic moment in the kung fu film when the hero tastes his own blood and is spurred on to greater acts of vengeance and violence, the women in *Heroic Trio* need a moment of recovery time when their blood is drawn. Because these displays of vulnerability are grounded in expectations of "feminine" behavior, they do more than merely humanize the superheroines— they establish and reconfirm the reassuring and inescapable "fact" of their womanhood.

The emphasis on the women's beauty and sexuality and the attention paid to their vulnerability may distract from the power they put on display, but it cannot negate it. All in all, *Heroic Trio* is a spectacular confirmation of female resourcefulness, intelligence, skill, and power, and the image of the violent woman it conveys is overwhelmingly a positive one. Indeed, the focus on the heroines' femininity does not only (or even necessarily or primarily) serve a derogatory function; it also renders them sympathetic and adds depth to their characters.

FIGURE 5. Thief Catcher (Maggie Cheung) strolls away from the havoc she has helped create in *Heroic Trio*.

Moreover, in the end the film seems fully aware of its own construction and perpetuation of traditional codes of the feminine, and it winks complicitly at its own dependence on and manipulation of those codes. In a gesture that is clearly meant as an ironic comment on what a woman "should be," the film closes with a cozy domestic scene of Wonder Woman sitting in her pajamas on the couch with her husband, watching a television broadcast describing her courageous exploits in saving the babies—and knitting a little white sweater.

Female Sidekicks

In this final section I look at an array of films in which violent women play secondary roles to male heroes. When a male hero carries the action, the violent woman tends to appear in a different light. She is often presented as a less capable fighter than the hero, and she will usually depend on the hero's help (rather than the other way around). In addition, unlike the films discussed so far, which present women's fighting skills as a given, the male hero–centered film will often frame the fighting woman as at least slightly unusual, if not as an outright surprise. Most importantly, however, the *context* in which the female sidekick appears affects how we "read" her violent behavior, because she is often the only female fighter in a film world populated by more conventionally "feminine" women. Instead of focusing in detail on just two or three films as I did in the previous sections, in this final discussion I will briefly touch on a number of films to show the different and often contradictory ways in which female violence is contextualized in male hero films.

First, it must be emphasized that the vast majority of kung fu films that feature men do not give women fighting roles. The recently rereleased *Operation Condor* (aka *Armour of God 2*), starring Jackie Chan, provides a good example: the three beautiful women who accompany Chan through the desert are not only completely incapable of defending themselves, but also an (inadvertent) menace both to him and to each other. Silly and stupid, they spend most of the film screaming, crying for help from Chan, and bickering poutily with one another. Although not all kung fu films condemn women so unequivocally, the brainless, bumbling beauty remains a conventional role (especially in many Chan films). Another typical role filled by women is that of the victim who needs to be rescued: in *Wheels on Meals* (1984; also a Chan film), Lola Forna plays a beautiful Spanish girl who must be rescued by Chan and his friends from an evil aristocrat. Forna enjoys one brief moment of competent self-defense; otherwise she is a classically helpless victim. In films in which women appear as fighting sidekicks, such conventional definitions of femininity in terms of weakness and helplessness are often embodied by the hero's love interest. As a result, the female sidekick appears within a narrative context that insists that strength, skill, and intelligence are not as desirable in a woman as beauty, a good body, and a lack of brains.

In *Supercop* (aka *Police Story III*, 1992), for example, Michelle Yeoh plays a mainland Chinese police officer who supervises and teams up with Jackie Chan to bust a drug ring. Although she does everything but steal the film from Chan with her fierce martial artistry and acrobatic stunts, she is framed within the narrative as serious and unsensuous. Chan's girlfriend (Maggie Cheung), on the other hand, is the all too familiar dimwit who inadvertently endangers the undercover police by blabbing about the operation to her girlfriend in an elevator. By splitting the functions of heroine and love interest, the film seems to reinforce the idea that helplessness and dependence are attractive qualities in a woman. Yet it also contradicts this message by simultaneously putting Yeoh's alternative form of female behavior on display as attractive. This doubleness can and should be read as a subtle form of self-mockery—while on the one hand the film takes quite seriously its own investment in the gender stereotypes that keep the genre ticking, on the other, it also knowingly and self-consciously parodies those expectations by juxtaposing them with clashing images.

Because the kung fu–comedy genre often derives a great deal of its humor from exploiting, manipulating, and mocking gender expectations from both sides of the gender divide, its use of conventional images of femininity can often lead to doubled and even tripled readings. For example, Chan's choice of a brainless beauty over the smart and confident cop is as much a comic reflection on mystified masculine desire as it is a serious comment on female attractiveness. In this film, as in many others, Chan parodies the erotic power beauty holds over men, playing a man whose infatuation with physical beauty has clearly blinded him to his lover's lack of intellect, personality, charm, and so on. Thus, rather than categorically condemning the images of women that conform to misogynist stereotypes, we should bear in mind the element of self-parody that is central to the genre. Frequently the buxom babe is already an exaggerated, self-conscious spoof of masculine fantasies about female sexuality (which are then often undermined by the woman's sudden display of extraordinary martial artistry). For example, in *City Hunter* (1993) Chan plays the comic book action hero Ryu Saeba in a filmed version of a Japanese cartoon character. This film features Chingmy Yau as a sexy and lethal antiterrorist operative. The first time Yau is introduced in the film, she and her big-busted friend are shown walking past Chan, who does a comic double take to focus attention on their fetishistically costumed bodies. By setting Yau up as a sex object first and foremost—and by thus intimating that she is another brainless beauty—the film achieves a healthy comic payoff when she reveals her ability to fight. But the film not only gives a satisfying reversal of expectations; it also provides a parody of the hypersexualized female body in the form of the busty friend. The extreme size of her breasts is a running joke in the film, culminating in the moment when her attempts to shoot a gun fail because the weight of the gun in front of her bosom pulls her off balance. That this is a parody, however, does not negate the fact that the film displays a conspicuously adolescent fascination with the fetishized female body. In other words, *City Hunter* is a good example of a film that presents and exploits the female body as sex object while simultaneously mocking that move, framing the woman-as-sex-object as an impossible joke, a ridiculous projection of masculine fantasy. That this film—and the genre as a whole—is in continual oscillation between representations of female power and stereotypes/parodies of femininity suggests an ambiguous attitude toward female sexuality, female desirability, and female power.

Finally, there is another manifestation of the female sidekick that frames female violence in a very different manner. In a number of films (particularly comedies) the hero's sidekick is his mother, and she is often as good a martial artist as her son (if not better). These films usually portray some version of the following family dynamic: a tyrannical father who beats his son and/or wife but who is not trained in the martial arts; a loving, supportive, and sympathetic mother who is a powerful martial artist and who is called on to use her fighting skills on behalf of her immature son and/or husband; and finally the mischievous son whose journey through the film involves maturing into independence through the mastery of his martial arts. What is most interesting about these films is the way they play with this family dynamic, representing the mother as a self-conscious performer of the role of submissive wife despite the fact that she holds much of the real power in the family. For example, in *Fong Sai Yuk* (1993) Josephine Siao plays the mother of the eponymous hero (portrayed by Jet Li). Although she obediently submits to her husband's authority and "allows" him to beat her in punishment, he is totally dependent on her and his son when his life is threatened. Twice during the film the mother and son fight side by side to save the father's life. By giving the mother greater physical power than the father, such a film calls into question the "natural" basis for patriarchal power, and hints that women need merely pay lip service to masculine authority. There is a similar dynamic in *Drunken Master II* (1994), in which Anita Mui plays mother to the Jackie Chan hero. Both films call attention to the real authority of the mother and her efforts simultaneously to undermine and uphold the appearance of the father's authority. The mother as sidekick is a curious phenomenon from a Western point of view (imagine a Hollywood action film that teamed together, for example, Bruce Willis with his character's mother), but in the Hong Kong kung fu comedy it comes across clearly as a satiric reflection on the power dynamic in the Chinese family, in which mothers traditionally hold a great deal of power within a larger social structure that puts nominal authority in the hands of men.

But what is crucial about the representation of the violent woman in the form of the mother is the way that it disconnects female violence from sexuality and places it in the realm of a quasimaternal instinct. The hero's love interest in these films virtually never fights, and so once again we have a split between female violence and desirability. In light of this split, the representation of the sidekick mother in *Fong Sai Yuk* becomes even more interesting: when at one point she cross-dresses as a young man in order to finish off a fight her son has deliberately lost, she becomes the object of another woman's desire. Thus the film displaces the question of whether or not the powerful woman can be the object of desire—the question with which I opened this article in my discussion of *Wing Chun*—by recasting the roles of "desirer" and "desiree." In other words, *Fong Sai Yuk* may come closest to the truth by depicting the powerful, violent, kung fu woman as attractive indeed—but only to another woman.

Kung fu films offer mixed messages about women, power, and sexuality. Although it is refreshing, exciting, and empowering to see the women of the Hong Kong martial arts films kick and flip their way in and out of danger, subduing huge evil thugs at every turn, we should also recognize and critique the extent to which the genre continues to perpetuate images of women as passive, as victims, and as sex objects. For as long as both "beauty" and the "drop kick" sell tickets, the kung fu film will put them on the screen together, in ways that provide both positive and negative images of powerful women.

Hong Kong Kung Fu Films Featuring Women: A Select List, with Actresses Featured

Ah Kam, written by John Chan, directed by Ann Hui, featuring Michelle Yeoh (1996).

Angel 2, written by Teresa Woo, directed by Teresa Woo and Raymond Leung, featuring Moon Lee and Elaine Lui (1988).

Blonde Fury, written by Sam Chi-Leung, directed by Mang Hoi, featuring Cynthia Rothrock (1987).

The Bride with White Hair, written by Ronnie Yu, directed by Ronnie Yu, featuring Brigitte Lin (1993).

Broken Oath, directed by Chang Cheung Wo, featuring Angela Mao (1977).

Butterfly and Sword, written by Chong Ching; directed by Michael Mak and Ching Siu Tung; featuring Michelle Yeoh, Joey Wang, and Brigitte Lin (1993).

China O'Brien, written by Sandra Weintraub and Robert Clouse, directed by Robert Clouse, featuring Cynthia Rothrock (1988).

A Chinese Ghost Story, written by Kai-Chi Yun, directed by Ching Siu Tung, featuring Joey Wong (1987).

City Cops, written by Barry Wong, directed by Lau Ka Wing, produced by Joe Siu, featuring Cynthia Rothrock (1988).

City Hunter, directed by Wong Jing and Ching Siu Tung, featuring Chingmy Yau and Joey Wong (1992).

Come Drink with Me, written by Ye Yang, directed by King Hu, featuring Cheng Pei Pei (1965).

Dragon Inn, written by Cheung Tan, directed by Raymond Lee and Ching Siu Tung, featuring Brigitte Lin and Maggie Cheung (1992).

Drunken Master II, written by King-Sang Tseng and Kai-Chi Yun, directed by Lau Kar Leung and Jackie Chan, featuring Anita Mui (1994).

Executioners (aka *Heroic Trio 2*), written by Susanne Chan; directed by Johnny To and Ching Siu Tung; featuring Maggie Cheung, Michelle Yeoh, and Anita Mui (1993).

Fong Sai Yuk, written by Jeff Lau, John Chan, and Tsui Kong; directed by Corey Yuen; featuring Josephine Siao and Sibelle Hu (1993).

The Heroic Trio, written by Sandy Shaw, directed by Johnny To and Ching Siu Tung, featuring Maggie Cheung, Michelle Yeoh, and Anita Mui (1992).

The Inspector Wears Skirts, written by Cheng Kam Fu, directed by Wellson Chin, featuring Cynthia Rothrock and Sibelle Hu (1984).

In the Line of Duty 1: Royal Warriors, written by Sammy Tsang, directed by David Chung, featuring Michelle Yeoh (1986).

In the Line of Duty 2–7: Writers/directors vary, series features Cynthia Khan.

Magnificent Warriors, written by Tsang Kan Cheong, directed by David Chung, featuring Michelle Yeoh (1987).

Midnight Angel (aka *Angel/Iron Angels*), written by Teresa Woo; directed by Raymond Leung, Tony Leung, and Ivan Lai; featuring Moon Lee, Yukari Oshima, and Elaine Lui (1987).

Miracles: The Canton Godfather, directed by Jackie Chan, produced by Leonard Ho, featuring Anita Mui (1989).

Moon Warriors, directed by Sammo Hung and Ching Siu Tung, featuring Maggie Cheung and Anita Mui (1993).

My Young Auntie, written and directed by Chia-Liang Liu, featuring Kara Hui Ying Hung (1981).

Naked Killer, written by Wong Jing, directed by Clarence Ford; featuring Chingmy Yau, Carrie Ng, and Svenwara Madoka (1992).

New Legend of Shaolin, written by Wong Jing, directed by Wong Jing and Corey Yuen, featuring Chingmy Yau (1994).

Outlaw Brothers, written by Frankie Chan, directed by Frankie Chan, featuring Yukari Oshima (1988).

Police Story, written by Jackie Chan and Edward Tang, directed by Jackie Chan, featuring Maggie Cheung and Brigitte Lin (1985).

Police Story III: Supercop, written by Edward Tang, Fibe Ma, and Lee Wai Yee; directed by Stanley Tong, featuring Michelle Yeoh and Maggie Cheung (1992/1996).

Project S (aka *Supercop 2*), written by Stanley Tong and Shiu Lai King, directed by Stanley Tong, featuring Michelle Yeoh (1993/1999).

Raging Thunder, written by Maria Elena Cellion, Roy Horan, and Keith Strandberg; directed by Corey Yuen; featuring Cynthia Rothrock (1989).

Righting Wrongs, directed by Corey Yuen, featuring Cynthia Rothrock (1986).

Shanghai Express, written and directed by Sammo Hung, featuring Cynthia Rothrock and Yukari Oshima (1986).

She Shoots Straight, directed by Corey Yuen, featuring Joyce Godenzi (1990).

Swordsman II, written by Tsui Hark, Hanson Chan, and Tang Pik-Yin; directed by Ching Siu-Tung and Stanley Tong; featuring Brigitte Lin (1992).

Swordsman III: The East Is Red, written by Tsui Hark, Hanson Chan, and Tang Pik-Yin; directed by Ching Siu Tung and Raymond Lee; featuring Brigitte Lin and Joey Wong (1993).

Tai Chi Master, written by Kim Ip, directed by Yuen Woo Ping, featuring Michelle Yeoh (1993).

Wing Chun, written by Anthony Wong and Elsa Tang, directed by Yuen Woo Ping, featuring Michelle Yeoh (1994).

Yes, Madam, written by Barry Wong, directed by Corey Yuen, featuring Michelle Yeoh and Cynthia Rothrock (1985).

Notes

1. Yeoh has also been known and billed as Michelle Khan. The roster of Hong Kong actors is a notorious confusion of names, because many actors go by different names in different markets (or adopt a "more marketable"—i.e., anglicized—name when they become better known). In all cases, I give the name by which actors would be most familiar to a U.S. audience, and give alternatives in the notes where appropriate.

2. I draw this particular formulation from Elizabeth Bronfen, "The Jew as Woman's Symptom: Kathryn Bigelow's Conflictive Representation of Feminine Power," in *Violence and Mediation in Contemporary Culture,* ed. Ronald Bogue and Marcel Cornis-Pope (New York: State University of New York Press, 1996), 73. Bronfen's investigation of a conflicted representation of violence and female desire in Kathryn Bigelow's film *Blue Steel* raises similar issues to the ones I investigate here, although she takes a very different theoretical approach.

3. Bey Logan, *Hong Kong Action Cinema* (Woodstock, N.Y.: Overlook Press, 1995), 149.

4. By "readily available" I mean obtainable at a video store in a relatively large urban market. Many of the films I viewed were quite difficult to track down. As a result, I have tried to focus the bulk of my analysis on those that were easiest to find.

5. E. Ann Kaplan, "Problematizing Cross-Cultural Analysis: The Case of Women in the Recent Chinese Cinema," *Wide Angle* 11, no. 2 (1993): 42.

6. Ibid.

7. Chris Berry, "China's New 'Women's Cinema,'" *Camera Obscura: A Journal of Feminism and Film Theory* 18 (1988): 9.

8. I paraphrase Kaplan here, who writes that Chinese scholars often complain when reading Western scholarship: "This is not the *Chinese* way of thinking" ("Problematizing Cross-Cultural Analysis," 41).

9. Stuart Kaminsky makes a similar observation and argues that the kung fu film fulfills a function for a ghetto audience analogous to the function of the musical for the white middle-class audience. See Stuart M. Kaminsky, "Kung Fu Film as Ghetto Myth," in *Movies as Artifacts,* ed. Michael T. Marsden, John G. Nachbar, and Sam L. Grogg Jr. (Chicago: Nelson-Hall, 1982), 137–45.

10. Tony Rayns, "Director: King Hu," *Sight and Sound* 45, no. 1 (winter 1975–76): 11.

11. Lisa Odham Stokes and Michael Hoover note the difference between violence in a typical Jackie Chan kung fu film and a Stephen Seagal Hollywood action film: "While the characters in a Chan fight rarely suffer serious injuries (in fact, there is often an absence of any blood), the physical punishment in a Seagal picture is graphically depicted and death is not an uncommon result. The latter's 'reel' fights are staged and shot to look and feel like 'real' fights, generally incorporating only a few moves into the filmed sequences. Jackie Chan's fight scenes, on the other hand, may integrate between twenty and thirty individual motions into a scene." See *City on Fire: Hong Kong Cinema* (New York: Verso, 1999), 122.

12. I advance that last generalization with some trepidation, because there are enough exceptional scenes of sadism, torture, and cruelty in any random sampling of kung fu films to render it untrue; my point is, however, that on the whole, the kung fu film frames violence in a way that is qualitatively very different from a film like Scorsese's *Casino,* which aims at a hypersensitive depiction of violence.

13. Logan, *Hong Kong Action Cinema,* 19, 96.

14. Cf. Stokes and Hoover, *City on Fire,* 90, 105.

15. Yukari Oshima has also been given the stage name "Cynthia Luster" (!).

16. In addition, the fact that the narrative centers exclusively on a woman and deals with a woman's dilemma is in itself significant; Yeoh claims that her work on films like *Wing Chun* has "opened the door for many other actresses to do action in Hong Kong." Stokes and Hoover, *City on Fire,* 106–7.

17. Chiao Hsiung-Ping, "The Distinct Taiwanese and Hong Kong Cinemas," in *Perspectives on Chinese Cinema,* ed. Chris Berry (London: British Film Institute, 1991), 161.

18. Leo Ou-Fan Lee notes that "the talent of Hong Kong's 'postmodern' filmmakers lies perhaps in their seemingly effortless probing and public representation (in the form of a commercial product) of the collective 'political unconscious' of the average Hong Kong resident and filmgoer." "Two Films from Hong Kong: Parody and Allegory," in *New Chinese Cinemas: Forms, Identities, Politics,* ed. Nick Browne, Paul Pickowicz, Vivian Sobchack, and Esther Yau (Cambridge: Cambridge University Press, 1994), 213.

19. For another reading of how the representation of masculinity in Hong Kong action films is tied to anxieties about reversion, see Julian Stringer, "'Your Tender Smiles Give Me Strength': Paradigms of Masculinity in John Woo's *A Better Tomorrow* and *The Killer,*" *Screen* 38, no. 1 (spring 1997): 25–41. Stokes and Hoover's *City on Fire* also contextualizes the Hong Kong film industry in terms of 1997.

20. Elizabeth Bronfen, "The Jew as Woman's Symptom: Kathryn Bigelow's Conflictive Representation of Feminine Power," in *Violence and Mediation in Contemporary Culture,* ed. Ronald Bogue and Marcel Cornis-Pope (New York: State University of New York Press, 1996), 92.

21. Natalie Chan Sui Hung, "The Transformation of Gender in *The Swordsman II* and *The East Is Red*" (Department of Literature, University of California, San Diego, 1995), 1.

22. Stephen Teo notes that the character of Asia is "a new type of hero/heroine, a gender-bending character so malleable that he or she bends not only genders, but all character types: Asia is a villainess, a romantic protagonist, and ultimately a character who wins the sympathy of the hero—and the audience." See *Hong Kong Cinema: The Extra Dimensions* (London: British Film Institute, 1997), 201. Teo links Hark's "gender-bending" to a trend toward "postmodernism" in Hong Kong films that propose "that ancient China had more liberal views toward sexuality" and suggest "that values or attitudes to be achieved in fact stem from somewhere in the very distant past" (251).

23. Stokes and Hoover read the figure of Asia somewhat differently than I do, attributing to her qualities of the "monstrous feminine" (*City on Fire*, 104–7). Rolanda Chu also sees Asia as representative of the "monster," but locates this as a source of pleasure and entertainment for the viewer: "If the utopian prospect is of a vision at least momentarily of the fluidity of gender options, then the most radical dynamic of pleasure put forth in *Swordsman II* is the prospect of loving the monster: the taboo of embracing the abject." "*Swordsman II* and *The East Is Red*: The 'Hong Kong Film,' Entertainment, and Gender," *Bright Lights* 13 (summer 1994): 35.

24. Lee, "Two Films from Hong Kong," 211.

25. Stokes and Hoover, *City on Fire*, 105.

26. Teo also comments on these films in terms of Hong Kong's identity in relation to China (*Hong Kong Cinema*, 250–51).

27. Craig Reed, "Those Wild Women of Fant-Asia," *Boxoffice Magazine* (Special Report, 25 March 1997), on-line: <http://www.boxoff.com/sneak2bfeb.html>.

If Looks Could Kill

Power, Revenge, and Stripper Movies

Jeffrey A. Brown

There is an ancient legend of the infamous "Dance of Desire" performed by Ishtar, the Sumerian goddess of love, sex, and war. As a reward for successful battles and generous patronage at her temples (where sacred cult prostitution was practiced), Ishtar would, on exceptionally great occasions, take human form as the most beautiful young woman in all the lands. In this guise she would perform her dance of desire for a select audience of sacred kings and the most powerful warriors. Accompanied by music only ever heard before by the gods, Ishtar would twirl and float with such grace that each man believed she was dancing only for him. The audience was held in a trance as her performance progressed and she shed more and more of her outer garments until, finally, she danced naked before them, a wonder to behold. Ishtar's dance was said to be so mesmerizing that after seeing it no man would ever desire to see anything else. Indeed, it *was* the last sight they would ever have since all of the men were so overcome by passion and lust that they died a blissful death humbled at the feet of pure pleasure.

Perhaps not surprisingly, by 1993 the fabled Ishtar would appear in a literary award–winning graphic novel, Neil Gaiman's *Sandman: Brief Lives*,[1] as a stripper. It was bound to happen sooner or later. The legend of Ishtar's dance of desire, loaded as it is with issues of erotic performance, scopophilia, fetishism, and ultimately death, is a perfect metaphor for the dynamics of modern striptease. Or rather, I should say it is the perfect metaphor for the dynamics of modern striptease as it is portrayed in contemporary films. From *The Blue Angel* (1930) to *Striptease* (1996) the filmic presentation of strippers has always been a particularly rich point for analyzing the role of the cinematic gaze in relation to gender and issues of power.

In this chapter I consider striptease as a symbolic act of gender and power negotiation that is played out as a very clear formula in a spate of recent stripper movies. Moreover, since the story of these films is very close to the rape-revenge formula set out by such scholars as Carol Clover and Peter Lehman,[2] I hope to show how the shift in the films' focus from horror to eroticism allows a different reading of gender and empowerment. In this reading, the avenging women are not reduced to the symbolic position of proxies for the male viewers, as mere "men in drag." Finally, I want to touch on the discrepancy between negotiations of power on the screen and negotiations of power in real life.

More than any other narrative subject stripper movies—or, as the French have dubbed them, "le cinema du strip"—lay bare the most traditional relationship of the sexes, and perhaps the most discussed dynamic in cinema studies: Men watch and do, women are watched and done to. Strippers, on film as in real life, are a quintessential example of Mulvey's famous concept of feminine value as "to-be-looked-at-ness."[3] "In their traditionally exhibitionist role," writes Mulvey, "women are simultaneously looked at and displayed, with their appearance coded for strong visual and erotic impact so that they can be said to connote *to-be-looked-at-ness.*"[4] Mulvey goes on to point out:

[T]he woman displayed has functioned on two levels: as erotic object for the characters within the story, and as erotic object for the spectator within the auditorium, with a shifting tension between the looks on either side of the screen. For instance, the device of the showgirl [or even more obviously, the stripper] allows the two looks to be unified technically without any apparent break in the diegesis.[5]

According to Mulvey, and the legions of critics who have subsequently built upon her groundbreaking work, women's role as the object of the cinematic gaze is tied up with a complex range of patriarchal motivations and disempowering film conventions.

What interests me here, though, is the character of the stripper. Though she is the ultimate object of a sadistic male gaze, her to-be-looked-at-ness is used as a way to advance the plot while simultaneously stopping the narrative. These films confound the traditional logic of voyeurism both within the narrative and for the male viewer in the real audience. In other words, the power of the masculine gaze is renegotiated in stripper movies to reveal the underlying control exercised by the object of the gaze. The fetishistic sadism of the look is exposed as ultimately masochistic.

Though enjoying more than its fair share of screen time in the 1990s, this concept of true power residing with the object of the gaze, which is almost always a woman, is not a new idea. It is at least as old as the legend of Ishtar's dance of desire. It is an archetypal myth, a morality tale warning about the deadly consequences of being entranced by desire. Long before straight-to-video thrillers cornered the market on seductive killer babes, the deadly dancer was a staple of literature and legend. Lilith, Judith, Circe, the Sirens, the Fates, Medusa, Cleopatra, Delilah, Mata Hari, Lolita—the list is lengthy and constitutes a "who's who" of castration anxiety. Consider, for example, the likes of Oscar Wilde's play *Salome* (1893), based on the legend of King Herod's sexually alluring stepdaughter who so captivated him that he offered to give her anything she wanted if only she would dance for him. Salome performs a striptease, the dance of the seven veils, but in turn she demands the head of John the Baptist delivered to her on a platter. Herod, though he loathes the task and knows it will prove his undoing, delivers up John's head to Salome.

Another classic example of the archetype is Victor Hugo's portrayal of Esmerelda, the gypsy dancing girl whose beauty throws an entire city into turmoil in *The Hunchback of Notre Dame* (1831). Hugo's famous description of Gringoire's first vision of Esmerelda is revealing:

In a wide space left clear between the crowd and the fire, a young girl was dancing.

But was it a young girl, or a fairy, or an angel? Gringoire, skeptical philosopher and ironical poet that he was, could not at first decide, so deeply was he fascinated by this dazzling vision.

She was not tall, but her slender lightsomeness made her appear so. Her complexion was dark, but one guessed that by daylight it would have been the beautiful golden tint of Andalusian and Roman women. Her small feet, too, were Andalusian, for they seemed at once tight yet comfortable in her dainty shoes. She pirouetted on an old Persian carpet, spread carelessly under her feet. Each time she twirled, her radiant face and her large black eyes seemed to glow for you alone. In the circle all mouths were agape and all eyes staring.

She danced to a Basque tambourine which she tinkled above her head, thus

displaying her lovely arms. She wore a golden bodice tightly laced about her delicate body, exposing her beautiful shoulders. Below her wasp waist billowed a multicolored skirt, which, in the whirling dance, gave momentary glimpses of her finely shaped legs. With all this, and her black hair and sparkling eyes, she seemed like something more than human.

"In truth," thought Gringoire, "it is a salamander—a nymph—a goddess—a bacchante of Mount Maenalus!"

At that moment one of the braids of this "salamander's" hair loosened, and a thong of yellow leather that had bound it fell to the ground.

"Oh no!" said he. "It's a gypsy!" All the illusion faded.

Hugo's description is doubly revealing because not only does it entail the mesmerization of the exotic dance that will drive men to fatal feats of passion, but it also demonstrates the falsity of the goddess illusion so willingly embraced by male viewers. Contemporary stripper movies give new life to all of these almost mythic themes—exoticism, seductive dances, worship, an underlying disappointment, and the male viewer's downfall or death. Their reemergence facilitates a different understanding of gender and power in a contemporary context.

"Lady, you got balls."
"Yeah, but it's a bitch keeping them hidden on stage."
—from *Dance with Death* (1993)

Strong female characters have gained tremendous ground in popular culture, whether in Hollywood action films like *Aliens* (1986) and *Terminator 2: Judgment Day* (1991), or foreign films such as France's *La Femme Nikita* (1991), India's *Pratighat/Retribution* (1988), or Hong Kong's numerous films like *The Heroic Trio* (1992) and *Robotrix* (1993). On television *Xena: Warrior Princess* has become the highest-rated program in the world. Likewise, the MTV cartoon *Aeon Flux,* about a futuristic female mercenary with dominatrix leanings, has developed a huge cult following, as has *Tomb Raider,* a computer game starring a scantily clad female Indiana Jones–type.

As a subset of this strong-woman theme, the stripper movies I will be talking about here fall into the category of avenging women. And, like the rape-revenge films discussed by Clover and Lehman, the stripper movies are almost exclusively the domain of the lower genres, namely straight-to-video thrillers and pornography. Even the big-budget versions *Striptease* and *Showgirls* (1995) seem like nothing more than expensive—and laughable—versions of their top-shelf predecessors including *Stripteaser* (1995), *Stripped to Kill* (1987) and *Stripped to Kill II* (1989), *Midnight Tease* (1994) and *Midnight Tease II* (1995), *Dance with Death* (1993), *Sunset Strip* (1993), *Angel of Destruction* (1993), *Lapdancer* (1996), *Lap Dancing* (1995), *Cover Me* (1996), *Blonde Justice* (1994), and *Blonde Justice 2* (1995).

Like the rape-revenge genre, stripper films are most closely identified with low-budget straight-to-video thrillers, but have on occasion appeared in every form from megabudget Hollywood productions to XXX-rated pornographic videos. The rape-revenge formula has been played out in mainstream movies such as Clint Eastwood's *Sudden Impact* (1983) and the Academy Award–winning *The Accused* (1988). Likewise, stripper movies have ranged from the failed mainstream film *Striptease* (for which Demi Moore received the highest salary ever paid to an actress: $12 million—or $6 million a breast, as many critics joked), through the many straight-to-video versions, to pornographic videos like the *Blonde Justice* series. Because the films are generally the domain of the low-budget thriller, their stories are more direct, and often more inventive and revealing than pseudoserious movies. The stripper-revenge movies cut directly to the core and deal specifically with gender issues in a blatant way. As with most cinematic genres that transcend their original niche, the core of the formulaic story remains consistent.

The plots of stripper-revenge movies mirror the rape-revenge films, but with a few significant changes. In the most formulaic of the rape-revenge films (e.g., *I Spit on Your Grave* [1977], *Ms. 45* [1981], *Eyes of a Stranger* [1981]), a harmless and innocent young woman is repeatedly harassed and then violently raped by one or more men, after which the system fails to do anything about the attack, forcing her to take matters into her own hands and kill the man, or men, usually in a dramatic and poetic fashion. The plot of the stripper movies, several of which I will be discussing in more detail below, usually goes something like this: A wholesome stripper (we know she is wholesome because she refuses to do drugs or turn tricks) is stalked by an unknown psycho/fan who has become obsessed with her, or the strippers from a particular club are being killed off one by one. The male authorities ignore the stripper's pleas for help because they think she must be a slut who willingly invites sexual predators. The disgruntled female cop (or journalist, or private detective, or a dead stripper's sister) disagrees, joining forces with the stripper(s) and/or going undercover as a stripper thus becoming a victim herself until she, or they, manage to kill the psycho by film's end. Not all stripper movies follow this story line of dance, be stalked, kill the stalker. These avenging-stripper movies are a subset of films that take strippers as their central focus. Other notable films like *Gypsy* (1962), *Portrait of a Stripper* (1979), *The Stripper* (1963), and of course, *The Blue Angel* deal with strippers in a different manner, though many of the themes of obsession and disrespect remain consistent.

In her incredibly thorough analysis of gender and horror movies, Carol Clover details the complex machinations of gender performance and audience identification across a wide range of subgenres including rape-revenge films. A key element in Clover's interesting and influential argument is her reading of the female heroines as symbolic proxies for the male viewer. The heroine, or the "Final Girl" as Clover calls her, is symbolically positioned as androgynous (she always has a boy's name, she abstains from any sexual activity, etc.) and through her actions—demonstrating mental and physical self-reliance, and killing the rapist(s)—she enacts masculinity, which enables male viewers to identify with her originally disempowered position and to enjoy her revenge. As Clover puts it:

[T]he willingness of the slasher film to re-represent the traditionally male hero as an anatomical female suggests that at least one traditionally heroic act, triumphant self-rescue, is no longer strictly gendered masculine. The rape-revenge film is a similar case, only more so; it is not just triumphant self-rescue in the final moments of the film that the woman achieves, but calculated, lengthy, and violent revenge of a sort that would do Rambo proud. (Paradoxically, it is the experience of being brutally raped that makes a "man" of a woman.) What I am suggesting, once again, is that rape-revenge films too operate on the basis of a one-sex body, the maleness or femaleness of which is performatively determined by the social gendering of the acts it undergoes or undertakes.[6]

Likewise, Peter Lehman's discussion of rape-revenge films claims that, on at least one symbolic level, the subgenre clearly "suggests that these avenging women are really men."[7]

Though I lack the space here to cover the complexities of Clover's and Lehman's arguments, I would like to question the suggestion that because women defeat the villain on their own they somehow represent men in drag.

(For a more detailed Freudian criticism of this point, see Barbara Creed, who writes, "[B]ecause the heroine is represented as resourceful, intelligent and dangerous it does not follow that she should be seen as a pseudo man.")[8] In fact, in the case of stripper-revenge, which is very similar to slasher and rape-revenge, the undeniability of the central character's femaleness is absolutely essential to the story. When the strippers, so clearly marked as women and as sexual spectacles, take up arms against their assailants, they are not enacting masculinity. Indeed, the accumulated emphasis on their being women denies the possibility of reading them as men. They exercise power over the men, both physical and visual/sexual power, in a manner that at least semiotically validates the possibility of female on-screen heroics.

The central story line of the stripper-revenge films almost exactly parallels that found in the rape-revenge narratives analyzed by Clover and Lehman. The woman is terrorized by a misogynistic male psychotic and when no one else is able or willing to help her she must take matters into her own hands with a "triumphant self-rescue in the final moments of the film." The distinguishing feature between the two formulas is the increased emphasis on the protagonist of the stripper-revenge film as an explicitly erotic spectacle. This crucial shift in occupation draws attention to the limitations of the "men-in-drag" thesis that has been so liberally applied to resourceful and independent female characters in recent years. To describe tough female characters as performing masculinity to the point of becoming "men-in-drag" undercuts the stereotype-breaking potential of these figures.[9]

By casting the heroine as a stripper the films can fully exploit the naked display of the female body and code it as desirable perfection, as quintessentially womanly. I am concerned specifically with the discrepancy between the gender semantics of the theory and what the audiences may see and understand of the intended narrative. As the above quotation from Clover mentions, the symbolic tranvestism of strong female characters operates on the basis of a one-sex body. The one-sex body, however, is a historical concept Clover borrows from Lacquer and denies both the physical presentation of these heroines and the perceptions of modern audiences.[10] Representationally, the masculinization of the modern heroine may make more sense with action heroines like Sarah Connor in *Terminator 2* and Ripley in the *Alien* series who embody masculinity through their muscular appearance.

The stripper-revenge films empower a completely different type of female body. The protagonist's body in these films is first and foremost a curvaceous, toned, and sexualized body, proportioned in the manner of a breast-implanted aerobics queen. The sexualized body of the stripper heroine, which is always abundantly shown naked and dancing (or in the case of the *Blonde Justice* films, actually having sex), is understood by audiences as ideally female despite whatever strong actions she may take to protect herself from harm. In the stripper-revenge films (and most other films with strong female leads) the heroine's heavily feminized body overrides the masculine connotations of "triumphant self-rescue." In other words, self-reliance and toughness hardly masculinize these women. Indeed, these films—as exploitative as they are—argue that such traits are accessible to heroes of either gender.

Dance with Death, a typical straight-to-video stripper movie, features strippers at The Bottom Line club in Los Angeles who are murdered gruesomely one by one. No one really seems to care—not the police, not the club's owner, and not the press. No one, that is, except for Kelly Crosby, an aspiring investigative journalist who has to convince her sexist boss to let her report on the story. Kelly goes undercover as a stripper and quickly meets the usual cast of characters and suspects: Art, the sleazy club owner; J.D., the horny MC who constantly tries to date the dancers; Henry, the nerdy knife wielder who always sits in "perverts row" but never tips; Jodie, the tough-as-nails lesbian dancer; and a variety of friendly stripper cohorts. Along the way Kelly also meets undercover detective Matt Shaugnessy, the rogue cop who actually shows an interest in the case.

A few more of the strippers are killed while Kelly and Matt review the long list of suspects, which it turns out also includes Kelly's boss who had been dating one of the first women killed. As Kelly becomes more involved with the world of striptease, she and Matt start to romance. Matt shoots Henry, the pervert, while trying to arrest him and begins to insist that Kelly give up stripping even though she still suspects her boss. Matt then shoots her boss, but while he comforts Kelly she notices the stone for Matt's ring is missing, the same stone that she found in the palm of Jodie's dead hand a few scenes earlier. "You're just a whore like all the rest!" Matt tells Kelly when he realizes he's been found out. He chases a screaming Kelly through back alleys and a nearby warehouse until she decides to fight back. And fight back she does, first tripping him with a telephone line and beating him in the head repeatedly with a two-by-four, then stabbing him in the chest with his own knife, then breaking his jaw with a lead pipe, and finally covering him in gasoline and setting him on fire. *Hey,* nobody said these movies were subtle.

Although *Striptease,* based on the best-selling book by Carl Hiaasen, was a major Hollywood production, its central narrative themes are direct descendants of the film's straight-to-video predecessors. Softened for mainstream audiences, *Striptease* is the story of Erin Grant, who is forced to take work as a dancer at The Eager Beaver club to raise money for her upcoming custody battle with her deadbeat ex-husband. She quickly becomes the club's star attraction and develops a loyal following of fans. In fact, Erin so captivates the men in the club that when an overly aroused patron jumps on stage to hug her, a U.S. congressman, David Dilbeck, rushes to her rescue by breaking a champagne bottle over the guy's head. In an interesting twist, *Striptease* exchanges the usual psycho for the loony congressman who subsequently becomes so obsessed with Erin that he pursues her relentlessly (even having an aide steal some of the lint from her dryer for a sexual fetish), tries to undermine Erin's attempts to regain custody of her daughter, and has his associates murder her most devoted fan. A lone cop and a mentally unbalanced bouncer serve as Erin's only allies against the congressman and her abusive ex-husband, Daryl, who begins to stalk her.

Frustrated by the lack of respect her case gets because she is "just a stripper," Erin takes matters into her own hands by kidnapping her daughter and manipulating the congressman, first at gunpoint and then through seduction, to confess all his crimes while she tape-records them. *Striptease* bombed at the box office during its much-hyped theatrical release but has done remarkably well in video release, suggesting that home video is where these narratives are meant to remain.

The "Adult Couples" video *Blonde Justice* was definitely meant for home consumption. Despite being pornographic movies, *Blonde Justice* and *Blonde Justice 2* (which is really a part two rather than a sequel) incorporate a great deal of plot relative to other hard-core movies. In fact, I agree with Linda Williams's excellent analytic history of pornographic film that to dismiss them as nothing more than flimsy narratives designed to link sex scenes together is to miss much of the complex meanings and pleasures on offer in pornography.[11] In *Blonde Justice,* Dominique, the feature dancer at an upscale strip club, is terrorized by what she assumes is a crazed fan, who sends threatening letters to her apartment and her dressing room. On the advice of Cara, Dominique's dancing partner and only friend at the club, she calls the police looking for protection. The police captain tells Dominique to call back after she's *really* been attacked, and he laughs her off as just another whore looking for attention. Fortunately for Dominique, a female cop named Karen McClousky, who is in her supervisor's office complaining about his ordering her to wear a miniskirt to serve drinks to police VIPs, overhears the call for help and volunteers her protection services. Despite Dominique's initial hesitation—she hoped for "a big strong cop"—she agrees to Karen's offer after she roughs up an obnoxious fan and chases the stalker through a back alley. Between sex scenes, including one with Dominique and Karen that culminates in Karen giving the dancer a gun of her own, a number of men and women are considered as suspects and then quickly eliminated. In the end it turns out the psycho is Giles, Cara's boyfriend, who is jealous of Cara's physical relationship with Dominique and who wants Cara to replace Dominique as the real star attraction. Ironically, in the last scene Giles shoots someone he thinks is Dominique, but who turns out to be Cara in a blond wig and a borrowed dress practicing a new dance routine. Dominique discovers Giles over the body and just before he can shoot her too, Karen bursts onto the scene, gun already drawn, and arrests him. *Blonde Justice,* one of the most popular XXX-rated movies my video store has ever stocked, spawned two more sequels, neither one of which had anything to do with strippers being stalked or avenging women.

Like Ishtar, Salome, and Esmerelda before them, the female protagonists of these stripper movies are beautiful women fetishized to an extreme, both for the male audience within the story and for the male audience of consumers the movie targets. Interestingly, the fetishization of these women obviously and directly connects to the punishment of the male voyeur and the vindication of the female object. The objectification of women in the cinema is not new—it is at the core of their to-be-looked-at-ness. Men's obsessive looking at women on display is the catalyst for the entire plot of the stripper movie. At least on the surface, the traditional power relationship between the sexes is cut to its most basic elements. But rather than portraying the voyeur as the bearer of power, as the one in control, he is shown as pathetic. After just one look at Erin in *Striptease,* Congressman Dilbeck declares that she is ". . . an angel. An angel of pure delight!" Others, like the drooling men in *Dance with Death, Blonde*

Justice, Stripped to Kill, and *Midnight Tease II,* are shown as slack-jawed idiots who either lose all control or sit motionless in complete awe as soon as they see the dancers.

Though this reversal of cinema studies' conventional wisdom about exactly who bears the power in relations of men looking at women is a staple of stripper movies, we can see clear examples of it emerging in more mainstream movies. The much discussed interrogation scene in *Basic Instinct* (1992), the scene that made Sharon Stone a star, is a prime example. When Catherine Tramell is brought in for questioning by the police, she is supposed to be the one on the hot seat as a team of male detectives grill her. Instead Catherine remains calm and collected while the men are reduced to sweaty, blabbering fools after she briefly uncrosses her legs and they get a glimpse of her pantieless crotch. More directly, Von Sternberg's *Blue Angel* was the epitome of and inspiration for this motif of the male's ruinous obsession with a showgirl. In this classic, the erotic performance of Lola Frohlich (Marlene Dietrich) so captivates a morally and socially upstanding professor, Immanuel Rath (Emil Jannings), that he marries her and turns into an obsessed fool, literally a clown and a laughingstock by the end of the film.

The Blue Angel also set the standard for accentuating the props used in erotic performance to heighten the fetishization of the woman as an object of the look. In her top hat, lingerie, exposed garter belts, black stockings, and sporting a cane, Deitrich's seductive performance as Lola personifies the fetishized woman. In fact, Gaylyn Studlar has documented this relationship between Von Sternberg, Dietrich, and the aesthetic elements of their films as revealing a masochistic impulse of overwhelming proportions.[12] The props of striptease are common fetishes made obvious through their inclusion in the erotic performance. They are the "furs, the fans, the gloves, the feathers, the fishnet stockings" that Roland Barthes described as costumes designed to reveal "nakedness as a *natural* vesture of woman."[13] The explicit erotic performance of striptease personifies Mulvey's description of the fetishistic pleasure of the male gaze.

Mulvey's supposition is firmly grounded in Freudian theory, which posits that the erotic display of women is influenced by the male viewer's horrific boyhood discovery of his mother's lack of a penis. Seeking to disavow that lack, that difference, the male projects onto the erotic image symbolic replacements for the missing penis. Thus a high heel shoe, or a leather bustier, or any other fetish, comes to represent a symbolic phallic adornment. The striptease dance is a ritualized spectacle performed for male scopophilic interests whereby the ultimate revelation both exposes what is not there—evidencing the absence of a penis—and eroticizes the female body itself as a phallic substitute. The plethora of fetish objects that accompany striptease performances as phallic compensation, and the ultimate fetishization of the female body, is an almost hysterically extreme example of the general principles of female representation in contemporary film.

Fetishization in the cinematic sense is supposed to function as a nullifier of the threat of castration supposedly posed by the female body. As Mulvey puts it: "Woman as representation signifies castration, inducing voyeuristic or fetishistic mechanisms to circumvent her threat."[14] But in stripper movies the complex processes of fetishization do not nullify castration anxiety; they enhance that anxiety. Ignoring, for the moment, the overall narrative structure of the films, we should consider the symbolically loaded image of women with guns offered by these films. I have discussed elsewhere ("Gender and the Action Heroine," *Cinema Journal* [1996]) the semiotic importance of guns as phallic symbols when employed by women in contemporary action movies.[15] There I was concerned with the female characters' use of guns as an ingredient of gender performance—in other words, as a semiotic device used in films like *Aliens* and *Terminator 2* to align the female leads with a clearly masculinized subject position. I argued there, as I do here, that reading these characters as merely "men in drag" because they appropriate certain props and behaviors traditionally associated with masculinity inappropriately simplifies gender. The image of women with guns in stripper movies operates within a different symbolic system. While the figure of a muscular Linda Hamilton wielding an oversized gun in *Terminator 2* (Figure 6) enhanced her position as a "masculinized" hero, the combination of guns and strippers, who are clearly marked as sexual spectacles, does more to eroticize the gun than to masculinize the woman.

This image of eroticized gun wielding is a rather loaded semiotic device. The symbolic use of guns in stripper movies encapsulates the male viewer's conflicted perception of the fetish in a much more direct manner than in horror or action movies, or in any other narrative form that emphasizes avenging women. In this case the fetish, the phallic woman, is clearly revealed as a fantasy that is both desired and feared. The imagery exposes this complex relationship through its often very rudimentary symbolism. For example, the video box cover for *Dance with Death* (Figure 7) is an extraordinarily clear illustration of phallic symbolism. It depicts a beautiful and busty blond woman, clad in a skimpy red bikini, sex-

FIGURE 6. Sarah sports the "masculine" look in *Terminator 2*.

ually embracing a gun that is larger than she is. The model's expression reveals pure pleasure as she caresses the barrel of the gun. The implication is difficult to miss. The woman (who is not an actress in the film) is displayed in the throes of phallic worship, reduced to a stock caricature of pornography: the all-accepting woman who desperately needs the (viewer's) phallus. The image for *Dance with Death* is almost identical to the famous series of paperback covers used in the 1960s and 1970s for Ian Fleming's James Bond novels. Each of the books featured a glamorous woman riding or lounging on a larger-than-life revolver (Figure 8). In their analysis of James Bond as a cultural icon Bennett and Woollacott point out that "in depicting one or more exotically but scantily clad women placed astride a large golden gun, the covers of this period clearly cue, as the central concern of the novels, the subordination of women to the regime of the phallus."[16] The same can obviously be said for the cover image of *Dance with Death*. But unlike the James Bond stories that feature a hero who literally embodies masculinity and phallic power, stripper movies, including *Dance with*

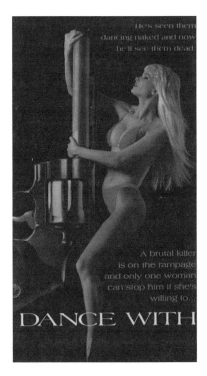

FIGURE 7. A woman in phallic rapture advertises *Dance with Death*.

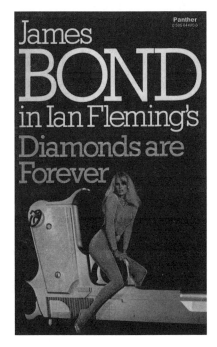

FIGURE 8. A Bond girl eroticizes the gun.

Death, ultimately deliver conflicting messages of women *not* subordinated by the phallus.

While the iconography of the posters may depict the eroticized woman as subordinated to the phallus, the narratives of these films deal with the woman's gradual mastery of (phallic) power. Rather than being disempowered through their role as the object of a fetishizing male gaze, and rather than being passive damsels in distress, these women exert power over the men in the film first through their control of the men's looks and secondly through their ultimate victory over the men who seek to terrorize them. Not surprisingly, when these women beat the villains in the final scene they usually do so at gun point or with some other phallic substitute such as a spear, a knife, or a two-by-four. So while at one level these films cater to male voyeurism in their excessive striptease scenes, they also reveal the darker implications of male scopophilia: they enact the threat of castration anxiety that necessitates women being fetishized in the first place. In other words, these films accentuate the desire and fear embodied in the voyeur's gaze of the female body. Jon Stratton's description of the dual implications of scopophilia is useful for our understanding of the dynamics at work in the stripper movies:

> **[The] fetishistic phallicisation of the female body has a dual effect on men's re-
> lations with women. The fetishistic context makes women both more sexually de-
> sired—their bodies appearing to acquire a heightened desirableness—and more
> feared—whilst simultaneously their bodies become the site of a fetishistic terror
> which complements, but is quite different in origin from, the fear of castration pro-
> voked by the recognition of women's "lack" of a penis. The cultural overdetermi-
> nation of cultural fetishism means that women may be constructed in two ideal-
> typical ways by men. First, and dominant, is the spectacle of the "passive,"
> phallicised woman, the woman who appears compliantly to express, for men, the
> spectacle of the phallicised body. Second, there is the spectacle of the "active,"
> phallic woman who, from a male perspective, reworks the phallic power attrib-
> uted to her into a spectacle which men experience as threatening to their own, al-
> ready lacking, feeling of phallic power.**[17]

The heroines of stripper movies transcend the two ideal ways fetishism constructs women for men. They appear to be the " 'passive,' phallicised woman" who exists merely for the viewing pleasure of the male audience, but they are also the "active" phallic woman who threatens, and in fact conquers, male phallic power.

The most interesting twist about stripper movies, in my view, is that the main female characters are a device for combining the two fetishized ideals of women—passive and active—thus revealing how the apparent passivity is also the source of activity, the source and the threat of power that male fantasy plays into. Obviously fetishized women, they are also, by extension, phallic women. But unlike other genres that highlight avenging women, the stripper movies ascribe the women's true power as the very quality that at first glance seems to disempower them. In other words, their seductive desirability is the real weapon, the phallic symbolism of the guns is just an external marker of the "activity" that can result from their inherent power. The real threat to male observers is not the masculine qualities that these women have taken on in defense of themselves and as a result of their objectification, it is the castrating power that they wield as seductive objects. A fitting metaphor for this form of desirability as a castrating threat is most clearly expressed in the subgenre of vampire-stripper movies. Though most of them are B movies, or pretend to be B movies, films like *Vamp* (1986), *Dance of the Damned* (1988), *From Dusk till Dawn* (1996), *Bordello of Blood* (1996), *Night Shade* (1996), and *Club Vampire* (1997) all feature vampires who perform as strippers in order to seduce their prey. It's hard to think of a more apt metaphor for the threat of castrating power strippers pose than that of vampirism. The female vamps literally sucking the energy and the life out of their enraptured, willing male victims—victims who initially thought they were in control of the situation because they were behind the look.

The duality of these phallic women as fetishized objects representing both activity and passivity is played out on another level in the villain's dual perception of the strippers. Harking back to the age-old stereotypes that position women as either saints or sinners, as virgins or sluts, the male psycho's motivation usually lies in what he sees as a disappointment. In *The Hunchback of Notre Dame* the illusion fades for Gringoire when he discovers Esmerelda is a gypsy, whereas in contemporary films the image is destroyed when the obsessed man discovers the stripper is not a chaste angel dancing only for him. In *Striptease* Congressman Dilbeck describes Erin as "[a]n angel of pure delight! She's so pure and clean . . . not like the rest of these whores." Likewise, in *Dance with Death,* when Matt turns on Kelly he declares: "I thought you were special, but you're just a whore like all the others." Within the narrative of the film the obsessive male voyeur initially perceives the woman as the ultimate passive object of desire. It is only when he discovers that the dancer is also an active phallic woman, particularly when she is sexually active with someone other than the psycho, that the dissonance drives the man to murderous actions. It is the discrepancy between the fantasy of the woman as passive, as saint, as accepting of only the viewer, and the reality of the woman's power and autonomy over her own sexuality that forms the crux of motivation for these stories.

"She takes the law into her own hands. What you take into yours is up to you."
—promotional copy for *Blonde Justice* (1994)

The morality tale played out within these stripper movies is really quite simple. On the one hand it is a tale of castration anxiety, and warns about the dangers of giving oneself fully to the seductive illusion of the beautiful dancers; on the other, it is a tale of powerful avenging women and a lesson in female subjectivity. The films make clear that the male voyeur's source of pleasure proves his ultimate downfall. Time and again, the male character who idolizes the erotic spectacle of the stripper to the point of obsession is driven to criminal and psychotic behavior when he realizes that she is not the perfect, all-accepting woman of his fantasies. These films usually try to stress that the strippers merely enact a stage persona of pornographic fantasy. This convention of trying to show that female strippers are "not just sex objects" may seem tenuous, but the technique typifies Hollywood's attempts to market exploitation as empowerment. In essence, these films repeatedly offer a voyeuristic fantasy and then condemn the fictional voyeur. Less clear are the complex layers of pleasure these movies offer to external male viewers, either in the theater or in front of the VCR. The stripper-revenge movies do not operate for male viewers in the way Mulvey and others have described mainstream films as working to nullify the threat posed by phallic women. The woman is not clearly brought back under the patriarchal system by the end of the film; rather her actions reveal the uselessness and the dangerous sexism inherent in the system.

These films do not conform to the "guys in drag" thesis at the root of the theories about the popularity of rape-revenge films among male viewers. Don't misunderstand me, I agree with much of Clover's and Lehman's readings of rape-revenge films, but the complex gender performances found in those movies that facilitate the Final Girls as masculinized proxies for male viewers are not found in the stripper-revenge movies. The strippers never enact masculinity. They may appropriate such phallic symbols as guns and knives; they may behave in an active, traditionally "masculine" manner defending themselves and killing the villains without male help—but their female sexuality is foregrounded to such an extent that it is near impossible to confuse these women with "men in drag." Moreover, their undeniably female identity is necessary for the story to work. If they are not firmly established as desirable women, then all plot motivation is lost, as are the very pleasures of looking that appeal to both the men within the film and those without. What, then, is at the root of these films' popularity with male audiences?

The most obvious answer to the question of why men enjoy these films seems laughably simple: "Naked babes, dude! Lots of naked babes!" I do not want to make the mistake of denying that the primary appeal of these films, for heterosexual men anyway, is that they provide a form of masturbatory pleasure. The million-dollar advertising campaigns for *Striptease* and *Showgirls* certainly pandered to male libidos as the primary audience for the films. Nor is it surprising that both of these films have enjoyed more success as videotape rentals than during their theatrical releases. It is no coincidence that, like hard-core pornography, these erotic thrillers cater to solitary home viewing. It would be ridiculous to underestimate the lure for many heterosexual men of seeing Demi Moore (*Striptease*) or Salma Hayek (*From Dusk till Dawn*) naked. Though I have generally been stressing the narrative plot of the films so far, it is important to remember that these films do present a great deal of eroticized female nudity. I would not want to skip over this undeniable fact for the sake of a purely theoretical analysis. Perhaps many men do use these films strictly as masturbatory aids, focusing only on the moments of erotic display and otherwise ignoring the plot and the ultimate punishment that the story consistently visits upon the voyeur. But even if this were the case it does not account for the repetitive nature of the formula. Why would the films always disparage the characters who most closely resemble the viewers?

Even the *Blonde Justice* films, which are hardcore pornography, provide clues that the pleasures available to men are more complex than the simple equation of voyeurism equals pleasure. As the promotional copy for *Blonde Justice* quoted above makes explicit, what the viewer takes into his own hands when watching the film is up to him—the promise is that the film will be so arousing that the viewer will not be able to resist masturbation. But as pornography, *Blonde Justice* is unusual. Susan Bordo has argued that the traditional critic's perception of porn as the ultimate "objectification of women" is not entirely accurate. Rather, Bordo argues, the fantasy requires a certain female subjectivity, one that allows the illusion that the women will be totally open to sex with the male viewer but in such a way that their voracious appetite for sex will always validate the male in ways that real women do not. Bordo surmises, quite correctly I think, that

[w]hat is desired, and what much heterosexual pornography provides, is a world in which women are indeed in a state of continual readiness and desire for sex, but one in which female desire is incapable of "emasculating" the male by judging or rejecting him, by overwhelming him, or by expecting something from him that he cannot (or fears he cannot) provide. What is desired is a sexual encounter that does not put manhood at risk in any way—neither through female indifference to the male (leaving *him* feeling sexually "too much," exposed, ashamed) nor through "too much" independent, unpredictable desire, will, or need on the woman's part (eliciting anxieties that he will be unable to satisfy *her*). In pornography women are indeed voracious, yet at the same time completely satisfied by anything the male has to give and non-needful of that which he cannot give.[18]

Yet, in *Blonde Justice,* the female lead does not conform to this basic acceptance of the male that would seem to be at the root of the male viewer's pleasure. In fact Dominique, the central character, is extremely active sexually, but only with other women. Rather than accepting any advances from male characters within the film, she rejects them and makes no effort to hide her belief that all of the males are idiots. In one telling scene, near the beginning of the first installment of the series, Giles (who turns out to be the stalker) walks in on his girlfriend Cara having sex with Dominique in their dressing room. Giles asks if he can come in, but Dominique snaps at him: "Fuck, no! Can't you see we're busy? Now get the hell out of here!" Hardly the response of a character "incapable of emasculating" the male. The fact that this scene runs directly parallel with the action in another dressing room where two strippers have been joined by the male manager only emphasizes that the typical pornographic response would have been to happily invite the male in for a ménage à trois.

FIGURE 9. Advertisers put Dominique in dominatrix gear for the advertisement of *Blonde Justice 2*.

On another level, this uncharacteristic rejection of the male in *Blonde Justice* is compounded for the viewer if he recognizes the actress playing Dominique is Janine Lindemulder—and it is likely that this may be the case because according to all reports she is currently the most popular starlet in the industry—who has a legendary "no guys"[19] clause in her contract. Thus, both within the film and perhaps through the viewers' extratextual knowledge about the star, the viewer finds a distinct variation on the supposition of an all-accepting pornographic pleasure. And if the direct, privileged, voyeuristic pleasure can be rendered problematic in a hard-core video, then what would seem to be the most obvious pleasures of the less explicit stripper movies might also be more complex. Rather than the all-accepting sex object, these rejecting and emasculating strippers have something of the dominatrix about them. This is made clear in the cover art for *Blonde Justice 2* (Figure 9). Although Dominique (and you can be certain this name was not chosen at random) never appears as a dominatrix in the film, the poster shows Janine dressed in leather lingerie and stiletto heels while she seductively holds a whip in her hands. Here the shift away from the mixed symbolism that implied the strippers were both passive and active phallic women is complete: there is no doubting the nature of the erotic pleasure derived from looking at these women. It is a pleasure that gives up power, a masochistic rather than sadistic pleasure.

In suggesting that for male viewers much of the pleasure derived from this particular form of phallic woman is, in a sense, masochistic, I agree with Gaylyn Studlar's argument that masochism may be as much at the root of the cinematic gaze as sadism is. Criticizing feminist film theory of the 1970s and 1980s for subscribing too narrowly to the idea that images of women are always subjected to a sadistic, controlling masculine gaze, Studlar points out that the "theory of masochistic desire challenges the notion that male scopic pleasure must center around control—never identification with or submission to the female."[20] Moreover, Studlar argues that because of their political agenda theorists of the sadistic gaze stop short of the logical conclusion that "would necessitate pairing masochism, the passive submission to the object, with fetishistic scopophilia."[21] Or as Rodowick put it (before Studlar): "Mulvey cannot admit that the masculine look contains passive elements and can signify *submission to* rather than *possession of* the female."[22] Stripper movies align, narratively and symbolically, with masochistic impulses, and in doing this they make explicit the association between the illusion of "possession of" and the fantasy of "submission to." Just as the character of the stripper transcends the positions of both passive and active phallic woman, so the visual pleasures available to male viewers transcend both looking at and submitting to. Where the voyeur within the story world of the film is driven to murderous impulses when his sadistic fantasy of possessing the ideal woman is frustrated, the voyeur in the theater or the living room is safely afforded the same fantasy of possession *and* the subsequent masochism of submission.[23]

Another possibility for the popularity of these films, one not premised as directly on psychoanalysis, is that the narrative structure allows the male viewer to have his cake and eat it too. Put differently, he can look at the women as sexual spectacles but he can also distance himself from the "bad" viewer within the film. The men within the films are always characterized as sleazy and obnoxious, or nerdy and perverted. Their point of view may be a necessary excuse to display often gratuitous portions of female flesh, but their obsession with the display is characterized as so unwholesome that male viewers can look down upon the men in the film. This device runs parallel to what Lehman describes in rape-revenge films where the "sexual desire these men have for the women must, in other words, be made to seem as far removed as possible from the male viewer's similar desire for her."[24] The films' nods to feminism may be merely tokenism—for example, when Dominique tells Karen "I don't get a chance to meet many strong women like you" in the middle of a pornographic video, it feels rather dubious—but in this era of political correctness, pretensions of being more liberated viewers may be just the saving grace needed for male audience members. In fact, it is amazing how many straight-to-video erotic thrillers openly take voyeurism as their subject matter. In addition to strippers, these videos have an inordinate number of models, photographers, filmmakers, and private eyes as main characters who spend their time either observing beautiful women or being beautiful women under observation. This apparent preoccupation with the morality and the dangers associated with looking in low-budget films is perhaps an interesting way in which this genre thinks out loud about itself, and it deserves more attention than I can afford it here. Within the stripper movies, as with erotic thrillers in general, male viewers can scorn the leering psychotics, at the same time that they themselves are caught looking, and align themselves through the narrative conventions with the female protagonist.

"That's what Erin's mother didn't understand about yuppie strip clubs: it wasn't the women who were being used and degraded, it was the men."
—from the novel *Striptease,* by Carl Hiassen (1993)

The narrative message of the stripper movies is clear, at least in a self-serving, superficial postfeminist sort of way: Ultimately the women exercise power over the men who look at them. But while this may be a common scenario in movies, its relevance to real life seems suspect at best. These films, like all films, operate in the realm of the symbolic, not the realistic. I do not want to be misunderstood here: I am *not* antipornography; I am not against women exploiting their sexual power over men for economic or more personal reasons. I believe that women are capable of producing and enjoying their own meanings and pleasures in a multitude of ways that conform to, challenge, and subvert societal norms. I *do* want to stress that the reality of gender and economic politics for women who work in striptease is more complex and problematic than it is on the screen. The films manage to encapsulate systemic misogyny within a few symbolic male characters who are ridiculed as ineffective leerers or portrayed as violent psychopaths eventually killed off by the heroines. That message probably comforts as many male viewers as female ones. If only it were that simple in real life.

"The feminist line is, strippers are victims," Camille Paglia told *Penthouse* magazine, which obviously has a vested interest in promoting extreme postfeminist views. "But women are far from that," Paglia continues. "Women *rule:* they are in total control. . . . [M]en in strip clubs are completely cowed." [25] I agree with Paglia in that many men I've seen in strip clubs fear the women and their open display of sexuality. The women control their interactions with the customers, many of whom are so frightened they don't even know where to look. But I would not go so far as to say this means women rule. The immediate interaction may grant all the symbolic power to the individual dancer, but this interesting revisioning of gender and power relations vis-à-vis the dynamics of looking should not blind us to the underlying system of control, the realm where real power is held, and usually held by men. For example, as Camille Paglia made her remarks—reinforced by a range of stripper movies and pseudojournalistic, autobiographical books like *Ivy League Stripper* and *Nine Lives,* which proudly describe strippers as powerful women in complete control of their working world—Toronto was embroiled in a dispute between judges and strip club owners on one side and dancers on the other.

The ongoing dispute began in Toronto on 10 February 1994, when an Ontario Provincial Court judge ruled the managers of an uptown club, Cheaters Tavern, were not breaking any laws by offering lap dancing in their establishment. The judge claimed that due to changes in laws concerned with pornography, lap dancing now fell within contemporary community standards of tolerance, which is the constitutional measure of obscenity and indecency. In his judgment he outlined the following dancer behaviors as innocuous if performed by a woman of legal age and with a valid, government-issued, striptease license: *(a)* being nude except for wearing an open shirt or blouse; *(b)* fondling her own breasts, buttocks, thighs, and genitals while close to the customer; *(c)* sitting on a customer's lap and grinding her bare buttocks into his lap; *(d)* sitting on a customer's lap, reaching into his crotch and apparently masturbating the customer; *(e)* permitting the customer to touch and fondle her breasts, buttocks, thighs, and genitals; *(f)* permitting the customer to kiss, lick, and suck her breasts; *(g)* permitting what appeared to be cunnilingus. Within days Toronto "gained the dubious distinction of becoming the lap-dancing capital of North America."[26] The ruling also made for interesting press coverage as pundits argued about the pros and cons of changing moralities.

A few weeks later somebody finally asked the dancers what they thought. Most of them, it turns out, frowned upon the changes—sure they could make a lot more money, but they had less control. This wasn't dancing, they argued, this was prostitution. The club owners were forcing the women to do lap dances despite protests about being groped and, many claimed, sexually assaulted. Several of the dancers tried to form a union to lobby the politicians and to provide some form of job security in the face of club owners who said, "You lap dance or you don't dance at all," and who reportedly began importing desperate Asian women willing to do almost anything for only a dollar a dance. So far the club owners are winning. The dancers have trouble getting the public to take them seriously.

Interestingly enough, the loss of power experienced by these real-life dancers occurred when the dynamics of striptease changed from looking to touching. Breaking the visual barrier alters the dynamics of power and control. With looking, control and subjectivity can be found on either side of the interaction; but with touching, fondling, and servicing, there is no room for illusion. The male patrons, and more importantly the male club owners, clearly control the women's bodies—economically, physically, and mentally. As one dancer said: "You know, I used to like it when it was table dancing, when there was no touching. But you don't see any happy faces anymore. None of us is happy anymore. Back when it was table dancing I use to have these fantasies about being really sexual in my real world. But now I can't do that. The touching really depresses me."[27]

When push comes to shove, dancers in real life find no easy solution, no single drooling villain whom they can stomp with a stiletto heel. In contrast, the stripper-revenge movies offer an idealized version of feminine power derived from mastery of the look. It's a good starting point and perhaps encouraging that at least in fiction our culture begins to recognize the consequences of misogyny and to accept women as heroes. But this does not necessarily mean that the real world has caught on.

Notes

1. Neal Gaiman, *The Sandman: Brief Lives,* DC Comics (New York: Vertigo, 1993).

2. Carol J. Clover, *Men, Women, and Chain Saws: Gender in the Modern Horror Film* (Princeton: Princeton University Press, 1992); Peter Lehman, "'Don't Blame This on a Girl': Female Rape-Revenge Films," in *Screening the Male: Exploring Masculinities in Hollywood Cinema,* ed. Steven Cohan and Ina Rae Hark (New York: Routledge, 1993).

3. Laura Mulvey, "Visual Pleasure and Narrative Cinema," in *The Sexual Subject: A Screen Reader in Sexuality* (New York: Routledge, 1992).

4. Ibid., 27.

5. Ibid., 27.

6. Clover, *Men, Women, and Chain Saws,* 159.

7. Lehman, "'Don't Blame This on a Girl,'" 111.

8. Barbara Creed, *The Monstrous-Feminine: Film, Feminism, Psychoanalysis* (New York: Routledge, 1993), 127.

9. For another criticism of the "men-in-drag" thesis, see Elizabeth Hills, "From 'Figurative Males' to Action Heroines: Further Thoughts on Active Women in the Cinema," *Screen* 40, no. 1 (1999).

10. Thomas Walter Lacquer, *Making Sex: Body and Gender from the Greeks* (Cambridge: Harvard University Press, 1990).

11. Linda Williams, *Hard Core: Power, Pleasure, and the Frenzy of the Visible* (Berkeley: University of California Press, 1989).

12. Gaylyn Studlar, *In the Realm of Pleasure: Von Sternberg, Dietrich and the Masochistic Aesthetic* (Urbana: University of Illinois Press, 1988).

13. Roland Barthes, *Mythologies* (Glasgow: Palladin Books, 1957), 92.

14. Mulvey, "Visual Pleasure and Narrative Cinema," 25.

15. Jeffrey A. Brown, "Gender and the Action Heroine: Hardbodies and the Point of No Return," *Cinema Journal* 35, no. 3 (spring 1996): 52–71.

16. Tony Bennett and Janet Woollacott, *Bond and Beyond: The Political Career of a Popular Hero* (New York: Methuen Inc., 1987), 59.

17. Jon Stratton, *The Desirable Body: Cultural Fetishism and the Erotics of Consumption* (New York: Manchester University Press, 1996), 144.

18. Susan Bordo, "Reading the Male Body," *Michigan Quarterly Review* 32, no. 4 (fall 1993): 707–8.

19. Mark Hudis, "The Sex Worker Next Door," *Gentleman's Quarterly* 67, no. 8 (August 1997): 172.

20. Gaylyn Studlar, "Masochism and the Perverse Pleasures of the Cinema," in *Film Theory and Criticism: Introductory Readings,* ed. Gerald Mast, Marshall Cohen, and Leo Braudy, 4th ed. (New York: Oxford University Press, 1992), 778.

21. Ibid., 783.

22. D. N. Rodowick, "The Difficulty of Difference," *Wide Angle* 5, no. 1 (1982): 7–9.

23. For a more thorough discussion of the complex nature of masochism in contemporary cinema, see Kaja Silverman, *Male Subjectivity at the Margins* (New York: Routledge, 1992); David Savran, *Taking It Like a Man: White Masculinity, Masochism, and Contemporary American Culture* (Princeton: Princeton University Press, 1998).

24. Lehman, "'Don't Blame This on a Girl,'" 112.

25. Melanie Wells, "Woman as Goddess: Camille Paglia Tours Strip Clubs," *Penthouse: The International Magazine for Men,* October 1994, 56–61, 132.

26. Joe Chidley, "A No to Dirty Dancing," *MacLean's,* 17 July 1995, 34–35.

27. H. S. Bhabra, "Ten Dollars a Dance," *Toronto Life,* May 1995, 52.

The Gun and the Badge

Hollywood and the Female Lawman

Carol M. Dole

The last decade has seen the emergence of a new breed of powerful women in film. Unlike the femmes fatales who used their sexuality to manipulate men in film noir, or the mother figures who attained moral power in maternal melodrama, these late-twentieth-century women appropriate male power in the forms of weaponry and physical prowess. Movies such as *Barb Wire* (1996), *The Quick and the Dead* (1994), and *The River Wild* (1994) feature female leads as sharpshooters, bounty hunters, and white-water daredevils, wielding guns for profit or self-defense. At the safe remove offered by science fiction, female fantasy heroes who combine musculature and military skills have scored big box office in such films as *Terminator 2* (1991) and the *Alien* series. This essay will examine the limits on representation of women in the world of everyday reality, in particular those women who wield the most potent combination of physical, moral, and institutional power. The violent women I discuss are triply empowered: by the central position in the narrative, by the symbolically potent gun, and by their status as officers of the law. What anxieties about gender might the licensed woman's assumption of the gun provoke?

Despite widespread support for strong images of women in the media, many mainstream film viewers and academic feminists alike have hesitated to celebrate

---

A portion of this essay is here reprinted with permission from "Woman with a Gun: Cinematic Law Enforcers on the Gender Frontier," in *Bang Bang, Shoot Shoot! Essays on Guns and Popular Culture,* ed. Murray Pomerance and John Sakeris, 2nd ed. (Needham Heights, Mass.: Pearson Educational, 2000).

cinematic women with guns, even those who uphold the law. In a controversy summarized by Jeffrey A. Brown in "Gender and the Action Heroine," academic feminists have sometimes derided action heroines as gender transvestites or complained of their fetishization.[1] Such popular women's magazines as *Glamour* have run debates about whether "female shoot-em-ups help or hurt women." Does every strong female movie character serve as "a validation of strength" and counter the victimization long modeled for women, or are female action roles just an occasion for women to "sink to the worst of macho men's behavior"?[2]

The problem for Hollywood, which aims to give audiences what they want to see, is that film consumers do not agree on the answers to these questions. Clearly the demands of the action genre dictate that the hero show courage and the strength and will to vanquish opponents. While most viewers praise courage in female characters, many—from all areas of the political spectrum—question whether violence suits women. Given this clash between generic expectations and gender assumptions, Hollywood has had trouble creating an action heroine with universal appeal. Obsessed as Hollywood is with the action film, its biggest moneymaker in the global market, the film industry has obviously found it difficult to place the troubling figure of the Woman with a Gun into the same narrative slot as the familiar Man with a Gun. In recent years Hollywood has experimented with various levels of violence, muscularity, and erotic appeal in the women's action film in order to achieve the mix that will produce big box office.

This essay aims to analyze more than to evaluate Hollywood's experiments. It takes as a testing ground one subgenre of the action film, the cop film, because there generic conventions guarantee that the armed and potentially violent woman, if she is the central character, must be a force for good. In this genre, therefore, traditional notions of the good woman—modest, faithful, virtuous, cooperative, and deserving of protection—come most clearly into conflict with expectations for the action hero—fearless, independent, physically dominant, and the protector of others. Moreover, I focus on films aimed at mainstream audiences (not those designed for the different sensibilities of, for instance, art house or teenage audiences) because those multigenerational, class-crossing audiences retain more traditional notions of womanhood.

I assume that Hollywood, particularly as corporate culture and filmmaking-by-committee have intensified in recent years, has sought to achieve high box-office returns by producing entertainment that will offend as few people as possible even while introducing fresh twists into time-tested genres—for instance, by producing female-centered action films. The degree to which Hollywood has succeeded in refashioning genres to the liking of audiences is, of course, hard to measure. Even box-office grosses cannot be considered fully reliable, since so many unrelated factors (such as star power, effectiveness of marketing campaigns, the skill of the director, timing of release, and many other variables) determine the popularity of a movie. Audience reaction to any single variable, such as the gender of the hero, or among a specific audience segment, such as female viewers, is especially difficult to isolate. Although scholars have begun to do such studies (see Jacqueline Bobo's study of the reception of Steven Spielberg's *Color Purple* among African-American women),[3] such information is available on very few films. Magazine and television movie reviews are sometimes cited as representative of popular taste; but the validity of such an approach is limited by the fact that most reviewers are educated cinephiles who react to films differently than does the average viewer. Note, for instance, the discrepancy between critics' annual "Best Films" lists and the "Top-Grossing Films" tallies for the same year. With no single reliable method of measurement available, I have in this essay tried roughly to gauge level of success based on a combination of factors: profits, reviews, awards, and anecdotal evidence of audience response, as culled from casual conversation and popular culture references.

In the course of its (generally unsuccessful) attempts to imagine an armed female protagonist with popular appeal, Hollywood has experimented in intriguing ways with the law-enforcer hero. Over the last dozen years, the woman-centered cop film has undercut its armed women with narrative devices that reduce the heroes' power; and it has used different tactics in different time periods. This essay will demonstrate that earlier female cop films (1987–91) frequently imitate the extreme violence of male action pictures while counterbalancing this masculine power with feminine psychological vulnerabilities, and that most later films (1995–98) tend to privilege intellectual over physical power and limit the woman's power by splitting strategies.

The First Generation

The first wave of films featuring armed female law officers as protagonists, rather than as the hero's partner or love interest, appeared in the late eighties and very early nineties. Just as female pioneers in corporate environments in the 1970s modeled their attire on men's, favoring blue or gray suits with white blouses, the female protagonists in these early cop films adopted behaviors associated with male movie cops. Most of these female law enforcers were tough-talking and hard-shooting, and some were sexually assertive. The more action-oriented films, replete with big guns and exciting chases, centered on female street cops. In *Fatal Beauty* (1987) Whoopie Goldberg played a street-savvy detective with a big gun and a comic edge, and in the darker *Impulse* (1990) hard-shooting Theresa Russell went undercover as a prostitute.[4] In *Blue Steel* (1990) Jamie Lee Curtis portrayed a rookie in trouble, both subject and object of recurrent violence.[5] Less violent but similarly action-oriented was *V.I. Warshawski* (1991), featuring Kathleen Turner as a gun-toting private investigator—a quasiofficial law enforcer cut from the same mold as her official sisters.[6] In a still less violent film, Debra Winger played an FBI agent in danger as she infiltrated a white supremacist group in *Betrayed* (1988).[7]

While they are similar in level of violence to male-centered action films, these films retain for their female heroes, however, both motivations and vulnerabilities associated with traditional femininity. Moreover, as if to sidestep any challenge to male dominance, they avoid pitting women against men. The five films adopt similar strategies for empowering women without disempowering men.

Hollywood deflected audience discomfort with the figure of the licensed-to-kill woman by incorporating into the film's dialogue the question of why a woman would place herself in men's turf. Although during the same era cops played by Bruce Willis or Mel Gibson did not justify their career choices, in *Blue Steel* Officer Megan Turner (Curtis) must explain to nearly every man she meets why she became a cop. Lottie Mason (Russell) of *Impulse* is forced to examine her motivations in the office of the department psychologist. And Detective Rita Rizzoli (Goldberg) of *Fatal Beauty* must explain how a personal tragedy had driven her to cleanse the city of drugs. Agent Cathy Weaver (Winger) of *Betrayed* has been chosen—plucked out of college by her FBI mentor—rather than pursued her own career.

In a bow to traditional notions about the propriety of women's arming themselves, these films construct the woman's will to (fire)power as defensive, not aggressive. Cinematic female law enforcers wish to protect those weaker than themselves: never men, but always women or children, ideally female children. Rita Rizzoli may blast people to bits every ten minutes of film time, but she does so under the cover of the stated maternal aim of protecting other children from the fate of her own young daughter. Megan Turner joins the force to protect women like her mother, who continues to be abused by Megan's father. Warshawski becomes the protector of a young girl whose own mother and step-father are trying to murder her. And though *Betrayed* focuses on Weaver's infiltration of an extremist group, the film ends on an unlikely emotional swell as Weaver gratefully embraces her target's orphaned daughter.

As Jeffrey A. Brown has shown in his analysis of action cop movies of the eighties and early nineties, male cops often defend their daughters, wives, and girlfriends.[8] But female cops of the same period have no husbands and sons to rescue. This absence avoids the dilemma of the armed woman who might be stronger than her husband—a potential affront to traditional views of the fam-ily. (This dilemma crops up in *The River Wild* [1994], in which the inept city-slicker husband must play a large part in the rescuing of Meryl Streep's adven-turous heroine.) Moreover, the elimination of a family limits the women's power by making them seem less fully adult. Male cops have commonly lost families to divorce; but these first-generation female cops answer to families of origin, one as a daughter (*Blue Steel*), another as an orphan, dependent on male mentors (*Betrayed*).

Their unmarried status also makes these women both sexually available—re-inforcing the erotic implications of advertising posters of seductive women with guns—and vulnerable through that sexuality. Although male movie cops sleep with their enemies on occasion, female law enforcers are routinely placed in danger through a sexual relationship, usually with an opponent. In *Blue Steel,* Megan Turner unknowingly dates the very murderer she tracks. The highly sex-ualized Lottie Mason of *Impulse* is endangered both by the come-ons of her boss and by her temptation to prostitute herself to a mobster whose execution-ers arrive while she is in his house. In *Fatal Beauty* Detective Rizzoli makes love with the bodyguard of a prosperous crook only hours before he is ordered to shoot her. Warshawski is almost killed as she attempts to learn who murdered the hockey player she picked up in a bar one night. And in *Betrayed* Agent Weaver, who has been assigned to infiltrate an extremist group by attracting one of its leaders, is further endangered when she falls in love with him.

By their ultimate triumph over their antagonists, these female law enforcers fulfill both generic requirements and the desire of some segments of the audi-ence for strong female characters. Nevertheless, these movies limit the discom-fort they may pose to traditionalist viewers by the invocation of feminine ideals (such as maternal motivations and sexual desirability) and by the elimination of direct competition for power with males other than villains. In spite of these limitations on female power, however, the female hero's possession of the phallic gun generates a castration anxiety that the more comic films attempt to defuse through humor while mimicking the joshing familiar between male partners in many comic buddy cop movies. Both Warshawski and Rizzoli belittle criminals and colleagues with witticisms on their penis size. The delivery of such remarks, often without obvious motivation, is particularly remarkable in *Fatal Beauty*, the first of these female-centered cop films. Moreover, these castration jokes are reinforced by threats of actual castration within the narrative. Warshawski squeezes information out of a thug by judiciously applying a nutcracker; and Rizzoli accomplishes a similar task by hanging a wounded drug dealer in a meat locker and pressing a gun to his testicles. The films also trade in metaphoric castration: Rizzoli takes obvious pleasure in her ability to remove a young punk's knife from his pocket without his knowledge.

Although the castration threat in *Blue Steel* is less overtly articulated, it is more fundamental. The castration theme arises early in the film when Megan interrupts her male colleagues as they enjoy a joke about a prostitute who accidentally bit off a client's penis in a taxi and then stitched it back upside down. But the real castration story is Megan's. She has to yield her phallic weapon first to Eugene, who causes Megan's suspension by pocketing the gun of the robber whom she shot because he was armed, and then to the police authorities. Indeed, Robert Self has found that "the image of castration constitutes the unsettling master trope of the film," which is organized around several plot strands which reveal the desire of male characters to take away Megan's gun and uniform, the signifiers of masculine authority.[9]

The film's transfer of castration threats from men to a woman is typical of the changes wrought by Kathryn Bigelow in her attempt to "recontextualize" the cop genre, to examine the ramifications of placing a woman at its center.[10] *Blue Steel* adopts the same mechanisms that other female-centered cop films of the era use to defuse the threat to gender hierarchies: infantilization of its female hero, questioning the woman's desire for a job with a gun, putting her in a position of defense rather than of aggression, and making her vulnerable through her sexuality. But it does so with a self-consciousness lacking in the other films.

This is not to imply that other filmmakers of the period were unaware of their own attempts to soften the challenge to men that a tough armed woman might be seen to represent. Television's earlier replacement of Meg Foster with Sharon Gless before *Cagney and Lacey* could get a regular spot in the 1982 fall lineup provided a notorious case in point. A CBS vice-president explained that with the original casting these female cops seemed "not feminine enough, too aggressive . . . too masculine."[11] In the film world, the production history of *V.I. Warshawski* offers an illuminating example of studio attempts to avoid offending potential customers by challenging gender stereotypes—even, ironically, in bringing Sara Paretsky's feminist hero to the screen. In Kathleen Klein's words, "Disney Studios and Hollywood Pictures bought the rights to one of the most provocative feminist private eyes in contemporary detective fiction and threw away everything about her which mattered."[12] Disney began with a script based not on one of Paretsky's popular novels but rather on the character herself, who was modified to be less threatening. According to producer Jeffrey Lurie, four writers were brought in to create a more palatable character who would not be "just a tough female who packs a gun." They purposefully emphasized V.I.'s sexuality, added humor, and "expanded greatly" the role of the little girl V.I. protects—changes consistent with the formula I have identified.[13] Although V.I. is an aikido expert shown in hand-to-hand combat, her competition with men is carefully regulated: she ultimately loses her fights with them, and fights her final shoot-out not with a man but with a murderous mother, a perverse representation of violent femininity. The film's indecisiveness about whether its female hero should be independent of men is evident in its treatment of her male buddy Murray. Murray arrives to save V.I. at the climax, but holds his (flaccid?) gun with so little conviction that the villain laughs and shoots him. Moreover, Murray was scripted to pull V.I. out of the water at the end, until Kathleen Turner insisted she be allowed to climb out on her own.[14] No wonder the *New York Times* reviewer Caryn James observed that the film "might serve as a guidebook: How to Create a Strong Female Character Without Offending Anyone."[15]

Blue Steel represents a self-consciousness of another order, one that produced limited box office and provoked widespread interest among feminist scholars. Both the early reviewers of the film and later analysts have found it difficult to determine whether or not *Blue Steel* constitutes "Progressive Feminism in the 90s."[16] On the one hand Megan Turner is a strong and courageous female protagonist; on the other, her violent reprisals against Eugene invite comparisons to a "Dirty Harriet" who replicates male violence.[17] Scholars also analyze how the casting of the "androgynous" Jamie Lee Curtis affects response to her character.[18] Curtis's screen history, as the star of *Halloween* and other slasher films, has identified her with the victorious female survivor whom Carol Clover has dubbed the Final Girl. This identification further complicates Megan's gendering since Clover sees the Final Girl as a character into which "the categories masculine and feminine, traditionally embodied in male and female, are collapsed."[19]

The self-consciousness of *Blue Steel* prevents it from being "a faithful cop thriller," but neither is it a "straightforward feminist revision" of the genre.[20] In Cora Kaplan's words, the film attempts "both to replicate and mock popular genre," exploiting the tactics of the urban thriller even while critiquing them through its awareness of the changes wrought by change of gender.[21] For instance, rather than use the regulation .38 caliber weapon issued by the New York Police Department, director Bigelow planned to arm her female hero with a larger gun; only Curtis's pleas for realism persuaded Bigelow to compromise with a larger, reconfigured .38.[22] The much discussed credit sequence, with its caressing close-ups of a gleaming Smith and Wesson, confirms that *Blue Steel*'s obsession is "not really with guns per se, but with their symbolic effects."[23] The gun's eroticization in these lingering close-ups "presents this phallic symbol as an object of desire."[24] But the sequence simultaneously recognizes "the disturbing implications of a fetishism surrounding women and guns" and invites us to share it.[25]

This invitation to a double response is typical of *Blue Steel*'s exaggeration of the recurrent motifs of first-wave women cop films. Megan Turner must explain her desire to be a cop not just once, as in *Fatal Beauty* or *A Stranger among Us,* but three times, a number suggestive of ritual. Moreover, the ambiguity of her answers demands reflection. Her joking response "I like to shoot people" comments on gender stereotypes and, as several critics have remarked, contains a grain of truth, since she covets the power that gun and badge give her over people like her abusive father. Megan's vulnerability through her sexuality is also overdetermined. In one scene she both makes love with her onetime antagonist Detective Mann (whose name suggests his symbolic universality) and is raped and almost killed by Eugene, whom she had earlier attempted to seduce. The movie also highlights Megan's childlike status, as in the graduation scene where her parents have abandoned her, or in the final shot where she is lifted limp from the car. Through such exaggeration, *Blue Steel* both strips bare the coping mechanisms of a genre threatened by gender shift and takes advantage of their dramatic effects.

In an era when the *Lethal Weapon* and *Die Hard* films raked large profits from audiences eager to see male cops in action, these woman-centered films died quick deaths at the box office. Indeed, *V.I. Warshawski* made it from theater to video store in only six weeks. This failure might at first seem odd in an era in which, as trumpeted in the popular press, "women got tough at the movies," a claim seemingly validated by the fact that 1991's biggest grossers—*Terminator 2*, *Sleeping with the Enemy*, and *The Silence of the Lambs*—featured women with guns.[26] However, in that same year the unexpected success and ensuing notoriety of *Thelma and Louise* sent a mixed message. While significant numbers of the moviegoing populace found it refreshing to see women retaliate against male brutality, many others were enraged by such "toxic feminism."[27] The very proliferation of films about armed women as heroes suggests increasing acceptance of physically dominant women. But the strident responses to *Thelma and Louise*, particularly to its depictions of violence against men, showed a cultural unease about the consequences for men of women's assumption of new modes of power.

What of the popularity of *Sleeping with the Enemy* and *Terminator 2*? How do they differ from the female cop films that met such limited success? The former, which portrays an abused woman resorting to the gun for self-defense only when flight and concealment have failed, poses little challenge to gender stereotypes. *Terminator 2* does break new ground in giving its female hero both muscles and munitions, but it also assigns her a traditionally feminine motivation (caring for her child) and surrounds her with cyborgs figured as male who are even stronger and even more relentless than she—the foremost played by marquee draw Arnold Schwarzenegger. More significant for this study—and, perhaps, for the evolution of women's action films—is the success of *The Silence of the Lambs*.[28]

The Silence of the Lambs found a way to catch the imagination of a mainstream audience, as is obvious from the film's impressive grosses and its raft of awards. Jodie Foster, in her acceptance speech for the Best Actress Oscar, expressed her pleasure in having played "such a strong feminist hero." In public discourse, as Janet Staiger has documented, "women—both straight and lesbian—uniformly defended [Foster] and the movie as a positive, powerful representation of a female."[29] In short, the public was ready to applaud the film's gender politics[30]—a very different reaction from the hot public debate that would rage over the two gun-toting heroes of *Thelma and Louise* just three months later.

How did the female hero of *The Silence of the Lambs* manage to meet with such acceptance, when her sisters Megan Turner and Rita Rizzoli had been derided even by female critics for acting as a Bronsonesque "one-woman vigilante force"[31] or for proving that a woman can be "just as loudly, obnoxiously macho as a man"?[32] *The Silence of the Lambs* defuses the threat posed by the female dick through a complex of strategies, some found in earlier films of its kind and some quite different. But the underlying approach is the same: the female hero's power is showcased but simultaneously contained.

Like her predecessors, Clarice Starling (Foster) defends women rather than men, as she seeks to hush the bleating of the lambs she failed to rescue in her childhood by rescuing the young women whom the psychopathic Buffalo Bill wants to flay. Also like most of them, she is positioned as daughter rather than full adult, subject to not one but three father-figures: her professional mentor Jack Crawford, her intellectual mentor Hannibal Lecter, and the slain father/cop who appears in her flashback memories.

But the film also introduces some changes to the pattern, among them avoidance of any sexual vulnerability. Although some viewers have read Clarice's failure to respond to the many (hetero)sexual invitations she receives in the course of the film as evidence of lesbianism, within the context of other films about female law officers it becomes clear that a more important function of her refusal of sex is to avoid the dangers posed by either sexual desire—which put Lottie Mason, Rita Rizzoli, Cathy Weaver, and Megan Turner at such risk—or sexual desirability. Clarice refuses to act as sex object, a role in which almost every male character tries to cast her, and so refuses to fall into the limiting categories of womanhood held by the men all around her.[33]

The movie limits her power, and thus her threat, by casting an actress of small stature. Clarice Starling's lack of physical power is established in the opening scenes of the film, where she pants and struggles through an obstacle course and then enters an elevator full of men who tower over her. Her lack of experience further undercuts her power; unlike Lottie Mason and Rita Rizzoli, cops with skills and status, Clarice Starling is still a student, and always addresses her (male) superiors as "sir" in a tone of respect. Moreover, as Joan Kotker points out, Jonathan Demme's film strips Clarice of the marksmanship and laboratory expertise that distinguished her in Thomas Harris's novel.[34]

The movie further contains the hero's power, and the anxieties surrounding it, by the use of a different mix of genres than in previous films. Whereas *Fatal Beauty* adds comedy like so many male-centered action-thrillers, *The Silence of the Lambs,* as Carol Clover has shown, mixes in the horror genre.[35] Thus it presents Clarice as potential victim, from the opening training scene in which the uneasy music and the camera angles suggest that she is being pursued through the woods, to the final confrontation where she finds herself drawn into the basement where the serial killer has victimized so many women before her. The horror conventions evoked by such scenes generate a strong sense of her peril and thus contain her power. Moreover, FBI films such as *Betrayed* and *The Silence of the Lambs* are primarily detective thrillers, a genre that requires far less violence than the cop film, with its standard chases and gunplay. Except in a training sequence so brief that it's hard to catch, Clarice never assumes the phallic gun except when stalked through the killer's lair, appearing through his point of view to be nearly helpless in the dark. The film thus constructs her use of the gun on a man as self-defense, which mainstream audiences find acceptable in female protagonists (for example, in *Sleeping with the Enemy* or *Jagged Edge*).

Counterbalancing these many controls on the female hero's power, however, were features that made it easy to read *The Silence of the Lambs* as empowering to women. The film offers several talented and successful female characters, including the classmate who helps Jodie Foster figure out Lecter's clues, the resourceful captive of Buffalo Bill, and a senator. Clarice is a resolute woman who can think under pressure, steel herself to face gruesome tasks, and decipher Lecter's most esoteric clues. The film avoids stereotyped markers of female hysteria and helplessness: unlike Cathy Weaver of *Betrayed*, who shrieks when startled by a bird, Clarice does not scream even "at the moments cued for screaming from the horror film tradition."[36] And the final triumph is Clarice's, a fact emphasized by the intercutting of her lone discovery of Jame Gumb with her male superiors' elaborate, and futile, storming of an empty house.

Hollywood Learns a Lesson

In the wake of 1991's blockbuster action pictures featuring female leads, studios gave the green light to several female-centered projects. By 1993, a *Newsweek* article titled "That's Why the Lady Is a Champ" cited a string of upcoming productions: Geena Davis in the big-budget pirate adventure *Mistress of the Seas* to be directed by Paul Verhoeven; Jodie Foster in the thriller *Trackdown;* Sharon Stone as a gunslinger in *The Quick and the Dead*. The article attributed these to the success of *Terminator 2* and the female-dominated baseball film *A League of Their Own*,[37] but also registered concern over gender stereotypes. It quoted *Die Hard* producer Joel Silver's fears that "the young male audience would not react well to a female lead," and noted that Steven Seagal's upcoming project *Dead Reckoning* was originally written for Michelle Pfeiffer.[38] Two years later Hollywood plans had changed: Foster's role in *Trackdown* had been rewritten for a man; Geena Davis's *Mistress of the Sea* had been rewritten for a stronger male lead and a teenage female pirate.[39]

Although the development history of these films and others demonstrates screenwriter Joss Wheedon's contention that Hollywood "hasn't yet figured out how to harness" the use of women in action plots, nonetheless certain directions had become clearer by this time.[40] A 1995 article mentioned the preference for teaming male and female action costars.[41] More important to the development of the female-centered cop film, Hollywood shifted from replicating male models to experimenting with female ones. Screenwriter Josh Freidman argued in 1995 that "the flinty heroines played by Sigourney Weaver and Linda Hamilton in the *Alien* and *Terminator* movies 'were well done, but they're outdated. They're the first evolutionary step in the female-action genre. I want to see women respond to danger and solve problems differently than men. Otherwise, what's the point?'"[42] *Broken Arrow* writer Graham Yost agreed: "Women have to be their own kind of hero, like Jodie Foster was in *The Silence of the Lambs*."[43]

Yost's citation of *The Silence of the Lambs* demonstrates its importance as a model for female-action films. In the wake of the financial and critical success of Foster's film, Hollywood adopted two of its most salient characteristics. One was to set aside the macho model of the action hero in favor of experimenting with varieties of womanhood. The other was to adopt *Silence*'s canniest strategy for making a female hero seem both independent and unthreatening: splitting. Splitting, which distributes among multiple personalities or characters the modes of power that would otherwise be concentrated in a single female hero, reduces the threat of each individual protagonist.

For many viewers, the most memorable character in Demme's film was Anthony Hopkins's Hannibal Lecter, the brilliant and psychopathic psychiatrist whose clues lead Clarice to the murderer. The film's most effective strategy for subtly limiting Clarice's power was to make her dependent on male advice even while using Lecter's incarceration to make her appear an independent agent.[44] Earlier films had been troubled by the difficulty of pairing their female heroes with a male partner, as the popularity of buddy cop movies seemed to demand. If he was strong, gender stereotypes demanded he rescue her; if he was weaker than she, gender assumptions were overturned and the audience potentially discomfited. In *The Silence of the Lambs,* the separation of these intellectual partners—through literal bars and through the demonization of "Hannibal the Cannibal"—provides the female hero independence in the physical world without seriously challenging gender hierarchies.

Heroes with a Difference

In the mid-nineties, Hollywood experimented with new modes of presenting female law enforcers. Though all these films hedged their bets through some sort of splitting strategy, two of the bolder efforts tried to craft a new female hero based on values associated with various brands of feminism. Jon Amiel's *Copycat* (1995), in teaming a female detective with a female adviser, introduced the feminist ideal of cooperation among women. The Coen brothers' *Fargo* (1996) ironized stereotypes about women through its sly presentation of an ungainly but shrewd pregnant detective, and tested them by combining the traditionally separate qualities of toughness and nurturance.[45]

Jodie Foster's wish that her film's financial success would spawn "copycat" films came true with the production *Copycat.*[46] This thriller, which reviewers compared to *The Silence of the Lambs,* adopted the earlier film's splitting strategy. This time, however, the incarcerated intellectual who helps the hero track a serial killer is another woman. Dr. Helen Hudson, confined to her apartment by a paralyzing case of agoraphobia triggered by a near-fatal attack, is, like Hannibal Lecter, an expert on serial killers persuaded to assist with a murder investigation spearheaded by Detective M.J. Monahan (Holly Hunter).

In several ways, *Copycat* gives women more power than does *The Silence of the Lambs.* Although this film too emphasizes its female cop's small stature, it winks at its own strategy in a sarcastic reference to "the wee inspector." Unlike Clarice, M.J. is experienced and in charge of the case; although she pays lip service to her boss, we know that she never means it when she says, "Absolutely, sir"; and she consults a female peer rather than a father figure. She proves to be a crack shot in a training scene where—in contrast to Megan Turner and Clarice Starling—she is trainer rather than trainee. Most significantly, for the first time in an action film two lead women work together in defense of the law. The pairing not only dares to approach the doubled power of the male buddy cops of the eighties, but also follows a feminist model of cooperation rather than individualistic competition. The two women combine their official resources (M.J.) and knowledge base (Helen) to learn the killer's identity. When he finally captures Helen, the two women cooperate to save each other: Helen hangs herself to distract the killer from the downed M.J., and M.J. shoots the man as he reaches Helen on the roof. They work together as equals, without male rescue.

Nonetheless, *Copycat*—with a title that alludes to its own generic origins as well as to the modus operandi of its featured killer—takes its experiments with gender and genre only so far. The improbable death of M.J.'s male partner, Ruben, just before the rescue sequence avoids the difficulty of positioning him as either rescuer (which would preclude the women's ascendancy) or impotent bystander. Moreover, the teaming of the two women not only provides them an occasion to conquer through cooperation but also allows the film to limit the strength of each. Though both women are admirable, M.J. is neither muscular nor especially insightful, and Helen suffers from agoraphobia and her resulting bitterness. By positioning Helen as potential victim in a horror plot, the film invites the viewer to contemplate its hero's vulnerability as well as her strength. Like Clarice in the basement, Helen becomes hunted as well as hunter, evoking horror movie conventions both by her position as Final Girl and by the casting of an actress famous as one of the first blockbuster Final Girls (in *Alien*): Sigourney Weaver. *Copycat*'s eroticization of Helen, who is first seen in a close-up of red lips and often costumed in slinky nightgowns, both emphasizes and replicates the objectification implicit in her role as "poster girl" of serial killers.

The most inventive spin on the female cop thus far comes, unsurprisingly, from independent filmmakers Joel and Ethan Coen. *Fargo,* though distributed by Warner Brothers and exhibited in megaplexes alongside more mainstream fare, has a quirky sensibility that escapes Hollywood formulas. *Fargo* takes the straightforward approach of making its hero an ordinary person who must deal neither with personal traumas nor with the careening cars and fiery explosions of so many cop films. Like *Silence* and *Copycat*, it leaves most of the violence (and there is plenty in this film) to the criminals; its female hero shoots only once, just to wound. Since the investigation relies on her sleuthing skills rather than on displays of physical force, *Fargo* can largely discount gender without ignoring it. Thus it answers the preference of some feminists that women be treated just as men are treated.

Brainerd, Minnesota, police chief Marge Gunderson (Frances McDormand), *Fargo*'s deliberate, good-natured hero, seems "the polar opposite of Frank Serpico, Popeye Doyle, and every other tough-guy cop to have achieved screen immortality."[47] Far from macho, Marge has many traditionally feminine qualities. A supportive and even nurturing wife, she is polite, friendly, and cooperative, neither maverick nor lone agent. Most noticeably, she is a very visible seven months pregnant. The image of a uniformed police officer holding a gun above her swollen belly complicates gendered categories. On the plot level, the film boldly assumes the irrelevance of its hero's sex: she may waddle as she pursues the murderer, but her ungainliness doesn't prevent a successful capture. Indeed, the film is edited to obscure any difficulties a very pregnant policewoman might have in performing her duties. The shot of Marge walking cautiously across the frozen lake to the murderer she has felled disappears in a dissolve to the road, so that we need never see Marge try to move the large, ferocious man into her police cruiser.

Marge's pregnancy provides an important element of the very different version of splitting used in this film. The strategy that enables the female hero to have position, success, firepower, and domestic happiness without threatening anyone is a split in tone rather than in narrative function. Marge's widespread popularity, with reviewers, audiences, and the Academy (surely part of the reason for MacDormand's Best Actress Oscar), owes much to a presentation at once affectionate and satirical. With her ungainly form, singsong speech mannerisms, chirpy demeanor, and relentlessly healthy appetite, the portrayal of Marge is "only a breath away from caricature."[48] Marge's quite ordinary oddities not only cohere with the film's comic presentation of its populace, but also defuse the threat of the potentially disturbing collision of gendered images, of mother and licensed killer, that a pregnant policewoman represents.

Marge is also the polar opposite of the cinematic female officers who preceded her. Indeed, the heroes of both *Fargo* and *Copycat* escape most of the limitations imposed on earlier policewomen. The glamorization of Lottie Mason is nowhere evident in Marge, who favors ruffled blouses and furry earflaps, or in businesslike M.J. Monahan. Neither policewoman is a rookie like Megan Turner and Clarice Starling, and Police Chief Gunderson answers to no one. Instead of playing the childlike role of orphan or daughter like so many of her cinematic forebears, Marge carries the markers of adulthood: a lined face, a house and husband, and a pregnancy. Although M.J. remains single, she answers to neither parent nor male mentor, and is clearly a grown-up. Nor is either policewoman endangered by her sexual relationships like the protagonists of early female cop films. Indeed, Marge has the ungrudging support of a husband who insists on cooking her a hot breakfast when she must leave in the night to investigate murder. And neither policewoman has to justify her profession to the world.

Nor do castration anxieties figure significantly. These later films feature none of the emasculating banter of *V.I. Warshawski* or *Fatal Beauty,* and neither policewoman loses her gun as in *Blue Steel*. The theft of Ruben's gun by a suspect suggests a lingering castration anxiety in *Copycat,* but it is countered by the reassertion of masculine values as M.J. adopts the macho magnum-force ethic that Ruben had been trying to teach her. On the whole, gender anxieties are much less in evidence in these films that make less effort to conform their female heroes to a male model. Indeed, *Fargo* seems not only to abjure the coping mechanisms of earlier policewoman films, but almost to parody them. It's even possible to read the film's most infamous scene, of a stiff severed leg being forced into a wood chipper, as an outrageous retort to the castration anxieties of films such as *Fatal Beauty* and *Blue Steel*.

Though neither *Copycat* nor *Fargo* could approach the extraordinary success of *The Silence of the Lambs,* both of these experiments at creating a less macho female cop found considerable acceptance. Both films received positive critical notice and made a tidy profit, and *Fargo* garnered several awards. However, both were, like *The Silence of the Lambs,* detective dramas. As such, they were free from generic pressures to include the spectacular action sequences characteristic of cop films that involve prolonged confrontation with the enemy, as in the *Die Hard* series. Moreover, because of their lower cost such detective dramas can turn a profit without drawing heavily from the large base of male fans of the action-adventure drama. For instance, the female-centered action extravaganza *The Long Kiss Goodnight* was considered a financial "miss" because it cost $65 million to make and market but grossed only $34 million in domestic box office. *Fargo,* which grossed just a few million more, earned a considerable profit because it cost only $7 million.[49] Because of their genre, then, *Copycat* and *Fargo* could easily avoid the repeated physical confrontations that often lead female action heroes to be derided as macho. Because they did not need as large an audience to recoup their costs, they could experiment with gender roles without extreme concern about offending the predominantly male audience that supports action flicks.

Split Personalities

Alongside these mid-nineties films that experimented with redefining the female hero as different from the male hero, other films tried to redefine the female law enforcer hero by separating her feminine and masculine attributes. Two of these—Sidney Lumet's *Stranger among Us* (1992) and Renny Harlin's *Long Kiss Goodnight* (1996)—offer the viewer two competing personalities within the same female protagonist.[50] The later Steven Soderbergh film *Out of Sight* (1998) places its female protagonist in two different genres.[51] Each of these splitting techniques avoids commitment to a single representation of heroic womanhood, an inconsistency evident in the incomplete closure of each film's ending.

Both split-personality films present a choice between a feminine persona identified with peaceful domesticity and a tougher but sexualized persona, reminiscent of early female law enforcers. *A Stranger among Us* begins with the tough cop. In this first manifestation, New York City detective Emily Eden might have come straight out of *Impulse*. Her spike heels and blond dye job foreground her sexuality, while the hints of emotional problems show her to be a true sister to Lottie Mason. Like Megan Turner, she has a troubled relationship with her father, an alcoholic who drove away her mother, and therefore remains positioned as a child like so many of her predecessors. She is also all too willing to use her gun; like Rita Rizzoli and a hundred male movie cops, she is a "cowboy" whom others fear to partner with, and whose boss tries to restrain her. And like Warshawski's, Eden's final confrontation is with a woman.

The Long Kiss Goodnight presents the tough version of womanhood in Charly, a CIA operative who has just emerged from eight amnesia-ridden years of a more domestic life. Strictly speaking, Charly is not a law enforcer, having been a government assassin during the lawless era of the Cold War—but the film bears consideration because it adheres to the same pattern as early female cop films, only writ large. This female hero, who can diverge further from the standard of goodness required of an ordinary police officer or detective, can therefore perform more violence. Indeed, Charly specializes in such active masculine heroics as throwing knives and shattering glass. Charly's emulation of male models surpasses that of late-eighties female cops. Like the male action heroes of the special-effects-ridden nineties, she miraculously and repeatedly escapes death through explosion, gunfire, and defenestration; she kills efficiently and often; and she even has a black male "buddy" (Mitch, played by Samuel Jackson) like Mel Gibson before her. As if to counterbalance these masculine activities (as well as to emulate the attention lavished on the hero's body in male action pictures), the movie makes Charly hypersexual. Like the tough version of Emily, she dyes her hair blond, wears provocative clothes, and favors lust over love.

For other audience tastes, however, the film offers a different version of womanhood: Samantha—mother, schoolteacher, and cookie-baker. With her long auburn hair and matronly clothes, Samantha embodies domestic womanhood: nurturing, affectionate, and homebound. The film even invites the audience to choose their version of heroine by scripting lines wherein Mitch announces which personality he favors at the moment.

A Stranger among Us marks Emily Eden's more traditional persona with a return to her natural brown hair color and adoption of more modest clothes, after her stay among the ultratraditional Hasidim transforms her. When her male colleagues first spot Emily in this garb, they make merry over having mistaken her for "a lady," a category of womanhood to which she will aspire by the film's end. The terms of her entry into this form of womanhood are telling: she switches from "lust" for her partner to love for a rabbinical student; and although she remains a police officer, she no longer shoots "perps" in the back or through the windshield of careening cars. The film's conservative implication that its female hero can find true happiness only as a "lady" (purged of overt sexuality and violence) is partly masked by linking each brand of womanhood with a different culture: toughness with the violence of the New York streets, softness with the peaceful community of the Hasidim. But Lumet's film does not meditate on the relative advantages of archaic religious and secular cultures as does Peter Weir's *Witness,* from which *Stranger* steals so heavily. The Hasidic world appears as an unabashed paradise (as implied by the film's original and non-U.S.-release title, *Close to Eden*).[52]

Although reviewers mainly lambasted its sugarcoating of the Hasidim, they also expressed discomfort with its vision of womanhood in their objections to casting Melanie Griffith, "with her baby-doll-on-helium voice, in the role of a pistol-packing cop."[53] Lumet declared that he chose Griffith based on her "vulnerability and openness," which were appropriate to "the third act of this movie."[54] But reviewers found the tough-cop Emily more credible than her feminized alter ego, since they lamented that Lumet had not cast Jamie Lee Curtis or Sigourney Weaver rather than an actress "who looks more worried about breaking a fingernail than catching lawbreakers."[55]

The very different casting of *The Long Kiss Goodnight* underscores its privileging of macho over domestic womanhood—a choice fairly demanded by Charly's generic position as action hero. Geena Davis brings to the film's female hero both athleticism and the force of her notorious role in *Thelma and Louise,* a film to which *The Long Kiss Goodnight* alludes. Harlin's film makes a nod to traditionalism by returning its hero to domesticity at film's end, but it has devoted so much time and energy to the spectacle of Charly's body and ruthlessness that the tough persona dominates.

Perhaps because it patterns its female hero on a male model, *The Long Kiss Goodnight* reverts to many of the devices of first-wave films to justify the woman's violence. Charly maintains a defensive stance, reacting to the attempt of associates from her past life to kill her; she defends women and children—herself and her daughter—rather than men.[56] She lives under the sign of the father, having been recruited (like Cathy Weaver) and even adopted by a male mentor after her father's death. She finds danger in a sexual relationship with a man who becomes her enemy. In this later film, however, the hero shows less deference to men: she rescues her male partner as well as being rescued by him, and in the climax kills her onetime lover in a vicious battle.

In spite of its somewhat more egalitarian view, the castration anxieties so obvious in early films erupt into *The Long Kiss Goodnight,* in the form of jokes about penis size. The female hero even yells, "Suck my dick." Moreover, in both *Long Kiss* and *Stranger,* the exchange of the phallic gun betrays castration anxiety and uncertainty about gender roles. Clarice Starling, M.J. Monahan, and Marge Gunderson all owned and held on to their own firearms, but the heroes of the split-personality films can't seem to keep guns of their own. During the final confrontation of Lumet's film, Emily Eden insists that the pacifist rabbinical student take her gun, figuring that no one will expect him to have it; this conservative film returns the phallic weapon to the male. In Harlin's film, Charly not only loses her gun at times but also seizes men's guns from suggestive locations, as when she fires Mitch's gun from inside his pocket or removes a gun from a dead man's fly. Whether the gun travels from male to female or in reverse,

FIGURE 10. Charly, the ferocious hero of *The Long Kiss Goodnight,* uses machine-gun fire to let the father of her daughter know what she thinks of him. Her bellow of murderous rage marks the outer limit of women's violence in cop movies.

the instability of ownership suggests the female hero's lack of a gun/phallus of her own.

These Hollywood containment devices familiar from first-wave films, however, didn't have much more success in satisfying the audience than they had had in the past. *The Long Kiss Goodnight* lost money and received mixed reviews. Although a number of critics confessed attraction to the slickness, speed, and smart banter of the film, they often complained about gross improbability and sometimes about the level of mayhem. Overt critical acceptance of the violent female hero seemed greater than in reviews of *Fatal Beauty* or *Blue Steel.* Still, reviewers were fixated on the collision of gendered categories. Janet Maslin sniped that Geena Davis is "able to shoot, slug and throttle without messing up her manicure"; and Roger Ebert advised Davis that it was a waste of effort for her to perform her own stunts in the film.[57] The occasional critic, however, resurrected the Dirty Harriet charge. The female reviewer from the *San Francisco Examiner* groused, "It must be a feminist statement. Otherwise why would an actress with Geena Davis' obvious ability want to keep making movies designed to demonstrate that women can be just as insensitive, bloodthirsty and repulsive in movies as men have been for years? . . . Remember [the pirate film] *Cutthroat Island? Thelma and Louise?*"[58]

The endings of both split-personality films respond to such lingering cultural discomfort with the image of the physically dominant female hero by temporizing. Both *A Stranger among Us* and *The Long Kiss Goodnight* leave audiences with a vision of a new and perhaps more complete woman who combines characteristics from the constellations represented by the two personalities. In the end, Emily Eden announces that she is a "new woman" who has learned from the Hasidim how to "feel soft on the inside" and is now renouncing sexual dalliance in preference to the search for a soul mate. Her natural hair color and modest but fashionable clothes suggest a compromise, but one dominated by Hasidic traditionalism. She does not, however, give up her profession; it appears to be acceptable that she be licensed to kill, so long as she is not too ready to kill. In the closing scene of *The Long Kiss Goodnight*, Charly/Charlene has reverted to Sam/Samantha (the very names embody the film's indecision), adopting once again her domestic persona as mother and mate—but with a difference. This compromise vision sports shoulder-length strawberry blond hair, midway between Charly's short platinum do and Samantha's long auburn locks. In bare feet and a flowing white dress, she avoids both Samantha's suburban frump and Charly's punk sexuality. Erupting into the family's country idyll is Sam's playful but practiced toss of a knife into a distant target—a sign that the female hero has not entirely set aside her toughness. Nonetheless, in Harlin's film as in Lumet's, the more traditionally feminine alter ego claims the powerful final moments of the film. These irresolute endings indicate a new strength and self-acceptance for the female hero, but they also revert to the familiar Hollywood formula, seen half a century ago in so many screwball comedies, of reinscribing the strong heroine into domestic values in the last scene.

An even more irresolute ending proved necessary in 1998's *Out of Sight*, which mixes incompatible generic formulas: romantic comedy, which demands that lovers be united; the cop film, which requires that criminals be apprehended; and the crime film, which directs sympathies toward bankrobber Jack Foley, played by the likable George Clooney.[59] The mix of genres demanded narrative indeterminacy from the start. As a cop, bound to nab her quarry, Federal Marshal Karen Sisko (Jennifer Lopez) shoots and jails Foley; as his lover, who must be reunited with him in the end, she is last seen with him in the prison van, setting him up with a cellmate who can help him escape. Although there can hardly be any rosy future together for an escaped con and a federal agent, the film does its best to have it both ways.

So too does the film improbably position its heroine both as tough cop and soft-hearted lover, not at different times—as in *A Stranger among Us*—but simultaneously. As tough cop, Karen is tough indeed, but less in terms of muscularity or exceptional skills than in terms of self-assurance. She knows her way around a gun, and is perfectly capable of defending herself by shooting a criminal or smacking a would-be rapist. Courageous without being foolhardy, she calls for backup but goes in herself when conditions deteriorate during a violent robbery attempt. She's much better at tracking the escaped convicts than are her bosses, and succeeds in most of her professional goals. And she is far more self-confident in manner than some of her cinematic forebears: when Foley marvels that she doesn't seem scared after being kidnapped, she dryly retorts, "What do you want me to do, scream?"

Perhaps because of its hero's toughness, *Out of Sight* employs most of the containment devices of first-wave female cop films. The hero defends women (Adele) and herself, and again must answer why "someone like you" would become a law officer. But the film also invokes some of the earlier motifs only to undermine them. The possibility of infantalization looms when Karen first appears in the company of her father, but recedes when she maintains a good-natured indifference to his advice. Likewise, Foley's sunny smile and Karen's safe emergence from a previous liaison with a crook dispel the threat implicit in her sexual relationship with a criminal.

Karen Sisko's sexuality, emphasized by the casting of Lopez, both limits and intensifies her power. The cop plot tempts her toward dangerous liaisons, all with married men or criminals, and so renders her vulnerable. Within the romantic comedy plot, Sisko's sexual attractiveness has a more complicated dual effect. On the one hand it sets the romance under way, and fuels much of the erotic energy for which reviewers praised the film; on the other, it also invites a reaction from characters and viewers alike that can overshadow the character's less physical attributes. The movie insists on her desirability to the point of improbability. (How many professional women head to work in short slit skirts and revealing necklines?) Exposure of the romantic comedy heroine's body also makes a joke of the cop hero. When she first confronts Foley during the prison breakout, the film makes high comedy out of the disjunction between U.S. Marshal Sisko's pronouncement that Foley is under arrest and cute Karen's flailing bare legs as the men hoist her sideways like a doll. Likewise, Marshal Sisko's complaints of FBI discrimination against female officers in the cop plot are counterbalanced by the traditionalist values in the romantic plot, represented by the gallant Foley, who marvels that shotgun-toting Sisko is "just a girl" and who feels obliged to rescue damsels in distress.

As in *The Long Kiss Goodnight* and *A Stranger among Us*, *Out of Sight*'s ambivalence toward gender roles surfaces in the exchange of guns. Again, the female hero cannot hold on to her phallic weapon. A scene that toys with gender expectations introduces Sisko as she opens a birthday gift from a gentleman, a gift that turns out not to be jewels from an older lover but rather a gun from her father. In her next scene, however, she loses both that gun and her shotgun to the unarmed escapees—a fact critically noted by her boss. The scene of the eventual return of her gun slyly remarks on its phallic nature: she awakes to find it on the pillow, in the place of her departed lover, after her night with Foley.

FIGURE 11. Hero Karen sports slit skirt and shotgun. She's dangerous but about to be kidnapped and romanced by the dashing criminal in *Out of Sight*. Glamour, vulnerability, and fighting skills combine in the female cop-hero package.

Although the female hero regains her gun (and the will to use it) by the end of the film, its slipperiness and its origin as male gift both call into question her inherent right to this masculine totem of power.

Like *A Stranger among Us* and *The Long Kiss Goodnight*, *Out of Sight* failed to generate much heat at the box office, in spite of generally favorable reviews and a number of awards (mostly for editing and screenplay). But neither did it generate the expressions of distaste for treatment of gender that the other films did. In casting its female hero role with an actress renowned for her sexual appeal, rather than one associated with tough roles (like Geena Davis) or feminine ones (like Melanie Griffith), it invoked a longtime Hollywood tradition of showcasing the female body. This move seemed less dissonant because of the film's use of romantic comedy as well as cop film structures. Moreover, it promoted gender values endorsed by a range of American viewers from diverse political positions, including equality in the workplace and male chivalry. Although competing gender visions and generic conventions cost it narrative closure, *Out of Sight* nonetheless envisioned a violent woman who would suit the taste of a wide audience.

Conclusion

By the late nineties, a decade after beginning its experiments, Hollywood still has not fashioned an armed woman who would meet widespread acceptance as a hero in the everyday world. Nonetheless, some general trends are clear. Films at the start of the decade generated concerns about gun-toting women masquerading as men, and sought to counterbalance their masculinity with a host of "female" motivations and weaknesses (*Fatal Beauty, Impulse, Betrayed, V.I. Warshawski,* and more self-consciously, *Blue Steel*). Later films, taking *The Silence of the Lambs* as a model, combined traits from the masculine and feminine constellations to create a more integrated hero, and some experimented with models of a specifically female heroism (*Copycat, Fargo*). Other films, using different splitting techniques, have allowed their viewers a choice of visions of heroic womanhood by offering alternate readings of the hero through two personalities (*A Stranger among Us, The Long Kiss Goodnight*) or two plots (*Out of Sight*). The films that have won most acceptance with critics and audiences have been those that emphasized their hero's resourcefulness and courage, rather than those showcasing the female hero's physical dominance. Audiences seem more willing to embrace female heroes who perform violence only on occasion, and prefer to let (male) villains rack up the action film's required body count (as in *The Silence of the Lambs, Copycat,* and *Fargo*). The limited box-office returns of most female-dominated cop films suggest that while some audiences embrace the spectacle of the female action hero coming to the rescue of others, the ultraviolent heroine cannot draw the large audiences necessary to turn profits for high-cost action extravaganzas like *The Long Kiss Goodnight.* These movies fail even when they offer the spectacular female body to appeal to the young men who make up the genre's primary fans.

In spite of the continuing uncertainties about gender manifest in Hollywood's female heroes, the industry's unflagging attempts to envision as admirable the woman with a gun signify a realization that consumers desire change in old gender categories. The experiments with female cop films testify to Hollywood's recognition of women's growing economic power and their influence in the industry, both as consumers ("Women are . . . driving the box office," says Fox Chairman William Mechanic)[60] and as producers (women directed *Impulse* and *Blue Steel,* and cowrote *Copycat*). The proliferation of women's action films increases the number and diversity of representations of women in popular culture, a change likely to erode stereotyped categories of femaleness. In challenging the exclusive right of the male to the institutional and personal power granted by the gun and the badge, these films, however cautiously, test the possibilities for women to insert themselves in arenas of power from which they have long been excluded.

Notes

1. Jeffrey A. Brown, "Gender and the Action Heroine: Hardbodies and the *Point of No Return,*" *Cinema Journal* 35, no. 3 (spring 1996): 52–71.

2. Mandy Johnson, "Women as Action Heroes," *Glamour,* March 1994, 153.

3. Jacqueline Bobo, "Sifting through the Controversy: Reading *The Color Purple,*" *Callaloo* 12 (spring 1989): 332–42.

4. *Fatal Beauty,* written by Hilary Henkin and Paul Reisner, directed by Tom Holland, produced by Leonard Knoll (MGM/UA, 1987); *Impulse,* written by John De Marco and Leigh Chapman, directed by Sondra Locke, produced by Albert S. Ruddy and Andre Marco (Warner Brothers, 1989).

5. *Blue Steel,* written by Kathryn Bigelow and Eric Red, directed by Kathryn Bigelow, produced by Edward R. Pressman and Oliver Stone (MGM/UA, 1990).

6. *V.I. Warshawski,* written by David Aaron Cohen and Nick Thiel, directed by Jeff Kanew, produced by Jeffrie Lurie (Buena Vista, 1991).

7. *Betrayed,* written by Joe Eszterhas, directed by Constantin Costa-Gavras, produced by Irwin Winkler (MGM/UA, 1988). This essay will not discuss *Black Widow* because, although the justice agent played by Debra Winger trains with a gun early on, she abandons it when she pursues her quarry, declaring that "she's not about guns." However, the film features several of the same mechanisms as the others I discuss: the female hero has little experience, being a data analyst rather than a field agent; she can seem somewhat juvenile, as insecure as a teenager about her sexual identity; and she becomes vulnerable through her sexual attraction to the criminal's fiancé. *Black Widow,* written by Ronald Bass, directed by Bob Rafelson, produced by Laurence Mark and Harold Schneider (20th Century Fox, 1986). Discussions of gender issues in this film appear in Teresa de Lauretis, "Guerrilla in the Midst: Women's Cinema in the '80s," *Screen* 31, no. 1 (spring 1990): 6–25; Marina Heung, *"Black Widow,"* *Film Quarterly* 41, no. 1 (fall 1987): 54–58; and Myra Macdonald, *Representing Women: Myths of Femininity in the Popular Media* (New York: Edward Arnold, 1995), 122–27.

8. Jeffrey A. Brown, "Bullets, Buddies, and Bad Guys: The 'Action-Cop' Genre," *Journal of Popular Film and Television* 21, no. 2 (summer 1993): 86.

9. Robert T. Self, "Redressing the Law in Kathryn Bigelow's *Blue Steel,*" *Journal of Film and Video* 46, no. 2 (summer 1994): 33.

10. Kathryn Bigelow, quoted in Betsy Sharkey, "Kathryn Bigelow Practices the Art of the Kill," *New York Times,* 11 March 1990, 217.

11. Quoted in Shari Zeck, "Female Bonding in *Cagney and Lacey,*" *Journal of Popular Culture* 22, no. 3 (winter 1988): 144.

12. Kathleen Gregory Klein, "Watching Warshawski," in *It's a Print! Detective Fiction from Page to Screen,* ed. William Reynolds and Elizabeth Trembley (Bowling Green, Ky.: Popular Press, 1994), 145–57.

13. Jeffrey Lurie, quoted in Anne Thompson, "What Happened to Warshawski?" *Philadelphia Inquirer,* 11 August 1991, L2.

14. Thompson, "What Happened to Warshawski?" 2L.

15. Caryn James, "These Heels Aren't Made for Stompin'," *New York Times,* 4 August 1991, 27.

16. Harriet E. Margolis, *"Blue Steel:* Progressive Feminism in the '90s?" *Post Script* 13, no. 1 (fall 1993): 67–76.

17. Ibid., 73.

18. Needeya Islam, "'I Wanted to Shoot People': Genre, Gender, and Action in the Films of Kathryn Bigelow," in *Kiss Me Deadly: Feminism and Cinema for the Moment,* ed. Laleen Jayamanne (Sydney: Power, 1995), 110.

19. Carol J. Clover, *Men, Women, and Chain Saws: Gender in the Modern Horror Film* (Princeton: Princeton University Press, 1992), 61.

20. Islam, "'I Wanted to Shoot People,'" 113.

21. Cora Kaplan, "Dirty Harriet/*Blue Steel:* Feminist Theory Goes to Hollywood," *Discourse* 16, no. 1 (fall 1993): 54.

22. Sharkey, "Kathryn Bigelow," 26.

23. Kaplan, "Dirty Harriet/*Blue Steel,*" 58.

24. Anna Powell, "Blood on the Borders: *Near Dark* and *Blue Steel,*" *Screen* 35, no. 2 (summer 1994): 146.

25. Yvonne Tasker, *Spectacular Bodies: Gender, Genre, and the Action Cinema* (New York: Routledge, 1993), 159.

26. Thompson, "What Happened to Warshawski?" 2.

27. John Leo, "Toxic Feminism on the Big Screen," *U.S. News and World Report,* 10 June 1991, 20.

28. *The Silence of the Lambs,* written by Ted Tally; directed by Jonathan Demme; produced by Kenneth Utt, Edward Saxon, and Ron Bozman (Orion, 1991).

29. Janet Staiger, "Taboos and Totems: Cultural Meanings of *The Silence of the Lambs,*" in *Film Theory Goes to the Movies,* ed. Jim Collins, Hilary Radner, and Ava Preacher Collins (New York: Routledge, 1993), 153.

30. All such references to mainstream reactions are, of course, generalizations; there are always individual and even group exceptions—such as, in this case, the gay activists who protested that the depiction of the film's monstrous serial killer promoted homophobia, and those who outed Foster in reaction to the film.

31. Caryn James, "Women Cops Can Be a Cliché in Blue," *New York Times,* 15 April 1990, 217.

32. Janet Maslin, review of *Fatal Beauty, New York Times,* 30 October 1987, C8.

33. As Linda Mizejewski explains, Clarice's refusal to engage in heterosexual exchange "clearly avoids the castrating threat of the female dick, just as it avoids the cliches of glamorization (consumable sexuality), fetishization, or monstrosity." "Picturing the Female Dick: *The Silence of the Lambs* and *Blue Steel,*" *Journal of Film and Video* 45, no. 2 (summer/fall 1993): 18.

34. Joan G. Kotker, "It's Scarier at the Movies: Jonathan Demme's Adaptation of *The Silence of the Lambs,*" in *It's a Print! Detective Fiction from Page to Screen,* ed. William Reynolds and Elizabeth Trembley (Bowling Green, Ky.: Popular Press, 1994), 199–200.

35. Clover, *Men, Women, and Chain Saws,* 232–33.

36. Mizejewski, "Picturing the Female Dick," 19.

37. Charles Fleming, "That's Why the Lady Is a Champ," *Newsweek,* 7 June 1993, 66.

38. Joel Silver, quoted in ibid.

39. Jeffrey Wells, "Ready for Action," *Philadelphia Inquirer,* 14 June 1995, E5. Geena Davis eventually starred in *Mistress of the Sea,* retitled *Cutthroat Island* and released in 1995 to dismal box office.

40. Joss Wheedon, quoted in ibid.

41. Ibid.

42. Josh Freidman, quoted in ibid.

43. Graham Yost, quoted in ibid.

44. Lecter is clearly more brilliant than is Clarice or her FBI colleagues; after all, they question him not because they suspect him of having a personal knowledge of the killer but because of his great intelligence as well as his (theoretical *and* experiential!) expertise on serial killers. Yet Lecter's genius does not undercut Clarice's intellectual standing. His very interest in Clarice, after he has rejected other overtures from the FBI, expresses his admiration for her intelligence. She is sometimes seen to manipulate Lecter, and only she can decode and apply his clues.

45. *Fargo,* written by Joel and Ethan Coen, directed by Joel Coen, produced by Ethan Coen (Polygram, 1996).

46. Jodie Foster, quoted in Lawrence Grobel, "Anything Is Possible," *Movieline,* October 1991, 32. *Copycat,* written by Ann Biderman and David Madsen, directed by Jon Amiel, produced by Arnon Milchan and Mark Tarlov (Warner Brothers, 1995).

47. Todd McCarthy, review of *Fargo, Premiere,* March 1996, 22.

48. Anthony Lane, "Republicans with Guns," *New Yorker,* 25 March 1996, 99.

49. Bernard Weinraub, "What Do Women Want? Movies," *New York Times*, 10 February 1997, C11.

50. *A Stranger among Us*, written by Robert Avrech; directed by Sidney Lumet; produced by Steve Golin, Sigurjon Sighvatsson, and Howard Rosenman (Buena Vista, 1992). *The Long Kiss Goodnight*, written by Shane Black; directed by Renny Harlin; produced by Renny Harlin, Stephanie Austin, and Shane Black (New Line, 1996). Action films that portray female heroes who are not law officers use similar splitting strategies. For instance, Edward Zwick's *Courage under Fire* (1996) sends a military officer on a quest for truth. He must judge four competing narratives of Captain Karen Walden's actions in a battle where she died. Three men from her ill-fated helicopter offer versions that represent three stereotypical reactions to women in combat. Her copilot describes her as "butch," foul-mouthed, and strident, but states his admiration for the way she did her job—a reading that finds conduct unbecoming to a woman even while appropriate to an officer. The medic paints images of efficiency and devotion, an ideal modeled on male heroes of war movies of the past. Sergeant Monfriez trades on stereotypes of women as hysterical and fearful. Although the fourth and apparently "true" account concludes that Walden deserves a medal, the film reaches that conclusion only after raising common objections to women in combat. Moreover, the corrected version of Walden's actions carefully balances masculine and feminine traits: Walden cries from nervousness but then takes a tough line. Most intriguingly, she justifies ignoring her own wound in rhetoric that combines military-man lingo with female experience: "I gave birth to a nine-pound baby, asshole, I think I can handle it."

51. *Out of Sight*, written by Scott Frank; directed by Steve Soderbergh; produced by Danny DeVito, Michael Shamberg, and Stacey Sher (Universal, 1998).

52. Sidney Lumet, *Making Movies* (New York: Vintage, 1996), 106.

53. Steven Rea, "Lumet Concedes the Boos, Stresses the Cheers for his 'Stranger,'" *Philadelphia Inquirer*, 19 July 1992, N2.

54. Quoted in ibid.

55. Desmand Ryan, review of *A Stranger among Us*, Weekend, *Philadelphia Inquirer*, 17 July 1992, 5.

56. In this rather incoherent film the hero's maternal motivations waver. As Samantha she devotes herself to daughter Caitlin, but as Charly she at first ignores the child's well-being. Nonetheless, by the end Charly defies death to rescue the girl, and the closing credits accompany a song that wails, "To save my child I'd rather go hungry . . ."—maternal devotion can overcome the resistance of even the toughest female hero.

57. Janet Maslin, "Muffin-Baking Mom or Gun-Toting Killer?" *New York Times*, 11 October 1996, C18; and Roger Ebert, review of *The Long Kiss Goodnight*, *Chicago Sun-Times*, 10 October 1996, online: <http://www.suntimes.com/ebert/ebert_reviews/1996/10/101104.html>.

58. Barbara Shulgasser, "Dirty Harriet's Latest Adventure," *San Francisco Examiner*, 11 October 1996, C3.

59. This essay's treatment of *Out of Sight* will concentrate on the movie's cop plot, centered on the female hero; and the romantic plot, in which she figures as half of the central couple. In the criminal plot, of course, she is only a secondary character. Though Clooney receives top billing in the film and commands more screen time, the story often proceeds from the female cop's point of view.

60. William Mechanic, quoted in Weinraub, "What Do Women Want? Movies," C11.

Caged Heat

The (R)evolution of Women-in-Prison Films

Suzanna Danuta Walters

The genre of women-in-prison movies, typically relegated to late-night sleaze-fest cable and offbeat guides to B favorites, can offer feminist cultural critics juicy fare for deconstructive antics. While presenting glimpses into the murky realm of "B" film making and exploitation schlock, these films also provide us with intimations of the unspoken, entrée into forbidden realms, insight into film's location as contradictory arbiter of changing social relations.

Women-in-prison films elaborate fully the creation of the marginal subject. Marginalized by gender, stigmatized by sexual preference, victimized by callous bureaucracies, physically isolated and preyed upon—these women are most assuredly the marked other. Because the genre itself assumes a certain otherness (criminal women)—differences literally explode and proliferate. Interracial friendships, lesbian sexuality, female rebellion, and violence all come into play. Women-in-prison films—in all their strangeness, their multiple marginality—often present images of women and women's relationships rarely found in more mainstream genres. Women in this world live together, love together, fight each other, and most centrally, fight back against the largely male systems of brutal domination that keep them all down. Unlike as in mainstream Hollywood films (e.g., *Thelma and Louise*), they often win. And, unlike more mainstream representations, the violent women of women's prison narratives are not inevitably punished for their violation of the (often unspoken) rule against female aggression. Kick-ass women are both glamorized and contextualized; their strength and power is key to their liberation from the forces of patriarchal darkness that keep them submissive. Patriarchal wrongdoing, indeed, often provides the motivation for the violence in the first place, so that female violence is seen as morally justified (as well as sexy). Like the rape-revenge genre in which female violence is justified through a prior victimization, there is often a certain celebratory air about these films. Indeed, as Judith Halberstam notes in her discussion of the prison film as site of the construction of "female masculinity," "[t]he scenes of rebellious women in prison films always allow for the possibility of an overt feminist message that involves both a critique of male-dominated society and some notion of female community."[1]

What is particularly interesting about this genre is how it manifests genre itself as always in flux, not simply driven by predetermined structural imperatives and symbolic motives. For example, while women-in-prison movies can be fairly categorized as B melodramas in the thirties and forties and even into the fifties, they quickly shift into the exploitation genre as the decades progress. The subject matter of the genre in its early cinematic manifestations witnessed the likes of well-known actors such as Ida Lupino, Shirley Knight, Ann Shirley, Eleanor Parker, and others, while in more recent years it has come to be the refuge of over-the-top camp stars such as Linda Blair and Pam Grier.[2] Played for high pathos or verité slice-of-life in the early days, it becomes almost exclusively played for sexual frolics and tongue-in-cheek camp sleaze in later years.

Yet, ironically, it is often these later, more clearly exploitative films that subvert the typical Hollywood endings and offer glimpses into realms of female empowerment. Indeed, these most marginal of representations (not only about criminal women but located in the larger context of exploitation action film) often explode with what Linda Williams has called (in another context) "the frenzy of the visible." But even the more staid early melodramas allowed for a discourse on female victimization and empowerment that pushed it away from its patriarchal moorings.

Women-in-prison films therefore constitute not one unitary genre but rather an odd and eclectic pastiche of many subgenres—from melodrama to teenage trouble to exploitation to protofeminist. And this (disunified) genre of women-in-prison films may also be seen in the context of the largely male-defined genre of prison dramas, a connection I am unable to explore in this essay.

This is not to say that these films are without structural continuities. Indeed, almost all women-in-prison films are characterized by a number of central elements, including some reference to lesbianism, violence between women, initiation of innocent victim into prison life, turning point where innocent victim becomes conscious and begins to rebel, struggle between prison heavies and inmates, riot, breakout, and of course, the inevitable shower scene. But, within these broad structural elements, there is a great degree of variation. For example, while lesbianism is clearly a central element in this genre (and possibly one central reason these films have any audience at all, given the prevalence of "lesbian" imagery in male-produced porn), it is alternately treated as mutual, loving romance and as violent, sadistic abuse. These genre shifts thus speak not only to the transformations of a cinematic language, but to the changing ways of "speaking" woman as outcast, woman as other.

Love Means Never Having to Be Locked Up: Incarceration as Melodrama

One of the earliest women-in-prison films incorporates the incarcerated woman into the transformative hands of the romantic melodrama. *Condemned Women* (1938) centers on a romance between the brave new psychiatrist and the victimized young inmate. Starring Ann Shirley as sweet and innocent Millie Hanson and Sally Eilers as bitter and tough Linda Wilson, this film is both a love story and a commentary on the battle between the entrenched bureaucracy of the prison system and the new "curative" ideas of a young psychiatrist, Dr. Philip Duncan. Importantly, the old-style bureaucracy is here represented less by the old-fashioned warden (who is rather benevolently paternal) than by the decidedly Victorian and superstern matrons, particularly the head matron, Clara Glover.

In an early scene, the warden speaks with the two matrons about their treatment of the inmates. While he is seated at his desk, the standing matrons take on an almost giantlike quality: large, imposing, and rigid in their immobility in the face of the warden's admonitions to liberality:

MATRON: But I can't discipline prisoners that way, Warden.

WARDEN: Nevertheless, you will continue to allow the prisoners to talk at work. Denial of the right to talk all day comes under the heading, I think, of unwarranted punishment.

MATRON: They're here to be punished.

WARDEN: Of course. But they come here bitter. We're better off if we don't send them out the same way.

MATRON: Twenty years ago we didn't worry about how prisoners felt when they went out.

WARDEN: You're right. But if we had the same women today in these modern prisons we'd have still less worry.

MATRON: You're not trying to tell me that women are different now?

WARDEN: They are. Full of tensions and nerves they never used to have. It's a hundred times harder for a woman to stand imprisonment today than it used to be. We must make changes to meet that.

These "tense" and "nervous" women of the postsuffrage era need not the iron hand of the callous state apparatus (here embodied in the oversize figures of the malicious matrons), but rather the gentle and soothing tones of the forward-thinking young shrink.

Bitter Linda is indeed brought back to life by the caring young psychiatrist, only to be told by the warden that she should give him up "for his own good." Upon that, Linda breaks out and escapes (innocent Millie dies here) with her former enemy Annie (who also dies). Linda gets caught, but is saved by her doctor/psychiatrist when he forces the warden to tell the truth and reveals the lies of the prison matrons, who claim Linda engineered the breakout. She is given one year and they presumably live happily ever after.

In this melodramatic rendering of women in prison, the system itself can be transformed once given over into the hands of the scientific "experts." Typically men, these experts are both representatives of the growing popularity of the "talking cure" and signifiers of a larger quest for moral redemption within the confines of the existing system. The women in these early narratives are largely innocent, toughened by the hard knocks of an unjust system, but rarely legitimately "locked up." And, importantly, while prison life is often characterized by the divide between the incoming "good" girl and the already hardened inmates, this film, like so many others, operates as a force of female reunification. In the world of women's prisons, the women know all too well which side their (moldy) bread is buttered on and most often end up, at least temporarily, reconciling differences in the service of battling the nasty wardens and corrupt system.

Women's Prison (1955) stars Ida Lupino as the hard-bitten superintendent of a women's prison separated only by "concrete walls and rifle bullets" from the men's prison. Jan Sterling plays Helene Jensen, the innocent young housewife brought in for killing a child in a car accident. As Helene cracks under the dual pressures of guilt and prison life, the good doctor (played with camp aplomb by Howard Duff) battles the mean superintendent Van Zant for the soul of Helene (and the integrity of the system). True to fifties backlash form, the evil is now firmly located in the lap of a frustrated and loveless woman. And who else but the benevolent doctor to inform the matron of her own psychopathology:

DOCTOR: May I tell you what's wrong with you? [*he sits on her desk*]

VAN ZANT: Do, by all means.

DOCTOR: You dislike most of the women here because, deep down, you're jealous of them.

VAN ZANT: That's absurd.

DOCTOR: You're feminine, attractive. You must have had opportunities to marry. Maybe you even *cared* for someone once in your cold way. [*reaction shot of Van Zant's fluttering eyes*]

VAN ZANT: How dare you! [*stands up*]

DOCTOR: But possibly he turned to somebody who could give him what he *really* wanted. Warmth. Understanding. Love. There's hardly a woman inside these walls that doesn't know what love is.

VAN ZANT: Yes, and that's why most of them are here.

DOCTOR: Exactly. Even the broken ranks have known some kind of love. And that's why you hate them.

VAN ZANT: What you call hate is complete understanding, Doctor. Knowledge gained by years of study and hard work. I know these women. All of them. And only a strong mind can control them.

The doctor goes on to call her a psychopath. Not soon after, the doctor's point is proven when Van Zant brutally beats a pregnant inmate, causing her miscarriage and eventual death. The prisoners rebel, Van Zant ends up crazy in a padded room (saved from the prisoners by the doctor), and Helene gets released and reunited with her husband. In this fifties narrative, working women are the carriers of bureaucratic abuse and—as in the earlier melodramatic prison stories—benevolent male doctors save the day. The unjustly incarcerated women are liberated less through the (almost obligatory) efforts of the prison breakout and more by the internal cleansing of a faulty (woman-centered) apparatus.

House of Women (1962) is characteristic of this melodramatic genre yet occasionally slips over into the more sensationalistic narratives that soon would dominate the women-in-prison genre. A remake of the classic 1950 film *Caged*, *House of Women* stars Shirley Knight as the innocent and pregnant Erica Hayden, picked up as an accessory to armed robbery because she happened to be with the wrong man at the wrong time. As in most women-in-prison films, the narrative centers on the trials and tribulations of the innocent prisoner (who often turns "hard" toward the end) in her battles to *(a)* get released or *(b)* keep her baby. Here, Erica gives birth in prison, and the rules dictate that the child can stay until his third birthday (a nice Freudian age!) and is then taken by the state. Erica is joined in her battle against the new and nasty warden Frank Cole by the drunken but compassionate doctor.

Erica's progress through the prison system takes many turns. After her child is taken from her a day early (and after a wonderful solidarity riot by the women), Erica is transferred to work at the warden's house. He invariably falls in love with her, and his meanness is revealed to be the result of his wife having convinced him to parole a prisoner who she then ran off with. Erica embarks on an "affair" with him (much to the chagrin of the doctor and the anger of the other women) hoping to enlist his sympathies in getting parole and being reunited with her son. But her plan backfires, as the smitten doctor argues against her parole, fearing she too will leave him. When she confronts him, he hits her and sends her back to the main prison, where another rebellion is fomented by friend Sophie ("We want a square deal!"). The warden cracks down, reversing the liberalization that occurred during his relationship with Erica. After Sophie's son falls from the roof of the children's dormitory and dies, Sophie takes hostages and all the women join in a breakout attempt. Hardened Erica at first aligns with furious Sophie (indeed, she leads them to the gun in the bedside table of the warden), but when Sophie attempts to kill one of the prison board members, the "real" (good-at-heart) Erica reemerges. The drunken but noble doctor rescues both Mrs. Hunter (the board member) and psychotic Sophie. The final image is a cut first to the humane Mrs. Stoughton (assistant warden), now firmly ensconced as the new warden, and then to the release of a chastened Erica.

In the aftermath of the Clarence Thomas–Anita Hill case, this film reads like a narrative on sexual harassment. It also confounds our expectations on a number of levels. First, we expect Erica to rehabilitate the stern warden, now that the source of his evil is revealed and located firmly in his ex-wife's errant sexuality. Yet she doesn't, he acts despicably in jettisoning her parole, and we don't have the heterosexual pairing neatly tied up. Rather, the failure of that narrative reinforces a rather different women's prison theme (men, particularly men in power, are dogs).

Compassion wins out over old-fashioned discipline as the film concludes with Erica paroled and reunited with her son. The final shot has Erica scooping up little Tommy with the doctor framed in the newly reconstructed (single-parent) family unit. Like in the 1938 film, the system itself can be "cured" of its excesses, almost always understood as the province of individual evil. Indeed, several other earlier films such as *The Wayward Girl* (1957) and *Girls Town* (1959) paint a rather benign picture of the penal institution—if evil is present it is seen in quite individual terms, rather than endemic to the institution or built in to the system. And, unlike later films, these melodramatic renderings keep intact the innocence of the unjustly incarcerated victim. She might be hardened (and thus compelled to act on her own behalf) but we never doubt for a moment her true "goodness" and status as victim of the vagaries of heterosexual pairings.

The Prison Metamorphosis: Born Innocent but Turned Tough

By the time we get to *Born Innocent* (1974), we have more explicitly moved into the realm of psychology and social work, now understood as not so easily victorious. Linda Blair, here beginning her penchant for roles in which she gets violated by inanimate objects, plays fourteen-year-old runaway Christine, given over by her parents to the state home for girls. Befriended by a do-gooder teacher ("I want you to know that I'm here if you need me"), Linda nevertheless goes through the genre ritual of rape and abuse, from which she emerges hardened. Christine's status as "inmate" is clearly understood as the result of some bad parenting: an abusive father and a cowed mother. Indeed, all of the girls are shown to be victimized both by parents and by a system that has little place for unwanted children. In this seventies narrative, the villain really *is* the system (plus bad parents). The administration is represented by either do-good social workers like the teacher, or well-meaning housemothers. The evil inside is literally the return of the repressed. And no happy ending is found here, as Christine's victimization by the system bonds her ever more fully to the reproduction of the same. Indeed, in so many of these narratives, the venality of institutional life, the evil of corporatist structures, and the duplicity of government are as taken for granted as the relentless violence and abuse. But, unlike mainstream counterparts such as *Rambo* and the *Alien* movies, whatever heroism exists is to be found in a collective resistance to structural oppression, rather than brave acts of isolated individuals.

Linda Blair stars in *Chained Heat* (1983) as (once again) the innocent (but soon-to-be-tough) girl thrown in jail with the frenzied monsters. This film, now in full exploitation mode, has it all: racial violence, sleazy male and female wardens and doctors, drug rings and double-crossings, lots of sex and violence, and one too many nude shower scenes. For an extra attraction, a male transvestite gets beaten by the girls in the holding cell, adding a certain frisson of gratuitous violence that so clearly distinguishes the exploitation film from its tamer melodramatic predecessors.

As born-innocent Carol, Linda Blair gets tough in the prison and foments rebellion against the perverted male warden and the deranged female matron, thus bringing together the warring leaders of the black and white gangs against the powers of the panopticon. While not as self-consciously aware of its status as marginal metagenre as Demme's *Caged Heat* (discussed below), this film nonetheless has several precious moments that, like so many of the films viewed, speak to the status of the film as cult production in a way that would make studied postmodern auteurs like David Lynch cream in their de rigueur black jeans.

For instance, the sexually obsessed warden manifests his deviance through an obsession with the image: he films the "girls" as they are forced to dally in the hot tub with him for drug payoffs. "Don't call me Warden," he gleefully yelps, "call me Fellini!" And when Carol is thrown into solitary the warden mockingly tells her, "Sorry we're out of sushi. Bon appetit."

Carol's abuse at the hands of this auteur/warden—and her horror at the abuse of her sisters—causes her to grow from innocent and scared little girl to tough and rebellious leader, as she tells her comrades after she gets out of solitary: "I've got the answer to our situation. A riot. That's exactly what I'm talking about. . . . By busting Taylor [the head matron] we have a fair chance to get good people to run this place. Which means better living conditions for us." Next thing you know, the leader of the black women (Duchess) and the newly empowered Carol successfully lead a revolt in which both the snitch Erica (Sybil Danning) and the nasty wardens get killed.

Not only is racism foregrounded and the black women located as moral agents (they refuse to deal drugs, as the white women do), but the leader of the black gang is an articulate Vassar graduate who speaks eloquently about the politics of sex and race in the prison system. The bad snitch and seller of girls Erica is a racist whose bigotry is part of what spurs Carol to consciousness and action. But in the end, snitch Erica is rehabilitated through the multiculti prison breakout, which focuses attention on the real evil of the warden and his various assistants (including Stella Stevens as the corrupt Taylor) and unites Duchess, Erica, and a transformed Carol into a sort of low-budget *Mod Squad.*

In 1986 a higher-budget, slicker version of *Chained Heat* came out that, once again, posited the innocent victim thrown in with the voracious wolves. *The Naked Cage* is a variation on the good-girl-done-in-by-associating-with-the-wrong-guy theme. Blond farm-girl Michelle gets thrown in jail when she inadvertently gets caught in a bank holdup with badboy ex-husband Willie. It just so happens that escaped con Rita (of the red boots and flagrant sexuality) has seduced poor Willie and planned the heist. Once again, we have the classic prison setup: perverted warden (this time, a beautiful blond masochist), rapist guards, and assorted hardened criminal elements. As in *Chained Heat,* the racial theme is central, as the leader of the black women (Brenda) is again depicted as the moral center of a drug-infested, duplicitous, immoral system.

When bad Rita is finally caught and returns to the prison, she vows vengeance on an unsuspecting Michelle. Meanwhile, a new warden has entered the system: an undercover cop committed to ferreting out the evil in the system. In the big breakout, racial tensions erupt, many women are killed (including the saintly, pacifist Brenda), and Michelle and Rhonda triumph, electrocuting nasty Rita along the way. The last image has Michelle jumping on her horse Misty and riding off into the sunshine, blond hair streaming behind her and prison life safely in the past.

Linda Blair returns in *Red Heat* (1984), in which she plays Chris Carlson, an innocent coed visiting her soldier boyfriend in West Germany. Chris's romantic weekend with her soldier boy is ruined by two events. First, Chris stalks out of their bedroom in the middle of the night after a tense evening in which boyfriend Michael reveals to her that he has reenlisted and their marriage plans will have to wait. Chris then witnesses the abduction of an East German defector, Hedda Kleeman, and is herself thrown into the back of the truck and taken to the East German prison from hell. This film is unique on a number of levels. First, it opens up the possibility of a coming-to-consciousness of naive Chris, which it does not fully explore. Nevertheless, while the East Germans are the stereotyped ugly monsters ("You are no longer an indeewidual. You are a property of the state"), the army and intelligence men of the West are shown to be little better, refusing to help Michael get information and leaving him to plan instead an elaborate rescue on his own. Chris gets rescued, but only after her own transformation—from adoring coed eager to marry her soldier boy to tough inmate who befriends the East German defector and takes on the lifer and prison gang leader Sophie. Porn star Sylvia Kristel also stars as the killer lesbian inmate who has the sadistic warden, quite literally, under her thumb.

In all three of these Linda Blair films we see the transformation occur—a transformation that is both necessary to her characters' own survival and essential to their development as agents of the narratives. For both *Chained Heat* and *Red Heat,* the metamorphosis of the main character from innocent victim to tough agent is accompanied by a concomitant rallying of the inmates against their common enemy: the system.

Seventies Self-Consciousness: The Genre as Parodic Protofeminism

Caged Heat (1974) is a sort of B-movie precursor to *Thelma and Louise.* But this time—in the feminist seventies—the women not only kick butt, they survive. Written and directed by Jonathan Demme, *Caged Heat* is one of the most feminist and self-conscious films of the women-in-prison genre. It is funny, fast, tongue-in-cheek, and exhilarating in its narrative of prison rebellion. Most striking here is the vision of interracial friendship—noted most for its refusal to problematize the "difference." These two prison buddies live and die for each other, without narrating their racial difference at all. Indeed, this film presents a vision of multicultural sisterhood that manages to address central issues of female consciousness with humor and insight.

Cult favorite Barbara Steele plays McQueen, the wheelchair-bound matron whose immobility is the sight/site for a strange sort of erotic frustration, particularly as she watches "her girls" perform a full drag burlesque revue. After a distraught McQueen shuts down the show, she returns to her room where she has a most curious dream in which she is a Deitrich-like character wearing sexy S/M-ish clothes as women come up to her to ask redemption for their sins. This image of the warden as both frustrated "sex kitten" and spiritual healer of wayward women cleverly parodies and thus contests the cinematic obsession with the virgin/whore dichotomy. In addition, while there is a "big breakout" scene at the end when the women escape, the film refuses any real narrative development—there are numerous smaller breakouts and scenes outside the prison when several of the women have escaped and then plan to return to liberate their sisters.

Such films are clearly tongue-in-cheek and quite self-conscious in their self-presentation as late-night TV fare. *Lust for Freedom,* produced by cult filmmaker Troma, necessarily falls into this genre of self-conscious exploitation. The self-consciousness with which films such as this one play on the sleaziness of the genre itself makes it amusing. In *Lust for Freedom,* an undercover detective (all blond and wide-eyed and long-legged) leaves town after her partner/boyfriend is gunned down in a drug bust. After the carnage erupts during the botched bust, detective Gillian Kaites walks out of the burning building, her voiceover saying: "Cops were dying all over the place and all I could do was act like a woman. I knew my days as a cop were over."

On the run from this sobering realization, Gillian is captured, drugged, framed, and imprisoned by a sheriff and his comrades in borderland "Georgia County." The warden runs an illicit slave trade, abducting young women and then selling them to "the doctor," who seems to both sell them into prostitution and make porno movies with them (as does the deranged warden). The "prison" is presided over by the deliciously evil Ms. Pusker and her thug "Big Eddie." As Gillian's voiceover says, "Mrs. Pusker was straight out of some low-budget prison movie. But this wasn't a movie, this was real." Innocent Gillian (pretty dumb even for a cop) finally realizes all is not right in Georgia County and manages to break out—liberating all the women and shooting up just about every one of the bad guys.

Several things stand out in this film. First, the obvious self-consciousness concerning the genre it both reproduces and spoofs is both funny and cinematically revealing. But for all the sleaziness and campiness of the film the women *are* liberated, kill all the bad guys, and the heroine is not married off or reunited with a male savior. As in so many of these films, Gillian's consciousness is raised by the suffering of her sisters, a consciousness that is here made both explicit *and* camp: "Why should I care about the screams of these women? It's true that in one sense, they were my sisters. But they were hardened criminals, weren't they? Besides, there were still screams of my own that I couldn't forget." When her new cellmate Sharon is framed, Gillian says, "Sharon had sparked the first embers of resistance in me." And later, after the death of a prisoner in a forced female wrestling match: "I couldn't just sit back anymore. I couldn't not respond to the pain of those around me. I vowed that Sharon and the other prisoners would go free."

And free they do go, as Gillian kills all the bad guys and liberates the women. The last shot of the film has Gillian in a freeze-frame, wielding a machine gun and blowing the baddies away. The preceding image—after the breakout— shows Gillian attending the engagement party of her sister-insider Sharon (who announces her plans to work for a victims' rights organization). Gillian's voice-over assures us that she "would never again lay down in submission" as the final image of a woman warrior fills the frame. And, while it seems for a moment that Gillian will "save" the sheriff from himself and lead him out of his own brutality, he in fact dies in the prison break (killed by the warden after attempting to take Gillian away). It becomes clear that our heroine had no intention of cozying up to the unsavable sheriff.

A great number of these films are clearly marked as exploitation and soft porn, produced as videos for the backroom crowd. Yet these films, as poorly made and violent as they often are, do not escape the humor that characterizes the higher-budget ones. *Women in Cell Block 7* is just such a bizarre hybrid. A 1986 Italian and American coproduction (dubbed horribly), this film opens with a direct address to the camera by "Sybil Danning" (star, incidentally, of *Chained Heat*) dressed in a tough, unbuttoned, warden's outfit, wearing black leather gloves, black leather pants, and wielding a large black nightstick. As she introduces us to "Sybil Danning's Adventure Video" she proceeds as if on a travel-ogue, tongue-in-cheek puns intercut with clips from the upcoming video. She ends with: "So tighten up your handcuffs. Put your nightstick where it feels comfortable. And let's blow the whistle on the bad guys as we do hard time with the women of cell block 7. And when you check out, if you're *real* good you'll get time off for good behavior. But if you're bad, then I'll meet you in solitary confinement." This film is beyond "B" but—even with its gratuitous violence, its obsessive parody of lesbian sexuality, its clichéd killer matrons—it manages to do what Hollywood fears to: have an abrupt and nasty ending. Both heroines die, the warden is shown to be an agent of the Mafia—that's the end. As Sybil says when she comes back on: "There. Whoever said that every story had a happy ending in the concrete jungle of adventure video."

Another badly dubbed production—this time French and Italian—is even more explicit in its soft-core focus. *Caged Women* is the most violent of all—with disgusting scenes of women being eaten by rats, rape, voyeuristic lesbian guards who watch and then viciously beat the women they force to have sex with each other, and everything else imaginable. But the underlying (thin) narrative line is amusing: A reporter working for Amnesty International has gotten into the prison to expose the atrocities that take place there. She is, of course, victorious—the bad warden and guards are arrested, and the good doctor/inmate (he was in for euthanasia of his dying wife) are united.

Jungle Fever: Cutting Cane and Kicking Ass

The three films with Pam Grier[3] almost constitute a genre in themselves. While the films have no sequel continuity, they are linked both by cast and by locale. All three take place in an undisclosed tropical third-world country (the films are actually Philippine/U.S. coproductions). So the prison mise-en-scène doesn't have that hard-boiled, urban, noir look of earlier films but rather the jungly, glary look of B adventure films.

What is significant about these three films is that, while there is a certain amount of innocence here, many of the women have committed "real" crimes: prison does not harden them—they are pretty tough to begin with. This is generally true of the postmelodrama films: the liberation of the women in these later films is not necessarily dependent on their "innocence" but is rather based on their brutal encounters with the powers of the sadistic prison system.

In the first, *The Big Doll House* (1971), Pam Grier is a "big dyke" prisoner (named Greer) who is joined in her cell by Collier (Judy Brown), Alcott (Roberta Collins), Harrad (Brooke Mills), and Bodine (Pat Woodell). New girl Collier is brought in for killing her husband, who was sleeping with the houseboy; when she returned the favor, jealous hubby got mad and she killed him before he killed her. She is greeted by Greer with the comment: "Green, scared, and pretty." Lucian, the warden, is a rather tall, tailored, Eurotrash kind of sadist. Bodine is a political prisoner—her boyfriend is in the hills, making the revolution; Greer was a hustler; and Harrad, a junkie, committed infanticide.

This film, like so many others, is replete with major torture scenes, performed by Lucian for the pleasure of herself and the watching, hooded, anonymous "General." All of the women in the cell get tortured. Then there is the superintendent Miss Deitrich—a very tall, buxom, Teutonic psychopath. After much ado, the women decide to break out, discover that Deitrich is the "General" who watches, break out, and make it to the hills. Collier evades the recapture, only to be picked up hitchhiking by a guy who, as the film ends, is taking her back to the prison. *The Big Doll House*—replete with numerous scenes of torture—thus ends on this bizarre note of glib irony, made even more incongruous by the game-show soundtrack that perks up the final image of Collier's silly recapture.

Women in Cages (1971–72) has Pam Grier as the nasty prison matron Alabama, who persecutes the innocent (but rather trampy) new white inmate Carol Jeffries ("Jeff"). She greets her with the memorable line: "This is going to be just like home. Only different." Jeff is a consort for drug-running government bureaucrats in this banana republic who is set up by her lover and then targeted for murder in the prison. In the end (after lots of torture and rape), Jeff escapes as all the others are brutally killed, including the bitter and deranged Alabama.

The third film, *The Big Bird Cage*, is the funniest of the trilogy, with Pam Grier now playing Blossom, a revolutionary whose boyfriend/revolutionary Django convinces her to go inside the jungle prison to liberate the women for their comrades in the hills. Needless to say, both Blossom and Django get killed while the white prisoner—Miss Terry Rich—makes it to the rebel camp and is given passage to freedom.

With all three of these films, as well as some of the others like *Lust for Freedom*, the high-camp parody is interspersed with the S/M porn motif to make for a cinematic rendering that gives pastiche a whole new meaning. Alternately hilariously funny (as in the parody of the Fidelistas in the hills in *The Big Bird Cage*) and nauseatingly violent, these films switch codes instantaneously, forcing the viewer to concede the illusory nature of image-making. Realist narrative is not simply dethroned, but is rather effectively deconstructed. And the ever-present specter of racial violence and antagonism is here played to the hilt, as when Jeff asks Alabama, "What kind of hell did you crawl out of?" to which Alabama replies, "It's called Harlem, baby." Grier herself, now in her role as inmate in *The Big Doll House*, speaks explicitly to what is the subtext of all women-in-prison films: men as dogs. "You're rotten Harry (she says to a would-be rapist delivery man at the prison). You know why? Because you're a man. All men are filthy. All they ever want to do is get at you. . . . That's why I'm in this dump."

The Philippines was not the only foreign locale to serve up women-and-prison tidbits for the hungry American public. The Italians seem to have gotten in on the act too, enlisting in the cause such notables as Maria Schell, Mercedes McCambridge, Luciana Paluzzi, and Herbert Lom in the bizarre tale of Sapphic seductions and failed liberations, *99 Women*. Also distributed under the title *Island of Lost Women*, this film combines a small dollop of Italian neorealism with a much larger dose of good old-fashioned S/M to create a narrative that gives full rein to the camp sensibilities of McCambridge. This film is characterized by the sensuousness of the numerous lesbian sex scenes (in contradistinction to the heterosexual scenes), the incongruous flashbacks to erotic images of 1920s-style lesbian bars, and the utter failure of the good superintendent (Maria Schell) to wrest control of the prison from the sadistic warden (McCambridge).

I have, of course, hardly begun to touch on these films—as prolific as they are funny, there are more of them than one would imagine. Many feature an international production staff, and constitute a peculiar hybrid with their bad dubbing and foreign locales. Many more are pure porno (e.g., *Whip-Chick Girl*) and seem to slight the specificity of prison narratives for the pornographic hegemony of the phallus and its tedious accoutrements.

This is not to claim for women-in-prison movies a privileged location as revolutionary agent in the brave battles against the patriarchal panopticon. Indeed, their marginal status inherently limits whatever mass-audience subversive effect they might provoke. Yet I think this brief glance at this genre can awaken us—once again—to the need to theorize genre films as particularly able to access the more repressed aspects of cultural and social life. Theorists such as Carol Clover and Isabel Pinedo[4] have elaborated the possibilities in these low-genre films, possibilities that include the articulation of female pleasures such as revenge, physicality, and violence. And both theorists—and others as well—have argued forcefully that feminism, women's victimization, and liberation are obsessively visualized in these apparently lurid tales of abuse and incarceration.

These films—so clearly beyond the realm of "art" and "high culture" (and, arguably, even beyond the realm of the popular)—are thus given free rein to unleash the perverse, the hybrid, the grotesque. As Randall Clark notes in his study of exploitation films, the genre lends itself to sociopolitical analysis in large part because there are "fewer restrictions placed on the content" than in Hollywood, commercial film.[5] Not trapped by the dictates of the classic Hollywood narrative, not driven by "lowest common denominator" demographics to produce the happy romance (indeed, driven more by the lure of the gutter than by the box office), these recombinant, genre-hopping, ironic tales of criminality and evil, lust and perversity are able blithely to traverse uncharted territories: to go where no filmmaker has dared go before.

So often, it is within the most marginal, most negated, most ignored aspects of the popular imagination that our worst cultural nightmares come back to haunt us. Female criminality, female violence, female desire—so firmly negated by mainstream popular culture—here emerge in all their overblown glory. Not only do these bizarre films explore the unexplored with humor and a certain postmodern verve, but they often allow women to be victorious over the forces of male violence.

Women's prison films have much in common with other genres where women take on nontraditional behavior—such as bodybuilding, fighting, enacting revenge. In this sense, this genre could be located within both the horror genre that writers such as Pinedo and Clover have written so forcefully about, or the action genre, written about by critics such as Yvonne Tasker. Yet, all of these women's prison films are low-budget, low-status films. To compare them with high-end films such as *Terminator* or *Thelma and Louise* seems a mistake. Certainly, the tough women of prison films have much in common with the neobutch, tough women of both early melodrama (e.g., Mercedes McCambridge in *Johnny Guitar*) and the new, more heterosexually tough women of contemporary action adventure films (such as Linda Hamilton in *The Terminator* and Sigourney Weaver in *Aliens*). A number of film theorists have written recently on the rise of "strong muscley women" films, films in which women are buffed up, kick ass, and wreak revenge. Films such as *Thelma and Louise, Terminator 2,* and the *Alien* movies have been noted for their depiction of women engaged in a kind of physical display atypical for film heroines. As feminist film theorist Yvonne Tasker notes:

It would be possible to see the centrality of action heroines in recent Hollywood films as posing a challenge to women's social role, and to her representation with the cinema's symbolic order. This is the terrain over which a developing debate is currently being conducted, within feminist film criticism, as to the significance of

the action heroine. Cinematic images of women who wield guns, and who take control of cars, computers and other technologies that have symbolized both power and freedom within Hollywood's world, mobilize a symbolically transgressive iconography. At the most fundamental level, images of the active heroine disrupt the conventional notion . . . that women either are, or should be, represented exclusively through the codes of femininity.[6]

Unlike the popular narratives of female resistance and struggle, such as the highly debated buddy film *Thelma and Louise,* women in these B movies fight back and (often) emerge stronger, tougher, united in female opposition to male brutality. They may learn sisterhood the hard way, but we often do actually witness the process of consciousness-raising occur, where women put aside their differences to struggle successfully against the overweening power of patriarchy. Many of these low-grade prison films share a similar interpretation of female violence with the more obviously feminist (or at least pseudofeminist) high-budget films such as *Thelma and Louise, Terminator 2,* and *Aliens.* In these high-budget tough-girl films, female aggressiveness is seen as responsive to male violence and other structural conditions. The heroines of prison films are not classic femmes fatales, nor are they the individualist heroines who mimic the stories of the lone gunfighter. And while they have much in common with the sister fighters of female buddy films, they are generally more communally constructed than reconstructed as the lone heterosexual or homoerotic pair (e.g., *Thelma and Louise*).

Their violence is radically contextualized, so that the tough but innocent good girls are seen as violent toward men who have done (or who desire to do) violence unto them, whereas the embittered bad girls are generally *not* the victims of the male-dominant system but are rather the tools of that system (e.g., killer wardens). Female violence is thus not "beyond the imagination," but is rather positioned as the understandable result of systemic injustice. This injustice is portrayed as both patriarchal and imperialist. The foreign setting of many of these films allows for a constant discourse on the relationship between the U.S. government and various third-world countries and liberation struggles. Often, as in *The Hot Box* (1972, scripted by Jonathan Demme) and *Caged Heat 2: Stripped of Freedom* (1994), the U.S. government is indicted for its imperialist repression of insurgent struggles, and our hapless heroines often find themselves on the wrong side of the government in local battles. While sometimes there is a lone U.S. agent who redeems the power of the institution (as in films like *Rambo*), just as often it is the rebels who provide any evidence of moral standing and ethical vigor.

In its problematizing of femininity and its simultaneous exploration of female violence as female bonding, "the prison film makes clear links between poverty, female masculinity, female criminality, and the predatory butch."[7] While it is true that, often, "a conservative message is embedded in this plot structure, namely, that female criminality must be contained because it erodes femininity, these films also make a hard-hitting critique of both class and gender politics."[8] That the critique is framed within the loose bonds of sexploitation is perhaps what allows the critique to emerge in the first place. To paraphrase the inimitable Pam Grier: "This is just like cinema. Only different."

Notes

1. Judith Halberstam, *Female Masculinity* (Durham: Duke University Press, 1998), 201.

2. Although it is true that what goes around comes around: Pam Grier's cult status has now been used to rehabilitate her as a "serious actor" in Tarantino films and Showtime series.

3. *Women in Cages* (1971), *The Big Doll House* (1971), *The Big Bird Cage* (1972).

4. Carol J. Clover, *Men, Women, and Chain Saws: Gender in the Modern Horror Film* (Princeton: Princeton University Press, 1992); Isabel Pinedo, *Recreational Terror: Women and the Pleasures of Horror Film Viewing* (Albany: State University of New York Press, 1997).

5. Randall Clark, *At a Theater or Drive-In Near You: The History, Culture, and Politics of the American Exploitation Film* (New York: Garland Publishing, 1995), 7.

6. Yvonne Tasker, *Spectacular Bodies: Gender, Genre, and the Action Cinema* (New York: Routledge, 1993).

7. Halberstam, *Female Masculinity*, 202.

8. Ibid.

Sharon Stone's (An)Aesthetic

Susan Knobloch

In 1992, Sharon Stone consummated twelve years as a little-known but steadily working Hollywood actress with a role as a bisexual, possibly murderous novelist in Paul Verhoeven's *Basic Instinct*.[1] About her performance the next year—in *Sliver*,[2] the first film built around her—*New York* magazine observed:

Sharon Stone, the current queen of Hollywood (she shares the throne with another non-actress, Demi Moore), has a funny, dazed look on her face, as if she had just gotten off a transatlantic flight and couldn't find her luggage.[3]

Three years later, Stone won a Golden Globe award for her (subsequently Oscar-nominated) work for Martin Scorsese in *Casino*. The *New Yorker* reported: "Stone went into the ceremony a goddess; she came out an actress—and incidentally raised her asking price from 12 million dollars a picture to 15. . . ."[4]

From 1992 to 1999, the English-speaking popular press was sure that Sharon Stone was a moviestar, but divided about the quality of her art as an actress. Reviewers seem just as fascinated by whether Stone's performances say anything new about women's sexuality. Thus *MacLean's* notes that "on screen and in person, Stone displays an aggressive candor, a wit that quickly undercuts the stereotype of passive glamour."[5] But *New Statesman and Society* finds that, "on film, Stone is the ultimate boy-toy-blonde."[6]

In the thrall of her glamour, popular reviewers make little of the fact that ten of Sharon Stone's thirteen starring roles in big-budget Hollywood movies from the 1990s feature her character both inflicting physical harm and variously receiving, witnessing, or defending others against it.[7] Richard Dyer theorized in

1979 that "star images function . . . in relation to contradictions within and between ideologies which they seek to variously 'manage' or resolve."[8] Indeed Stone's persona builds upon four sets of (what from some vantages would seem or need to be) opposing terms: masculine/feminine; heterosexual/not-quite heterosexual; wielder of violence/victim of violence; and trustworthy helper/liar (or "liar for others" versus "liar to others"). Some Stone vehicles, which I would call gynocentric, emphasize the violent woman's just purpose and reason. The androcentric ones point up her immorality and victimhood. Stone's star image works, I believe, because viewers can use both feminist and antifeminist, "backlash" reading strategies to make sense of her violence.

Stone's stardom, like her personas' affinity for violence, feeds off of her ability as a screen actor to throttle her characters' emotions: both to choke them off and to modulate them with a precise control. Periodically and glaringly, Stone adopts artificial mannerisms (an uninflected voice, stiff or exaggerated movements, lack of connection to her costars). Stone's modulated use of nonrealistic acting helps deliver a unique type of meaning, though reviewers reject while relishing its effects. For example, the *New Yorker* claims:

Her acting is daringly stylized, constantly poised on the brink of self-parody; [the 1996 film] *Diabolique* **pushes her over the cliff. . . .[9] [S]he makes an impression, and just as inevitably, she becomes ridiculous. . . . The way Stone is used in** *Diabolique* **implies that . . . a wised-up, sexually confident American woman is some kind of freak.**[10]

To (type)cast an actress who slips away from the codes of realistic acting that have dominated Hollywood undermines (at least for the critic), via connotations of poor quality, any positive expressions around her of physical female power. In the same vein, even positive reviews of *The Quick and the Dead* (1995)[11] call Stone's attempts to play a female gunslinger of the Old West laughable: "You have to laugh at first. Yet . . . Sharon Stone has the tall, lean body of the Western hero, and she's developed an amusingly minimal, narrowed-eyed style."[12] Or: "The grossness of the movie is somewhat mitigated by its laughableness. . . . [Stone] is not called upon to do much acting, but the way she narrows her eyes to a slit and hisses out a sarcasm redounds to her credit."[13] However, the ideology informing both Stone's physical choices and the stories told around her seems to run as follows: the culture cannot, from an angle either feminist or not, quite conceive of a violent woman who is convincing in her emotion. Realism in Hollywood performance must, like other self-effacing codes of filmmaking, draw spectators into a certain "normal" vision of reality. Hence star roles, such as violent women in the movies, which do not easily fit a status quo (as conceived by anyone, feminist or not), would not mesh easily with codes of the serious and the real.

Stone Typecast: The Structure of Her Star Image

In Stone's work we can investigate the intersections of thirty years of recent feminism with the archetypal Hollywood figure of female violence, the "spider woman," [14] or femme fatale. Defined on American screens in the films noir of the 1940s, the femme fatale incorporates violent tendencies posing as vulnerability, voracious heterosexuality, rampant mendacity, and inscrutability to males. Stone's most publicity-gathering revision to the character type lies in her hypersexualization of it, adding nudity and bisexual overtones; she also adds an athleticism lacking in female stars of earlier decades. Postmodern genre-bending finds Stone playing a femme fatale–type not just in the expected murder mysteries and mob films, but also in science fiction, action adventure, and the Western. The plots of her films also lean hard upon the contemporary notion that male violence toward women and women's families provokes and sometimes justifies female violence. But the element of Stone's persona most distinctive of her times is her films' obsessive suggestions that her characters are both violent and justified, both deceitful and honest. All of her films negotiate the legitimacy of this combination, and the most distinctive of them never resolve it. Most Stone films center on questions of when, for, and to whom her characters lie. In Paul Verhoeven's *Basic Instinct,* the film that established her stardom, Stone's character is either a lying killer or a cold-hearted artist. As *Time* noted,[15] "[T]he film breaks faith with the most inviolable convention of the whodunit—refusing to state firmly which of the two women dunit [*sic*]." [16]

Stone's breakthrough came in Verhoeven's sci-fi action adventure, *Total Recall* (1990).[17] She plays a key supporting role as Laurie, Doug Quaid's (Arnold Schwarzenegger) wife, soon revealed as a government agent sent to guard his former-interplanetary-spy-turned-amnesiac-construction-worker. The story never quite makes it clear to the audience whether Stone's character has misrepresented herself to her husband. The action could all be his psychotic dream.

Of all her work, this film demands the most athletic-looking violence from

Stone.[18] Laurie engages in judo-style hand-to-hand (and foot-to-body) combat with both Quaid and his dreamworld girlfriend Melena (Rachel Ticotin). They fight in escapist, balletic fashion, amidst wisecracking from participants, with minimal injury. Quaid does not provoke Laurie's violence and responds as necessary rather than with sadism: he punches Laurie in the jaw and later shoots her dead, both times (only) after she tries to distract him with sexual or romantic conversation, while we (but not he) see reinforcements arriving behind her, or her reaching for a back-holstered gun.

The ambiguity of the film's storytelling seems the formal equivalent of the movie's ambivalence toward women's violence. As many of Stone's subsequent stories do, the narrative structure of *Total Recall* incorporates—without completely accepting—the central idea that feminist critics of the seventies raised about the femmes fatales of the forties:[19] that the violent on-screen woman is just an image in men's minds, and in some senses a mirror image of men's violence. *Total Recall* plays down the possibility that Laurie is Quaid's blameless wife, onto whom his nightmare projects his own anger and violence. But even such a low-key unsettling of the story structure—the suggestion that there is more than one way to look at the film's events—introduces the idea that the heroine may have a point of view of her own, separate from the hero's. From there one might begin to see the woman's violence as heroic, or acceptable on its own terms. Some of Stone's later vehicles pursued this very idea.

Femmes Fatales as the Images of Men

Stone's characters in her star vehicles serve as the means whereby males define themselves and fight their battles with each other. For example, in both *Last Dance* (1996)[20] and *Basic Instinct,* the story and the direction explicitly double her character with the male hero. This provides narrative extension of her "lean," muscular, and agile physicality, which in the 1980s became womanly but had been boyish. In *Basic Instinct* and *Diabolique,* her characters' doublings with men find expression and confusion in her characters' male-serving bisexuality. Because, as Dyer has shown, Hollywood star images work more to "manage" than to reveal or change the terms of ideological contradictions, the androgynous doubleness of Stone's persona suggests Hollywood's confusion between masculine projections and feminine images—a confusion that Stone's star image embodies rather than defeats.

Thus, although *Last Dance* was Stone's star vehicle and gave her top billing, Rob Morrow's prodigal lawyer enjoyed more screen time and a happier ending. Stone's death row inmate represents lost opportunities and the nearly criminal disasters of *his* past. *Basic Instinct* reverses the situation but retains the doubling: billing Michael Douglas as star and Stone's Catherine Tramell as his character's evil double, but allowing her to overwhelm and bamboozle him. The most famous scene of the film, Stone's interrogation at the hands of a roomful of policemen, recurs with Douglas in the hot seat; and Stone has explicitly compared Catherine to a man. She told *MacLean's* magazine, "Catherine is a very male kind of character. . . . Playing her, I started to think how hard it must be to be a guy, to get up every day and win, to have the best girl, be the strongest." In the same article, Michael Douglas expressed his approval of Stone herself in conventionally "male" terms: "[S]he has a great sense of humor, almost a jock mentality."[21]

Stone plays a new kind of femme fatale because, like traditional male movie heroes, her women wield violence (or control violent men) morally, at least sometimes. Christine Holmlund names this character a "deadly doll," the central figure in a 1980s–1990s cycle of Hollywood films.[22] As in most deadly-doll films, the justification for Stone's female—in all her postfame, violence-tinged

FIGURE 12. Catherine Trammel offers smoke-screened inscrutability and contempt, maybe with and maybe without the femme fatale's homicidal habits, in *Basic Instinct*.

starring vehicles (*Sliver*, *The Specialist* [1994], *The Quick and the Dead, Casino, Diabolique, Last Dance, Sphere* [1998], and *Gloria* [1999])—includes male violence against women or women's families.[23] On the level of generic formula this swaps the gender of the avenging protagonist; yet the femaleness of Stone's violent heroes prevents their simple assumption of heroic status: only in four of her starring vehicles does her characters' active, self-determined violence mark them as self-sufficient heroes—as figures whose actions are rewarded or at least not punished and seem positioned to satisfy the audience as much as scare it. This is not the case in *Sliver,* where Stone's character kills a murderous man ("only") inadvertently. Nor is it so in *The Specialist,* where her character manipulates and is manipulated by three violent men and winds up a romantic leading lady to Sylvester Stallone's violent hero, her physical power subordinated to his. In *Last Dance* and *Casino,* her characters die for their violent ways, just like the violent women of forties Hollywood.

Last Dance divides female violence from female innocence more sharply than any of Stone's other films. Cindy Liggett (Stone) has killed years ago, and we see her homicidal violence only in flashbacks, which obscure Stone's features in makeup, clothing, and tinted images. The Cindy of the present embraces goodness, having kicked drugs, learned drawing, and made sisterly connections in prison. Stone plays Cindy with heavy signifiers of realism (an adopted southern accent, the impression of no lipstick or other makeup, hair more brown than platinum) while dwelling upon her definitive themes. Reviewers found Stone's acting in *Last Dance* convincing: most identify the movie as a blatant move for the sex-goddess star to continue gaining respect as an actress, and many grant it to her, one comparing her positively to Meryl Streep.[24] The same equation holds true in the more low-budget *Gloria* (1999), which finds Stone with a well-turned Brooklyn accent attempting to turn her titular gun moll into a good mother figure.[25] Thus, in these two films acting adjudged "quality" goes hand in hand with the punishment or renunciation of her characters' violence.

In Stone's most prestigious project, *Casino,* she does violence as a victim; men do worse violence around and against her, a violence less fun than gory, relentless, and demoralizing.[26] If other Stone films use violence as metaphor for male and sometimes female self-empowerment and self-definition, this film uses it as a metaphor for self-eradication and pathological self-interestedness, a metaphor for the slow death of the heart in business and in love.

We first see Stone as Ginger from the vantage of men watching the casino on security video: the filming reaffirms her as a construct, mediated by men like the Vegas mobsters Ace (Robert DeNiro) and Nicky (Joe Pesci), who tell the story in voiceovers. An early shot sums her up by focusing on her purse clutched against a dice table at crotch level. Pretending to reach for her lipstick, she slips into the purse a coin stolen from the man for whom she's shooting dice. Freud didn't dream a clearer image of woman as lying, money-sucking sexpot. When the gambling man objects to Ginger's skullduggery and refuses to give her what she perceives as her rightful cut, she flings his winning chips into the air for other gamblers to grab.

However, Ace tells us that Ginger is, like the mobsters around her, a professional criminal skilled, in her case at "hustling" in the casinos, playing the games and the men for money, sex, and drugs. Ginger tells Ace fairly that she doesn't love him when he promises to set her up for life—once she bears his kid. She stubbornly wants Lester (James Woods), a pathetic drug-using pimp. Ace and Ginger's wedding toast to each other is shot in slow motion, a traditional filmic way to render violence. And the men are all violent to her. Lester and Ace and Nicky variously yell and curse at her, drag her across the floor, and manhandle her down a flight of stairs. Ginger remains male-defined even when she lies to escape Ace's monitoring of her; she starts an affair with Nicky, whom she thanks for telling her what to do.

The movie shows us Ginger's abysmal mothering and her rotten performance as Ace's lover. With Lester she does a line of cocaine in front of her little girl and later ties the girl up and leaves her alone in the house. After freeing his daughter, Ace goes after Ginger at Nicky's restaurant: he upsets her drink, bangs the table off her, and threatens her life. The next morning she drives her car into his and into the yard, cursing and yelling. She then lies to cops, convincing them to help her grab what she calls her possessions from the house and the bank. As Ace's bemused but bitter unresponsiveness suggests (she's a drunk and a drug addict, he dismisses), the scene shows us less a woman's liberation than a man's view of a crazy, violent, divorcing wife. Ace mentions Ginger just once afterward, to describe her fatal overdose. *Casino* won Stone acclaim as a good actress[27]—and so connected "good" acting with androcentrism.

"Bad" acting, gynocentrism, and positively valued violence conversely link up around Stone in most of her movies. *The Quick and the Dead* and *Diabolique* both star her as killers whom one might read as innocent or justified, with a mix of masculine and feminine, as well as some "unnatural" acting choices.[28] In both these films, Stone stays on-screen nearly every minute, and she plays her androgynous, violent, self-determining characters in an antirealist style, judging from the reviews I've quoted above.

Acting Principles: Playing Them as They Lie

For James Naremore, studio-era Hollywood actors achieved believability in "true" displays of feeling by showing their characters being "false." They used physical signs of stress and strong indications of falsity in the script and direction. By "emphasizing certain of the characters' lies . . . [they show] us [by contrast] how 'true' emotions are expressed."[29] Naremore borrows the term "expressive coherence" from sociologist Erving Goffman to explain how actors achieve this clearly marked falseness. Expressive coherence describes the congruence expected by observers between all elements of a person's self-presentation: Naremore argues that Hollywood acting represents lies by violating that expected congruence.

Virginia Wright Wexman notes a sharp change in the seventies, when Hollywood scripts incorporated unresolved ambiguity and actors took up antirealist techniques, radically confusing true and false displays. Wexman traces the polysemic connotations one could assign to actress Lindsay Crouse's flat vocal inflection in the David Mamet film *House of Games;* but she does not explore further examples of the denotative physical techniques underlying post-1970s Hollywood antirealism. Wexman also raises but leaves open the question of how nonmainstream acting tools affect ideologically weighted representations, especially of gender.[30] Unlike the actors analyzed by Wexman, Stone is a star, but it seems that she brings certain (formerly) avant-garde techniques into her 1990s genre thrillers—since, as much as the nonmainstream films and the theater Wexman explores, they center upon questions of her characters' interiority, whether they have feelings, and if so what they might be.

The writings of Russian actor and director Constantin Stanislavski formed the theoretical bedrock of norms of twentieth-century acting. In America, Lee Strasberg promoted the most famous variant of Stanislavski's "System" of acting, the "Method." A popular imagination links the System and the Method with realistic acting, and then with "good" or "normal" Hollywood acting. Teachers of Stanislavskian ideas do argue against this as limiting and inappropriate. Writing in 1958, another American disciple of Stanislavski, Harold Clurman, summed it up: "Though there is an historical or chronological correspondence between the realistic school of dramaturgy and the Method, the Method relates to every kind of acting—good acting—and not narrowly to realistic acting as such."[31]

However, Stanislavskian ideas help us understand what actors do. In studying Stone, I find that Stanislavskian principles aptly describe much of her work, though sometimes in terms of her abandonment of them. (I describe such principles as realistic, bearing in mind that the more precise term would be "realist-connoting.") Stanislavski thought actors responsible for conveying ideas with the details of body and voice.[32] In discussing Lindsay Crouse's refusal or omission of it, Wexman has identified one of the most important physical tools by which Hollywood actors represent believable characters: varied intonation. To use his voice in a convincingly realistic way, an actor must employ a wide range of (as we will see, narratively) ordered variety, not only in vocal pitch but in volume and texture.[33] Quick, constant, coordinated changes are necessary on visible bodily axes as well as vocal ones: the actor needs to tell stories by moving the parts of his body that the audience can see.

Stone's performance style stands out for her selective departures from and embraces of norms of believable screen acting. With Stone, sudden bursts of "bad" acting under Stanislavskian terms (jerky movements, stiff physical connections with costars, lack of vocal inflection) appear beside textbook applications of Stanislavski's fundamental principles; old-fashioned, broad, melodramatic gestures appear next to quick, small movements used as modern, TV-influenced, physical comments on the story. It is her sometime combination of old-fashioned moviestar acting, Stanislavskian precepts, and the needs of the contemporary screen acting and the occasional absence of all this—that constitutes her particular aesthetic.

Stone represents her characters' lies about and in the face of violence and violent intentions (her own and others') in three ways: so that everyone knows, so that only the audience knows, so that no one knows. The first occurs in *The Specialist* with a conventional Hollywood violation of expressive coherence. Stone's character May is Ned's (James Woods) pawn, we have recently learned. She has for the first half of the film only been pretending to need Ray's (Sylvester Stallone) help; really, she has been setting Ray up for Ned to kill. Now May has begun a double-cross, however, letting it seem to Ned that Ray accidentally killed her. She has also enjoyed steamy sex in the shower with Ray, whom we now know—or think we know—she really loves. But then Ned sees her in the hotel lobby.

We see Stone stop and take a breath behind a column where Woods can't see—cueing that her character is about to perform. Then, confronting him, she becomes very active both bodily and vocally. She moves her weight back and forth at her shoulders, providing lots of movement on a set mark. And she varies her vocal pitch, volume, and texture by tossing in high notes, occasional softly spoken syllables, and various gasps and pants for breath. This nearly amounts to a hyperrealization of the realistic acting norms: too active, too busy, revealing the character's nervousness. The simultaneous playing of the character's lie and the character's acknowledgment that both she and her interlocutor know she lies comes out even more plainly when Stone takes off her sunglasses as she walks up to Woods. She puts her hand to her jacket pocket, takes off her sunglasses, and finally puts them in her pocket. The doffing of the shades also works like the opening of a curtain to imply to him that she is putting on a show—a show of being exceptionally real and honest, of showing him the "true" self behind the mask.[34]

The second type of lying—Stone's lying to a character who does not know it, though the audience does—usually occurs in her work by means of the monotone, when Stone goes flat and dead on certain lines, which could be interpreted as part of her character's deadpan humor. Often Stone will use such a lack of inflection when her character mocks the powers-that-be (who are usually men) around her. She often combines her flat voice with a bodily display of her femininity and her moviestarness, implying that the role of the woman requires as much fakery as that of the would-be killer. For instance, earlier in *The Specialist,* she pretends to be Tomas's (Eric Roberts)[35] girlfriend in order to get close enough to avenge her parents' murder, which he committed. Stone insults Roberts's character "jokingly" in a dead tone and then aggressively crosses her miniskirted legs. The display of female sexuality might soften the insult for Tomas, but the viewer knows that he is being set up. The connection between femininity and an open masquerade unsettles in a way that one might expect of a femme fatale. But Stone's coldness and cockiness, which seem to be attitudes of flirtation, are also her character's true and justified feelings, masquerading as jokes. The deadening of her voice and her body—the reduction of both to a very small set of possibilities and movements—thus represents both the way the character feels and the state she wants to reduce the man to. (Kneeling at her feet as she lounges seductively in a chair, Tomas goes on to say, "When I look at you, I see something I like very much . . . me.")

To represent moments whose "truth" is forever unknowable, Stone works with both realist and antirealist signifiers at once. An early scene from *Diabolique* takes place at the teachers' table at a boys boarding school. Chazz Palminteri's character Guy has just been forcing his wife Mia (Isabelle Adjani) to eat the terrible food he buys. Stone's Nicole is having an affair with Guy—and plotting with him to scare Mia to death with the results of Mia and Nicole's pretend-killing of Guy—but here she stands up for the victim of his psychological terrorism.

Stone prefaces a drop into extreme antinaturalism by moving very naturally through the frame. She performs a three-part gesture, very quickly, but with great thought. She moves her left hand toward the salt shaker, but picks her hand up as if to rub her nose—then she moves her right hand up to the shaker and pulls it back to hold in both hands. The fake with her left hand at once allows the movement to have a (realist-connoting) beginning, middle, and end form—and it hides Nicole's grabbing of the salt shaker from Guy. Nicole goes on to loosen the shaker's lid, and then she "accidentally" spills all the salt into Mia's food.

The script never makes clear whether Guy and Nicole have set up this entire performance to make Mia think that Nicole is on her side. Guy might be gratuitously nasty and Nicole might really feel moved to thwart him—an impression that the rest of the movie fosters. Either way, Nicole—the character, as differentiated from the actress—goes on to give a performance. The actress makes a choice to emphasize the performed nature of the character's act, as she absents inflection from her voice—although a tight harsh note of contained rage, typical of Stone, lingers. "Oh. Look what I did. . . . Wasn't that fun?" Nicole asks, in an extremely flat tone. "Don't you wish you had that on tape?" she asks the film crew who are making promotional tapes for the school. We are reminded by the film's self-referentiality that it is not only Nicole but Stone who is performing. Wexman notes that this awareness of being part of a presentation, not an unmediated view through the fourth wall of a representation, differentiates realist from antirealist acting styles.

A Woman's Violent Acting

Stone takes a dead tone of voice and a frozen bodily mien to deal with violence again and again—whether men's or her own. In the more gynocentric vehicles, her use of dead tones accompanies her characters' own violence, representing the violence as liberating and repressing to these women: they lose (feminine expressiveness) even as they gain (masculine authority) by it. An early scene from *The Quick and the Dead,* however, tips the scales toward a celebration of the antisexist female avenger. The shambling, busy gait and effusive speech of the saloonkeeper who tells her to go look for a room with the other women (the "whores next door") sets off Stone's stillness. She opens his mind by kicking his stool out from under him. Stone's silence and stillness—down to her limited pitch and volume range—accompany an ever-increasing activity of both a bodily and vocal nature by her supporting actor. She smirks toward the camera as he

FIGURE 13. Ellen enjoys a drink after putting a man on the floor in *The Quick and the Dead.* Her underplayed violence has just changed his mind about a woman's proper place. In the background stands a little girl for whose forced prostitution Ellen later retaliates.

ends the scene with a singsong, bouncy rhythm to his speech in counteraction to hers.[36] This scene encapsulates the theme of the film, which Stone produced and which centers upon and celebrates her nameless heroine's violent yet principled retribution in collaboration with principled men against the uncontrolled violence of one town's unprincipled patriarchy.

In contrast, *Diabolique* is Stone's one film focused on women. It provides an atypically verbal role for Stone, who does a lot of talking as the sardonic, self-mocking, and self-emptying Nicole. As discussed above, Nicole makes Mia think that she and Nicole have killed Mia's husband Guy, with whom Nicole has been having an affair. But, as anyone who has seen the Henri-Georges Clouzot original (France, 1955) would know, Nicole and Guy have really been setting Mia up, hoping the shock of his return from the dead will kill her. The Stone version of the story differs from the original in two ways: Nicole becomes more concerned with Mia than with Guy, and the detective brought in to solve the case is female. The violence shown by both films remains more psychological than physical: the lying that the lovers do to Mia (designed to be deadly to her)—and at the end of the Stone version, also the lie (actually deadly to Guy) that Nicole doesn't love Mia, or loves Guy more. Nicole lies both ways at once to Mia through sexual gestures, kissing her cheek or her wrist (as though she were Guy, she says—though Mia says he wasn't that tender).

As Nicole rethinks her lies, Stone modulates over the course of *Diabolique* from an artificial to a realistic style, a transition precipitated by her character's decision to switch allegiance from Guy to Mia, from the male to the female other in the deadly con that she runs. This process begins with the entrance into the film of Kathy Bates as private detective Shirley Vogel. Bates carries connotations of "quality" acting, with her theatrical background and Academy Award, and she lends this "good" undertone to a character—a private investigator and former cop—whose violence, seemingly in opposition to that of Stone's Nicole, comes with legal sanction.

The infusion of realism from Bates—the idea of the very convincing, yet aggressive and commanding female character—allows the gender politics of *Diabolique* to lean toward the woman-centered. More than any other element in the film, the acting drives the viewer toward the idea that Nicole and Vogel become doubles at the end of the film, as sister avengers of antifemale violence. The film suggests that Nicole will not find happiness this way, because her motives for violence are impure (Stone's films never represent women's violence as completely justified or satisfying). Similarly, in *Diabolique,* Stone never assumes a "convincing" pattern of acting. Nicole and Detective Vogel become rivals for the attentions, and latently the affections, of Mia. They are doubles: both smoke, order Mia about, and generally act tough.[37] At the very end of the film, Vogel lights up a cigarette just after she has helped Mia and Nicole get away with murder.[38] Vogel walks up and punches Mia, but her socially acceptable female violence has turned toward the same ends as the other two women's unsanctioned brutality. Vogel tells Mia that it'll be easier to claim self-defense with a mark on her face.

At the level of the actors' uses of their bodies and the script, Stone and Bates make their characters rhyme. Stone uses a two-beat gesture—two claps of her hands, two raps of her fist, two claps on the back of a supporting character—as Nicole's sole, and hence distinguishing, hand movement. Nicole's gesturing is stiff and digital—she makes two clean beats and then stops, with no raggedness, no carryover. In her first scene, however, Bates links Detective Vogel to Nicole—and sets her up as a looser version of Nicole—by rapping her hand in an analogue fashion (1-2—1-2-3) as she also looks around and shifts her weight, making the gesture less obvious. Vogel holds an unlit cigarette in her hand as she raps out her complex and multilayered rhythm: the links between the Stone and Bates characters in the script appear by the acting, as Bates naturalizes what Stone has played artificially.

When Bates and Stone first play face to face, Stone chooses nonrealistic bodily and vocal (lack of) rhythms: she fails to make any transition between a line intended for Isabelle Adjani (the actress playing Mia) and one intended for Bates, for instance. Meanwhile, Bates changes her address from Adjani to Stone with an intake of breath, a move of her shoulders, a small smile. But by a certain point in the film, Stone begins to be as realistically fluid as Bates herself—when, we are led to believe retroactively, Nicole might be in some sense falling for Mia, or else (contradictorily) when she might for the first time feel truly afraid that the detective will discover her plans with Guy.

In a sequence with Bates and Adjani in the schoolyard, Stone—for the first time in *Diabolique,* and for one rare instance in her performing life as a star—makes extensive comments without words. She moves her head, changes her expression, and varies the pitch in her voice with small murmurs in excess of the dialogue as Nicole attempts to outmuscle the detective in front of Mia. This fits Stanislavski's belief that actors must listen and react to each other, but seems out of character for Nicole and the studied stillness and deadness Stone has used for her to this point in the film.

In this sequence Stone also employs vocal variety, in order to be as "real" as Vogel is for Mia, and to set up a more obvious doubling between Vogel and Nicole herself. When Stone says "Oh?" in a high pitch, Bates echoes Stone's feminine register on her next word, before dropping back down to a deeper, "businesslike" tone for the rest of her line. The acting realizes the characters' woman-to-woman connection. Soon after, Stone sighs before a line that questions Vogel, a sudden deployment of an analogue, colloquial transition such as Stone had shunned to this point.

We might read the above scene as Nicole's deployment of the tools of believability in order to deceive Vogel and Mia. But the rest of the film suggests that Nicole comes closer to revealing and attaining the aims of her real emotions the more realist Stone becomes. Nicole's failure to attain her ends seems sad because Nicole cannot connect with Mia no matter how profusely Stone employs the strongest conventional means to connect with her costars.[39]

By the end of the film, Nicole's attempts to be true to her only friend and to save their friendship fail. In the last sequence, Nicole protects Mia: by lying to Guy (that Mia is safely dead); by hitting him and bearing his punches so that Mia can flee; and by slugging him in the head with a rake in the film's goriest moment, so that the two women can finally drown him for real. But even as Nicole tearfully apologizes, Mia tells her good-bye. The movie prepares this break with an earlier misunderstanding, one marked as an instance of ineffective communication by Stone's Stanislavskian style. Telling Mia that she must take her medicine, Stone moves from a high pitch, as she mothers—or at least pretends to mother—Mia, to a slightly deeper, more ragged register, speaking with a jaunty rhythm that she emphasizes by an excessive finger waving in front of Adjani. Then, when Adjani speaks in a deep tone, Stone first employs a similar pitch but then goes to a pitch higher in comparison, following a slight break in rhythm—all in order to inject vocal variety into her reading of the word "okay" so that it sounds as though Nicole is being playful and comforting to Mia as well as irritated by her. This moment features Stone's most natural-sounding line reading as well as the moment when Nicole loses touch with Mia—who refuses her thereafter.

Stone's blanking or freezing of realist norms expresses a "true" ambivalence within her modern female characters who adopt conventionally masculine means to women's own ends. Stone links her departures from realist acting with her characters' violence, or with violence against them, and with her characters' lies to others by means of their conventional feminine posturing. Conversely, Stone reserves "convincing" displays of tenderness for weaker men or for other women and children: only for them does she become "more real." Thus she foregrounds gender roles by her playing; and though I see no unambiguous feminist thrust to Stone's work, I do see a shaky insistence on women's subjectivity.

Conclusion

Stone appeared at a fundraiser for breast cancer research presented by the cable network ("for women") Lifetime. She went onstage to talk about a friend of hers who had died of cancer—until tears momentarily silenced her. She said she took something to prevent such an outburst, using the dark joke to recover herself and finish her tribute, which brought women in the audience to tears as shown in the televised version. This moment sums up Sharon Stone's aesthetic and appeal as a moviestar. She makes a show of not quite deadening her emotions by "unnatural" means, moving huge audiences, telling stories about and through the mortal, female body. She seemingly can represent the pain, confusion, hope, and desirability of this body with no more realism for modern eyes.

Sharon Stone, the 1990s sex-goddess, stars in a post-1970s genre of unresolvable mystery stories; and her acting revolves around these questions: Does her character lie, and if so, to or for whom? Does the actress portray human experience correctly or incorrectly? Does she express false or true emotion? Because her scripts do not always resolve such questions within the stories (or do so only in their final shots), Stone's acting must provide the answers, or at least the hints. The morality of the fictional violent woman comes down to the clench of her jaw, her stare, her use of pauses and inflection, or their absence from her speech. The formulaic plots and obvious dialogue of her genre films in this late era need something from an actress that classical Hollywood did not. She must discard codes of proper speech, movement, and facial expression and become unfeeling or unreal. She must both mock and confirm the audience's ideas about the scariness of the femme fatale.

Virginia Wright Wexman has suggested that people expect Hollywood screen acting to be realistic, yet find in movies various styles of antirealistic acting, the most significant of which she finds to be monotone speech. I suggest that this post-Stanislavskian, post-TV code of "good" acting consists of specific physical habits. Stone's case suggests that actors of different types and situations have different access to the realistic for ideological reasons that manifest in their physical work and personae. Hollywood in the 1990s responded with ambivalence to Stone's femmes fatales, although one might infer progress in the increasing confusion. Stone's mayhem-dealing characters reveal at least flickeringly "true" hearts and comprehensible minds, despite the evidence in her films that Hollywood still seems unable to conceive of a violent woman—a functioning fighter, a sexual subject—who is fully "real."

Notes

1. *Basic Instinct,* written by Joe Eszterhas, directed by Paul Verhoeven, produced by Allen Marshall (TriStar, 1992).

2. *Sliver,* written by Joe Eszterhas, directed by Philip Noyce, produced by Robert Evans (Paramount, 1993).

3. David Denby, *"Sliver,"* New York, 7 June 1993, 55.

4. "The Big Picture," New Yorker, 25 March 1996, 72–78.

5. Brian Johnson, "A Role No One Wanted," MacLean's, 30 March 1992, 55.

6. Andrea Stuart, "A Touch of Taboo," New Statesman and Society 6, no. 265 (13 August 1993): 32.

7. *Total Recall, Basic Instinct, Sliver, The Specialist, The Quick and the Dead, Casino, Diabolique, Last Dance, Sphere, Gloria* feature violence. *Intersection, The Mighty,* and *The Muse* do not.

8. Richard Dyer, *Stars* (London: British Film Institute, 1979), 38.

9. *Diabolique,* written by Thomas Narcejac, directed by Jeremiah Chechik, produced by James G. Robinson and Marvin Worth (Warner Brothers, 1996).

10. *New Yorker,* 1 April 1996, 102–3.

11. *The Quick and the Dead,* written by Sam Moore; directed by Sam Raimi; produced by Joshua Donen, Patrick Markey, and Allen Shapiro (Columbia/TriStar, 1995).

12. David Denby, review of *The Quick and the Dead, New York,* 27 February 1995, 108.

13. John Simon, review of *The Quick and the Dead, National Review* 47, no. 5 (20 March 1995): 75.

14. This is Janey Place's term from "Women in Film Noir," in *Women in Film Noir,* ed. E. Ann Kaplan (London: British Film Institute, 1980), 35–54.

15. Richard Schickel, review of *Basic Instinct, Time,* 23 March 1992, 65.

16. Unfortunately, the film also engages deep misogynist and homophobic currents by making all of its murderers, potential and established, bisexual women. If Beth (Jeanne Tripplehorne) has killed the rock star and the cop in the present, she probably killed her husband in the past when she was rumored to have a girlfriend. Two other women with whom Stone's character Catherine engages in more or less obvious physical affection (a young one she lives with and an older one she calls honey and pats on the shoulder in a way that seems upsetting to our hero Nick) also have past records: (per-

haps) like Beth, they killed family members "for no known reason"—the film's implied reason being their desire for other women. Adding insult to injury, the bisexual ladies are more interested in Nick (Michael Douglas) than in each other, whether he's their rival or their love object or both. *Diabolique* also equates lesbianism with murderous desire—not to mention adultery, embezzling, and general nastiness when the husband trying to kill his wife with his mistress's help tells her that he suspects she's been sleeping with that mistress herself, and that such "sin" makes her just like he is. However, *Diabolique* differs from *Basic Instinct* by leaving room for the viewer to imagine that the male character is wrong, and that the women's mutual feelings are stronger and more important than any involving him—with the death in the film thus resulting not from lesbianism but from heterosexuality.

17. *Total Recall,* written by Ronald Shusset, Dan O'Bannon, and Gary Goldman; directed by Paul Verhoeven; produced by Buzz Feitshans and Ronald Shuset (TriStar, 1990).

18. Stone herself publicized *Casino* (in France) as her most violent film yet; but as we will see, the violence there is mostly against rather than by her character. Béatrice Demol, "Sharon Stone: 'Je n'ai jamais ete aussi violente que dans *Casino,*'" *Le soir illustré,* 25 February 1996.

19. See the essays in *Women in Film Noir,* ed. E. Ann Kaplan (London: British Film Institute, 1980).

20. *Last Dance,* written by Ron Koslow, directed by Bruce Beresford, produced by Chuck Binder and Steve Haft (Buena Vista, 1996).

21. Johnson, "A Role No One Wanted," 55.

22. Christine Holmlund, "Cruisin' for a Bruisin': Hollywood's Deadly (Lesbian) Dolls," *Cinema Journal* 34, no. 1 (fall 1994): 31–51. Holmlund notes that the underground "mother" of the deadly-doll cycle in mainstream thrillers and domestic dramas of the nineties was the "rape revenge" cycle of low-budget seventies horror films theorized by Carol J. Clover in *Men, Women, and Chain Saws* (Princeton: Princeton University Press, 1992).

23. *The Specialist,* written by Andrew Seros, directed by Luis Llosa, produced by Jerry Weintraub (Warner Brothers, 1994); *Casino,* written by Nicholas Pileggi and Martin Scorsese, directed by Martin Scorsese, produced by Barbara De Fina (Universal, 1995); *Sphere,* written by Kurt Wimmer; directed by Barry Levinson; produced by Michael Crichton, Barry Levinson, and Andrew Wald (Warner Brothers, 1998); *Gloria,* written by Steve Antin, directed by Sidney Lumet, produced by Gary Foster and Lee Rich (Columbia, 1999).

24. Boyd Tonkin observes that the movie "brings to mind those oh-so-sensitive numbers that Meryl Streep used to do on Po' White Trash parts. Yes, Stone does impress." See review of *Last Dance, The New Statesman,* 16 August 1996, 43. Stanley Kauffmann notes that "[t]he Southern accent isn't difficult; for anyone with the slightest talent. But there are colors in Stone's performance, shades of self that I've never seen." See review of *Last Dance, New Republic,* 20 May 1996, 26.

25. The character Gloria even lies in a good way by "taking the rap" for a crime her gangster boyfriend committed, but then breaks up with him after she gets out of jail. To save a child whose parents he killed, she knees one of his men in the groin and holds up the gang with his gun, taking all their money and leaving them stark naked. Gloria then bonds on the run with the child, who has a computer disc the gangsters want, with lots of androcentric talk about how the young kid is "the man" and how she is just looking for "a man who likes to win" to take care of her. Gloria is quite a traditional lady, exercising violence in service of the male child, whose male pride becomes the focus of several scenes. No one mentions that the child is Latino and Stone white, liberal notions of the integrative power of motherly love triumphing.

26. The homophobic, homoerotic, misogynist nature of the men's violence comes out early when Vegas mobster Nicky reduces a man to "a little girl." Nicky defends the honor of a friend, who has been told to stick a pen "up your ass." Nicky goes on to torture a man to death, finally popping his head in a vise; shoot dozens of people; and die horribly beaten himself.

27. Karen Jaehne writes, "Stone's flawless physique makes her a vertiginously high-class hooker, a perfection of plasticity she effectively undercuts with the edgy insecurity of the gambler who knows there's nothing left to lose but self-respect." See review of *Casino, Film Quarterly* 49, no. 3 (spring 1996): 43.

Another reviewer notes that "[t]he actress here displays a range that earlier roles never permitted." See Richard A. Blake, review of *Casino, America* 173, no. 19 (9 December 1995): 24.

28. *Sphere* features no human-on-human violence. Instead, after three scientists enter a sunken deep-sea spacecraft, an alien object "manifests" each character's fears as real perils (weapons, creatures, and fires) for everyone. So Stone's typical deadliness and disbelievability come into play in a muted form, and her acting is never artificial. "You tried to kill me," Dustin Hoffman's Norman says. "She's lying about everything," Samuel L. Jackson's Harry says. He goes on to tell Norman that the undersea environment plus Beth (Stone) equals "one bigass bomb." Which it literally does when her fears lead her to ring the alien craft they study with explosives. She triggers it with her mind in a suicide attempt after she remembers that all of the men question her credentials. Everyone in the cast has to play both dangerous and scared, unknowing and menacing in turns. No one can know who's lying or who's telling the truth, on-screen or off until the end. Then the three come together as a team to forget their discoveries as soon as the Navy brings them back to the ocean surface. Here Stone is also not sexual except in the mental realm (of memory). Gender becomes an issue only when the men imply that Beth is crazy (she was once a patient of psychiatrist Norman and attempted suicide) or incompetent or too angry at Norman (who became her lover in the past without telling her he was married and then dumped her) to be rational. However, characters raise and then overcome these common male/female nonsexual relationship blockers once the group notices that all of their fears are coming out and being projected onto each other. For example, Norman first believes her to be too angry at their past, but later he says that she may have a right to be.

29. James Naremore, *Acting in the Cinema* (Berkeley: University of California Press, 1988), 71.

30. Virginia Wright Wexman, "Epilogue," in *Creating the Couple: Love, Marriage, and Hollywood Performance* (Princeton: Princeton University Press, 1993), 210.

31. See Robert Lewis, introduction to *Method—Or Madness?* (New York: Samuel French, Inc., 1958), xii.

32. In *An Actor Prepares,* Stanislavski writes, "The significance of physical acts in highly tragic or dramatic moments is emphasized by the fact that the simpler they are, the easier it is . . . to allow them to lead you to your true objective" (142). All subsequent citations of Stanislavski are from *An Actor Prepares,* trans. Elizabeth Reynolds Hapgood (New York: Theatre Arts, Inc., 1939).

33. Stanislavski (218) recommends that actors modulate their volumes to appropriate levels by thinking about the variety of pitches and volumes one would use at varying distances from one's lover in life. He writes that actors fail by speaking too loudly in order to reach the balcony: "[Y]our first duty is to adapt yourself to your partner" beside you onstage.

34. From role to role, Stone varies her deployment of her star tools, namely her looks: both how she costumes and moves her physical features, face, and body; and how she acts with her eyes alone

in an otherwise frozen face. Like many Hollywood stars that came before her, Stone's stare defines her, in the clarity and concentration of its immobility.

35. The Caucasian actors Eric Roberts and Rod Steiger play Latino crime bosses, although Latino actors play the lower-ranking criminals in their gang.

36. In *Acting in the Cinema,* Naremore notes that the nonleading characters—and often those nonwhite, nonmale characters—are more active in both speech and movement, "busier" than the star players in classical Hollywood (43). In Stone's movies the extra level of activity among other actors does not always mean that they are subordinate to her, perhaps because she is a woman, and definitely as a sign that norms of what constitutes an actorly power have changed since the studio era. Kathy Bates is more active and "realistic" than Stone in *Diabolique,* we will see, and so is Gene Hackman as the villain in *The Quick and the Dead.*

37. People talk about cigarettes in the film: Bates's character complains about trying to quit, while Stone's sweeps the one cigarette Adjani tries to put in her mouth away, saying, "You can't pull that off."

38. Female rebellion coded with this adolescent signifier of cool links that rebellion to self-destruction: smoking.

39. In 1980s and 1990s Hollywood film and television often represent professional female characters at work in long takes, which permit the actresses to pair their own professional powers with their characters. *Diabolique* features a long take just after the schoolyard scene. Stone builds from Bates's actorly command in a long take wherein Bates delivers a long stream of dialogue punctuated by a few lines and several well-placed glances by Stone. Stone's professional potency is underlined in this scene not only in terms of her ability to pull off a continuous shot like this, but in terms of her star image. Vogel makes a veiled reference to AIDS—and Stone drops her forehead to stare moodily at the ground. The film thus invokes Stone's offscreen role as honorary chairperson since 1995 of AmFAR, raising money for AIDS research. Stone's acting choice is realistic, both in terms of its responsiveness to the other character, and in that it points to the politics of the real world by means of her star intertext.

Part II

• • • • • • • •

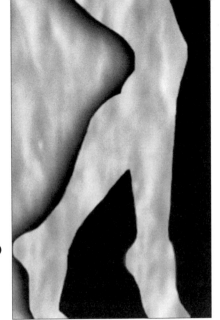

New Bonds
and New Communities

• • • • • • • • • • • • • • • •

Sometimes Being a Bitch Is All a Woman Has to Hold On To

Memory, Haunting, and Revenge in *Dolores Claiborne*

Laura Grindstaff

"Sometimes being a bitch is all a woman has to hold on to." So says querulous old Vera Donovan to her maid and companion, Dolores, in the 1995 film *Dolores Claiborne*.[1] Many years later Dolores repeats the phrase to her daughter Salena, who, by the end of the story, adopts it as her own, offering it back to her mother as both a justification for her own "bitchy" behavior and a grudging token of respect for the two older women.

Adapted from Stephen King's novel of the same name and directed by Taylor Hackford, *Dolores Claiborne* does not fit easily into any genre, though it comes closest to the "woman's film" in the tradition of *Terms of Endearment, The Color Purple, Thelma and Louise,* or *Fried Green Tomatoes.* It features three generations of women, demonstrating their courage and strength, loves and loyalties, blindnesses and inadequacies. It's a film about violence, particularly domestic and sexual violence, and the painful cycle of repression and self-destruction that often results. With its emphasis on the sacrificing mother and the mother-daughter bond as well as violence, revenge, and murder, it encompasses the melodrama, investigative crime thriller, social issues film, female buddy film, and female revenge film.

Dolores Claiborne is also a feminist ghost story, one about memory and haunting in which the terror of the past intrudes on the present and forces a painful reckoning. Refusing to stay in its place, the past demands acknowledgment and redress: it imposes a deadly architecture on the unconscious lives of the characters that shapes and directs their behavior, an architecture illustrated formally through repetition and flashback. The flashbacks foreground the forceful, insistent, and very *real* nature of the haunting, for while the present-day scenes remain dull and colorless, shrouded in fog and mist, the flashbacks glow with sunshine and falsely bright colors, thereby reversing the cinematic codes typically used to make such temporal distinctions. That all the flashbacks save one belong to Dolores tells us not only that we watch her story, it also tells us of the unavailability of the past to Salena, and of the displacement and repression forced into play by the girl's experience of incest. With Vera's aid, Dolores helps Salena escape her poverty and abusive father, Joe. Salena grows to be a beautiful woman, attends an elite college, and makes a name for herself as a celebrated journalist. But she also exhibits symptoms of incest survival: she is a bundle of compulsions and addictions, her hard-driving ambition, like the drinking, drugs, and sexual promiscuity, another form of self-medication. Like Dolores, Salena is bound by the past, and only deliverance of a mother-daughter exorcism can "cure" her.

Violence operates in the film on many levels beyond the characters' actions. As Vera Donovan says to Dolores, it's a depressingly masculine world out there—hence one must often be a "high-riding bitch just to survive." Vera is a wealthy woman and Dolores her maid: thus, at the same time, it's a depressingly class-stratified world, and while the film privileges the common bond of gender oppression over class difference, the two women experience the violence of patriarchal culture in different ways, with different effects and consequences.

This chapter traces the violence in the film and places it within a larger framework of gender- and class-based inequality in the United States, especially as it relates to battery and incest. In offering us a qualified feminist text on these issues, the film reworks genres that take as their subject matter women's victimization in a patriarchal order. In both form and content, *Dolores Claiborne* pushes the boundaries of the woman-as-victim trope, and in so doing joins a growing number of contemporary films that express women's rage. In the case of *Dolores Claiborne*, resistance becomes a collective effort. For despite the attempts of the state (embodied by Detective Mackey) to convict Dolores (as much for being a strong, independent woman as for being a murderess), she walks free because she has the loyalty, love, and support of other women.

There's No Place Like Home: Dolores Claiborne, Gothic Romance, and the Maternal Melodrama

Set on a small island off the coast of Maine, *Dolores Claiborne* opens with Vera's death, ambiguously shot so as to suggest that Dolores (Kathy Bates) has deliberately pushed Vera (Judy Parfitt) down the stairs. Dolores's daughter Salena (Jennifer Jason Leigh) is a journalist in New York, and arrives on the scene to question Dolores and uncover the "truth" of the situation—as does the state prosecutor in the case, Detective John Mackey (Christopher Plummer). But both Mackey and Salena already believe Dolores guilty, and their investigative efforts work less to uncover truth than to confirm what they think they already know: that Dolores Claiborne has not only killed but killed again. For both also believe that Dolores murdered her husband Joe (David Strathairn) some fifteen years earlier during a solar eclipse, but due to a lack of evidence was never convicted of the crime. Yet as the narrative unfolds we learn of another, more horrendous crime, an unspeakable crime of husband against wife, father against daughter—a crime only Dolores remembers and for which there is no adequate "official" mechanism of accounting or retribution. We also learn that what constitutes "evidence" is not always visible or a matter of official inquiry. As the truth of the past surfaces and reshapes the truth of the present, the relations between mother and daughter, and also between Dolores and Vera, characterized at the beginning of the film by sharp antagonism, are gradually refigured as life-saving, if not always happy and idyllic, alliances.

Indeed, the importance of female bonding and solidarity in the face of brute misogyny links *Dolores Claiborne* to contemporary "women's films" such as *The Color Purple, Thelma and Louise,* and *Fried Green Tomatoes.* But its emphasis on the home, domesticity, and familial relations also links the film to older generic forms about, and for, women such as the gothic romance and the maternal melodrama. Indeed, these genres "haunt" the film just as the film itself relates a haunting of its own. From the gothic romance, a subcategory of the gothic horror film, comes an emphasis on the evil husband (who may or may not be redeemed in the end) and the home as a potential site of violence, danger, and entrapment; from the maternal melodrama we get the primacy of the mother-daughter bond and the importance of maternal sacrifice.

The opening shots establish "home" in all its complexity. Accompanied by soft, ominous music, the camera moves slowly over an expanse of gray water and comes to rest at the base of a hill, revealing a large Victorian house at the top, partially obscured by trees and mist. One might recall the first glimpse of Manderley in Hitchcock's *Rebecca,* or the Bates Mansion in *Psycho*—the original "evil mansion on the hill" reprised in countless contemporary horror films. One might also think of Orson Welles's *Citizen Kane:* as we track forward, a series of slow dissolves bring us closer and closer to the house. We see the front door is made largely of glass, and a simultaneous track forward/dissolve gets us inside. As with *Kane,* the camera penetrates and investigates, fostering a mood of mystery and suspense: what secret lies within? In each case we witness an old tyrant's death, Vera's body tumbling down the stairs and "smashing" not unlike the glass paperweight that falls from Kane's hand as he dies. With Vera's last breath goes the answer to the secret to which the rest of the story points: Did Dolores do it?

Although the conventions of the gothic romance—and of the noir/detective genre from which the film also borrows—require that appearances can (and probably do) deceive, at this early stage we could easily think that Dolores did it—a matter to which I return later on. Because the movie features not one death but two, Vera's is not the only home harboring a secret. Indeed, *Dolores Claiborne* employs the mansion-on-the-hill trope more as a red herring than anything else, for there is another, decidedly humbler house in the film that, far more than the Donovan mansion, bears the imprint of past evil. This house—the home where Salena grew up—functions much as the Victorian mansion of gothic/noir films like *Rebecca, Gaslight,* or *Suspicion:* as the site of violence and women's potential victimization. The postwar films of the gothic tradition—sometimes pejoratively referred to as "paranoid women's films"—suggested in no uncertain terms that, contrary to the view of domesticity offered by most musicals and melodramas of the period, the home can be a dangerous place for women.[2] And while the male violence or threat of male violence in the postwar gothics appeared entirely in psychic terms, Andrea Walsh argues that this provided a narrative substitute or displacement for what movies could not show at the time: rape, battery, sexual abuse.[3]

The fact that the family home in *Dolores Claiborne* has been abandoned and suffers disrepair is a metaphor for the broken family, particularly the fractured relationship between Dolores and Salena. In gothic tradition, the moment of entry into the house after a long absence triggers Dolores's initial flashback, the first in a series of flashbacks that tell the story of the real crime in the film. Dolores and Salena have just come from the police station to find the front window smashed and the word "bitch" painted across the outside wall. Dolores crosses the front porch and tries to open the door, also covered in graffiti, but it's stuck and will not yield. "Let me do it," Salena says, pushing past her. Dolores then turns and looks out over the surrounding fields. Suddenly the scene suffuses with bright light and color and she "sees" the search party combing the fields for Joe's body fifteen years earlier. Salena is a young girl of thirteen. Her face shows suspicion and distrust; she is poised to run. "Salena! Get in the house! Get in the house right now!" Dolores commands her.

"I am in the house," adult Salena replies, breaking the reverie. Like Paula in *Gaslight,* Salena is more than a little spooked by what she sees. Dolores notices this and says to her, "The longer you stand there, the more boogery it's gonna feel." In a later scene when Salena is reluctant to mount the stairs to the upper floor, Dolores urges, "Go on, it won't bite ya." Clearly it will be an enormous task to clean house, to exorcise the ghosts and restore the home (and by implication, their relationship). But Dolores is nothing if not an expert at cleaning—after all, she does it for a living. And while cleaning other people's houses is not the same as cleaning one's own, Dolores has already proven herself strong-willed and determined, unlikely to give up on Salena without a fight.

The film aims to restore the relationship between Dolores and Salena; and this focus, along with the primacy of maternal sacrifice, links *Dolores Claiborne* to the maternal melodrama. It also differentiates the film from the original novel, in which Dolores not only has two sons, but Salena neither returns to the island nor reconciles with her mother. Whereas the book tells Dolores's story and hers alone, the film tells the shared story of mother and daughter. As Janet Walker observes, the maternal melodrama centers on the mother-daughter bond, its ambivalences and conflicts as well as its intimacies and rewards.[4]

In the classic films of the genre, successful resolution of the mother-daughter conflict requires considerable sacrifice on the part of the mother. The title character in *Stella Dallas* serves as an example. When Stella realizes that her working-class roots embarrass her daughter, Laurel, and prove an obstacle to the girl's upward mobility, she feigns disinterest in motherhood and sends Laurel to live with the father and his new, upper-class female companion—even though it breaks Stella's heart to do so. Mothers not properly asexual and self-effacing (like the ambitious actress Lora Merideth in *Imitation of Life*) will be punished, typically by the "bad" behavior of a daughter. *Dolores Claiborne,* too, foregrounds maternal sacrifice. Dolores works her fingers to the bone as Vera's maid in order to send Salena to college and give her a better life. It is for Salena and Salena alone that Dolores kills Joe. And when Salena rejects her, Dolores carries on in the only way she knows how: by continuing to work for Vera, developing the kind of close relationship with the older woman she cannot have with her own daughter. What begins as a kind of substitute relationship (the aging Vera replacing Salena as Dolores's "charge") grows into something intimate and fulfilling on its own terms.

While *Dolores Claiborne* is self-consciously feminist in a way that classic melodramas are not, the older films do not present simple family relations. One can read the maternal melodrama as satisfying patriarchal demands for an idealized mother-figure who prioritizes the needs and desires of others over her own (see, for example, Ann Kaplan's essay "Theories of Melodrama: A Feminist Perspective"),[5] but the genre also dramatizes the need for women to be persuaded and convinced of the naturalness and rightness of this ideal. Indeed, a number of scholars consider melodrama *the* genre for exposing the ideological contradictions of marriage, home, and family, despite the genre's seeming celebration of them.[6] *Mildred Pierce* provides a good example. In this noir/melodrama hybrid, Mildred fails at motherhood, though not for lack of love, sacrifice, or hard work; rather, she fails in part because she loves her daughter too much, overindulging the girl and failing to reproduce in her the feminine values of domesticity and self-denial. Mildred runs a successful business as well as her own household, and thus dooms the family from the outset.[7] At one level, then, the film cautions middle-class women to marry and stay home. However, it also suggests the inadequacy of a patriarchal order. As Pam Cook observes, films such as *Mildred Pierce* articulate the need to reconstruct patriarchy—a project one wouldn't need if the patriarchy worked to begin with.[8]

Melodrama brings ideological contradictions to the surface and re-presents them in aesthetic form, giving voice to "private" fears and desires unacknowledged in public discourse. In doing so, "it accesses the underside of official rationales for reigning moral orders—that which social convention, psychic repression, political dogma cannot articulate."[9] *Dolores Claiborne* combines this melodramatic impulse with the investigative structure of a noir crime thriller and a contemporary feminist consciousness. It speaks the unspeakable (incest) and shows how "the family" and "the home" harbor conflict and violence as well as domestic harmony and marital bliss.[10]

Unlike conventional melodrama, however, *Dolores Claiborne* makes no last-minute attempts to smooth over the contradictions it exposes, or to rehabilitate the traditional nuclear family—a stance that, along with its narrative structure, also aligns the film in important ways with classic noir.[11] As Salena herself says to Dolores, "Let's not pretend we're in some goddamn Norman Rockwell family reunion, here." The moral order appears not only flawed but perverse, the father's sexual abuse of the daughter providing but an extreme example of the pervasive oppression of women by men, an oppression in which the "official" state proves part of the problem rather than part of the solution.

We see plenty of conflict among the women as well. Vera is a selfish, demanding woman who makes life hellish for Dolores, barely paying her a living wage. Dolores and Salena themselves remain at odds until the concluding moments of the narrative. In fact, because the girl retains selective memories of her father, she remembers Dolores as the violent parent, not Joe. She thus presumes Dolores guilty from the moment she hears of Vera's death, and pursues a private investigation of Dolores as prosecutorial in tone as Mackey's public, official one—a move that hurts Dolores deeply, since Salena's judgment matters to her. "Do you think I give a fiddler's fuck what anybody else says about me?" Dolores asks her daughter. "It's you, what you think, that's the only thing left that's important." Dolores commits one kind of crime to save Salena from another, but Salena does not thank her for the sacrifice.

All in the Family: Gender, Class, and Violence

Salena is not grateful for the sacrifice because she does not remember being abused. In fact, successful repression of the incest depends partly on her valorization of the very person who abused her. Consequently, Salena harbors a great deal of anger toward her mother, as do many actual incest survivors,[12] but this anger stems not from the mother's unwillingness or inability to do anything about the incest, but because Salena sees no legitimate cause for Dolores's aggressive behavior toward Joe. In fact, Salena remembers not Joe's but Dolores's violence. She recalls Dolores hitting Joe and threatening him with an ax.

Dolores recounts this scene in flashback as she and Salena sit at the kitchen table the first night of Salena's return. Dolores has made dinner but Salena smokes and drinks whiskey—her father's brand—instead of eating. As Dolores's gaze drifts past Salena to the front door, she "sees" Joe enter, take off his boots, and hang his coat on a peg. The camera swings behind Dolores, the back of her head obscuring the door from view. When the camera emerges on the other side of her the scene has suffused with color and we're "in" the past. We learn in this sequence that Salena and her father have a very close relationship — she adores him, in fact. She has cooked a special dish for him and he praises her effusively, commenting on her smile ("There's that St. George smile. Don't you look just like my mother!"). He tickles her, she steals his cap and giggles. She is flushed and excited in his presence, their banter mildly flirtatious and childishly innocent, at least for Salena, a fact underscored by her school-girl attire and little-girl pigtails.

We also learn that Dolores did indeed strike Joe, in retaliation: he hits her first, suddenly, brutally, across the small of the back with a heavy slab of wood, to punish her for laughing at a rip in the seat of his pants. (Salena is upstairs doing homework by this time.) We learn that Joe has made a habit of hitting Dolores, but this time he's gone too far. As he sits in his chair drinking whisky and watching television later after dinner, Dolores smashes a china pitcher against the side of his head. He lunges from the chair, blood gushing from his ear, but Dolores pushes him back down, ax in hand.

FIGURE 14. After years of both suffering and standing up to his abuse, and without the money to leave, Dolores Claiborne will kill her husband. This approach to marital conflict will make her a permanent murder suspect.

"You better sit back down, Joe, if you don't want this in your head," she hisses at him.

Salena awakens and descends to the foot of the stairs, asking if everything is all right. Dolores stands with her back to the girl, trying to shield Joe from sight. She tells Salena to go back to bed, that she and Joe are just having "a little discussion." Then when Salena leaves, Dolores goes nose to nose with her husband.

"You want to run me down?" she asks in a furious whisper. "Go right ahead. You can be as mean and hurtful as you want. But this is the last time you will ever hit me. You do it again, one of us is goin' to the boneyard."

Joe, subdued by Dolores's threat, turns his "attentions" to their daughter. But Salena retains only the memory of her mother as a threatening woman, a violent woman, a woman who might kill if provoked. The ax provides a key symbol of this aggressivity and appears twice more in the film: when Dolores smashes the remaining shards of glass from the front window broken by the town hoodlums, and later when she confronts these boys as they drive by the house late at night, yelling obscenities and firing gunshots into the air. The scene is ugly, with overtones of a stoning or lynching, and makes clear that Detective Mackey and Salena are not the only ones persecuting Dolores.

The difference between Salena and the others is that Salena's own violent past is intertwined with her mother's and thus is also at some level "on trial." As in much film noir, the crime that constitutes the "dark secret" of the film and provides its emotional charge also provides the narrative justification for the film's use of repetition and flashback. *Dolores Claiborne* recounts not one crime but three, each one a kind of decoy for the others. Vera's death is but an excuse for Mackey to avenge Joe's; Joe's murder in turn hides another, more sinister transgression. The crime of incest that lies at the core of the film is therefore everywhere and nowhere at the same time; it instigates a violent chain of events with dramatic and visible effects but is itself hidden and repressed, never fully emerging until the end when Salena finally recovers her memory and "sees" the truth.

Thus, throughout most of the film Salena and Dolores remain at odds ("estranged" is the word Dolores uses repeatedly in the novel), the distance between them underscored by their different last names: Dolores goes by her maiden name, Claiborne, while Salena uses "St. George," Joe's last name, which further

FIGURE 15. A mother and daughter estranged but later united by recognition of the role of bloodshed in their lives in *Dolores Claiborne*. Such women do not always get along, but they eventually discover their common need for violence.

aligns her with Joe. So estranged are the two women that Dolores does not even recognize her daughter when Salena comes to fetch her from the police station. Later as they eat dinner at the house, Dolores tries unsuccessfully to draw Salena into conversation, to find out about her work and her life. When she comments on Salena's drinking and smoking and makes a comparison to Joe, Salena gives her mother an angry warning: "Let's face it, mother, we barely know each other. We haven't spoken in years, and that's as much your doing as it is mine. If you didn't kill Vera, great, you've got nothing to worry about. If you did, you deserve whatever comes. . . . I'm sorry, Ma, but that's where we are."

Because Salena has repressed memory of her father's abuse and because she remembers Dolores as the aggressor, she answers Dolores's efforts to talk about the past and correct her vision with anger and denial. But recovery depends on exposure, and Salena cannot be "cured" until she acknowledges the crime. Until she does that, mother and daughter cannot reconcile, nor can Salena escape the self-destruction that incest has spawned. As a result, the flashbacks serve dual functions: they not only reveal what happened, they show how the present repeats the past. In psychoanalytic terms, if repetition attempts to master trauma, then the characters will repeat the past until they "get it right." While Freud himself refused to consider what happens to the little girl going through the Electra complex when she does in fact "get" the father as her romantic partner, the consequences become increasingly clear as the film progresses and as the flashbacks get progressively closer to "the secret" at its core.

One good example of this repetition occurs immediately after the town hoodlums drive by in their truck harassing Dolores. Salena is deeply upset by the incident and retreats to the bathroom, crying, fumbling for her pills. She downs several with water from the tap and then remains crouched on the floor, arms hugging her knees. Dolores, who knows Salena has been drinking, becomes concerned and confused. "What good are those going to do?" she asks, referring to the pills. She then hears the phone ring, and when she turns to look, she sees Salena, now thirteen years old, pick it up. It's a prank call; on the other end of the line are voices that, just like those of the teenage boys in the truck, make fun of Dolores, and accuse her of murder. Young Salena begins crying and Dolores grabs the phone, shouting back into the receiver just as she shouted back at the hoodlums in the present-day scene. Meanwhile, Salena has begun taking ornaments off the Christmas tree and smashing them against the wall.

"Salena, stop that!" Dolores entreats her. "Honey, it's gonna be all right!"

"It won't!"

The ornament in Salena's hand breaks, and she deliberately slices her throat with a shard, drawing blood.

"Salena!" Dolores cries in anguish. At this point the flashback ends, and adult Salena leans against the bathroom wall, staring at her mother. The pills and the drinking are but more sophisticated versions of the broken ornament—tools of self-destruction, Salena's method of "speaking" her pain.

Later on, another flashback reveals the similarities between the way young Salena responds to Dolores's initial discovery of the abuse and the way adult Salena responds to Dolores's attempts to make her remember it. In both situations, Salena, offering a customary response to incest, refuses to believe, and instead lashes out at the mother's crazy ideas. The two scenes are linked across time by a slap: young Salena slaps Dolores on the ferry and this initiates the cut to adult Salena slapping her as they sit at the kitchen table.

"You bitch!" Salena yells, springing from her chair. "You crazy old lying bitch! You're a fucking psychotic! Do you know how insane that is? Does this shit actually come to you or do you work on it?"

"No! For god's sake, do you think I'd make up something like that?" Dolores rises and follows Salena around the room. "How could you not remember? How is that possible?"

"I remember you hitting him. That I remember. I remember the blood coming down his face, I remember the drinking, I remember the fighting—but this?"

"Salena, you're not responsible!"

"Mackey's right. You are dangerous. Fuck you!"

In both the present and the past, Salena responds by running away. In the flashback sequence, Dolores chases her through the fields adjacent to the house, and discovers the abandoned well by almost falling in herself. Thus in the very midst of "losing" Salena, Dolores finds the solution to their problems with Joe. In the present-day story, however, Dolores knows better than to run after her daughter. Instead she has packed Salena's bags and makes no protest as Salena leaves for the ferry.

These sequences illustrate the difficulty of Dolores's position in choosing to handle matters all on her own. She does so because she sees, correctly, that the "official" channels of retribution are, like the family itself, corrupt. Dolores neither reports Joe to the authorities nor (understandably, given the historical framework and lack of a feminist discourse about incest) insists that Salena seek "professional" help. Rather, she plays therapist, revisiting the scene of the crime that prompts memory. This not only allows the film to skirt the thorny issue of so-called "implanted" or "false" memories triggered by professional intervention, but also makes Dolores responsible for the outcome of what happens to Salena, and leaves her vulnerable to rejection and blame.

The distance that separates Dolores and Salena—a distance that appears insurmountable throughout most of film—results not only from the girl's victimization but also from class difference, largely the consequence of Salena's Vassar education and New York career. The family thus serves as the site of class as well as gender conflict—an intersection not uncommon in classic melodrama as well.[13] *Dolores Claiborne* tends to go further than classic films of the genre, however, in attempting to locate the personal and familial within a larger social and political context. According to Gledhill, "[M]elodrama touches the sociopolitical only at that point where it triggers the psychic, and the absence of causal relations between them allows for a short-circuiting between melodramatic desire and the socially constructed world."[14] *Dolores Claiborne* complicates this circuitry to some degree by playing to both registers: the family fractures along class lines; and, as in *Stella Dallas,* this difference limits the mother's ability to understand and protect her daughter. Dolores's experiences in the community also demonstrate how her working-class status compounds the injustices of gender inequality, and vice versa.

Aside from her conflicts with Detective Mackey (discussed later), this becomes most obvious in the scene where Dolores confronts the bank manager about the money Joe steals from Salena's account—$3,000 that Dolores has painstakingly saved for her daughter's education. Dolores goes to the bank to withdraw it so that she and Salena can make their escape from the island, only to find that Joe has already been there and closed the account, claiming to have lost the passbook. Dolores is furious that Joe has done this without her knowledge or consent.

"It's because I'm a woman, ain't it?" she hisses at the bank manager, tears of anger and frustration standing in her eyes. "If it'd been the other way around, if I'd been the one passin' off a fairy story about how I'd lost a passbook and asked for a new one, if I'd been the one who started drawin' out what took eleven years to put in, you woulda called Joe."

Joe himself frequently underscores the connection between class and gender when he belittles his wife as much for her "lowly" station as for being a woman. In the first flashback when Dolores laughs at the ripped seam of his trousers, Joe not only complains about her general domestic/feminine incompetence ("my mother warned me you'd let yourself go. Fat ass, lousy cooking, that goddamn mouth"), he implies the ripped seam is evidence of her "preference" for wealthy Vera Donovan over her own family, and he warns Dolores that she better not forget her humble roots.

"What's the deal, huh?" he asks, his tone belligerent. "You kiss that rich summer ass all day long you got nothin' left for me. Just remember, your father used to scrape my old man's boat. So don't get high and mighty on me."

Dolores points out that if Joe still had the boats she wouldn't need to work for Vera, and this is when Joe slams her in the back with the slab of wood. Later when Dolores expresses concern over Salena's slipping grades, he says with contempt, "Why don't you leave her alone already? It's not like you were some great genius at school. Claibornes! You weren't even born in a hospital for Christ sakes!"

Joe thus builds himself up by putting Dolores down because he has been emasculated both by his wife's assertiveness ("that goddamn mouth") and his failure to provide adequately for his family. His weaknesses, like Dolores's strengths, appear mainly in individual rather than structural terms. He seems lazy, shiftless, and alcoholic in contrast to hardworking and self-sacrificing Dolores. No one mentions the depressed Maine economy, or the loss of fishing as a stable source of regional wealth, both of them structural conditions that put families under stress and may lead to alcoholism and domestic violence. Instead these conditions form an unspoken backdrop that serves to heighten the contrast between Dolores and Joe; whereas he responds to hard times by giving up and growing weak, she gets a job and makes the best of a bad situation. And, as in urban contexts where male joblessness results from local deindustrialization in a global economy, poor and working-class women remain more employable than men because of service and domestic work.

Of course, nothing prevents men from taking domestic jobs too, except disdain for "women's work"—a point the film makes more explicitly. In both the humble St. George household and in the ostentatious Donovan mansion, the home offers to men relaxation and recreation, regardless of how much, or little, they do outside of it. Thus Joe sits on the sofa drinking whiskey and watching television, while Vera's husband Jack plays golf. For women the situation differs, and the poorer the woman, the more physically demanding work/home becomes. Vera gives orders and runs the household but Dolores sweats and toils, both in Vera's home and her own. Not surprisingly, then, the class difference between Dolores and Vera, like so much else in the film, figures primarily in domestic terms, underscored by the contrast between the two houses and the female labor performed therein.

Dolores cleans for a living, and faces the biggest challenge of fixing the broken family. Indeed, when Salena first arrives at the police station to fetch Dolores and the constable takes her upstairs, they find Dolores cleaning the room. "Jesus, Dolores, you're a suspect not a maid!" Frank exclaims in exasperation. That class and cleaning are inextricably linked is a story best told in the film by Dolores's hands, the film's symbol of her working-class status. Decades of domestic service have left her hands so cracked and callused that Salena gasps in astonishment when she first sees them. Having begun paid housekeeping at the age of thirteen, Dolores is well equipped to become Vera's maid. Nevertheless, she knows going into the job that it will be hell, for Vera is rigid and particular in her ways—so particular that none of Dolores's predecessors could endure her. Vera insists the tubs be scrubbed daily with vinegar and baking soda. The presence of mildew is grounds for firing. All the linens, the tablecloths, napkins, and handkerchiefs must be hand-washed, ironed, and starched. And the sheets have to be line-dried, even in the dead of winter.

"Hell, ain't something you get thrown into overnight," Dolores tells her daughter, recalling the past twenty-two years with Vera. "Nope, real hell comes on you slow and steady as a line of wet winter sheets. Snot leaking off your nose, your hands so cold and raw you start wishing they'd go numb. You know by February that skin's gonna be cracked so bad it'll break open and bleed if you clench a fist."

For this Dolores is paid $40 a week, every cent of which goes toward Salena's education so that Salena can take a very different sort of job and lead a very different sort of life. But the sacrifice, etched into Dolores's hands, also separates mother and daughter by class and deepens the rift between them, a rift subtly underscored by Salena on three separate occasions (two of them involving heated arguments with Dolores) in which she grabs lotion from her purse and rubs it vigorously over her own soft, uncallused hands. This class conflict between mother and daughter is further overlaid by a rural/urban opposition. Dolores was born and raised on Little Tall Island, her life filled with the daily struggles and challenges of raising a family in a small, economically depressed town. Salena is an educated career woman, an award-winning journalist who rubs shoulders with the social and political elite.

Ultimately, however, the common bond of gender oppression transcends whatever class antagonism exists between Dolores and the other two women. Vera might be a millionairesse and Dolores her maid, but when Dolores collapses, sobbing, on the piano in Vera's front parlor, and confesses to Vera that Joe has been "messing" with Salena, it changes the relationship between them forever. Vera's normally impassive countenance shows emotion for the first time. Her eyes grow hard and steely as Dolores talks, and then tears gather in anger and sympathy. Vera scoffs at Dolores's scheme of running away with Salena— even if Joe had not stolen their money. "Where will you go?" Vera wants to know. "How long do you think it would take Joe to find you?" As Vera reminds her, "It's a depressingly masculine world we live in, Dolores."

Because it's such a world, women's options for justice are depressingly limited. This much Vera knows from experience. And she does not hesitate to share her wisdom with her less-worldly maid, thereby giving Dolores the seeds of the solution to her problems with Joe.

"Husbands die every day, Dolores." Vera says, voice calm and gaze intense. "Why, one is probably dying right now while you're sitting here weeping. They die, and leave their wives their money. I should know, shouldn't I? Sometimes they're driving home from their mistress's apartment, and their brakes suddenly fail." Vera pauses, and then adds ominously, "An accident, Dolores, can be an unhappy woman's best friend."

The very next day Vera throws a lavish party to mark the solar eclipse. She is in high spirits, and has hired extra help so that Dolores can leave early to "celebrate" with Joe. She and Dolores both know that this will be the one opportunity to kill him, for the entire town will be distracted, gathered at the harbor for the event. It is when Dolores gets cold feet and whispers to Vera that she can't go through with it that the older woman tells her matter-of-factly, "Sometimes, Dolores, sometimes you have to be a high-riding bitch to survive. Sometimes being a bitch is all a woman has to hang on to."

"Thank you, Vera," Dolores whispers back.

From this moment on, the relationship between them is characterized by a new closeness and camaraderie. Vera is no longer "Mrs. Donovan," but "Vera," and Dolores, though still an employee, is no longer just her maid. Similarly, when Salena finally has her own flashback and learns the truth about Joe, suddenly the differences—in class, in education, in lifestyle—that have stood between mother and daughter melt away under the force of the revelation and the new bond it creates between them.

Women, Violence, and the Law

Dolores's refusal to conform to conventional standards of white, middle-class femininity compound her guilt in the eyes of her accusers. She is an independent, assertive, working-class woman who speaks her mind and whose primary relationships are with other women rather than men. She is also physically large and not above using violence when necessary. In other words, Dolores Claiborne may or may not be guilty of murder, but she is certainly guilty of violating the cardinal virtues of "true" womanhood mandating passivity and submissiveness,[15] as well as heterosexuality, and one gets the impression that Mackey and the town hoodlums are more concerned about this "crime" than the deaths of Vera and Joe. In addition, Kathy Bates as an actress has a prior "record" of violent behavior: in *Misery* (another Stephen King adaptation) her character is not only strong, aggressive, and decidedly unfeminine, but unapologetically monstrous, and the ax used to subdue Joe in *Dolores Claiborne* recalls the sledgehammer used by Bates to torture the male protagonist in the earlier film.

Of course, the violence in *Misery* is associated with the woman's individual psychosis and is therefore unjustified, while in *Dolores Claiborne* the woman's use of violence is ultimately shown to be the rational response of a protective mother to poverty and male violence. Nevertheless, the film self-consciously dramatizes the conflation of criminality with gender nonconformity, and the ways in which the female offender marks the limits of cultural femininity. In the original novel, Dolores herself explicitly recognizes this. Knowing that her ability to remain on the island after Joe's murder depends more on the judgment of the townsfolk than the results of the official inquest, and that this judgment in turn depends on an appropriate display of wifely grief, she is forever grateful for the single tear she spontaneously sheds during her initial conversation with the shrewd and suspicious John Mackey. She is even more grateful that Frank was present as a witness, and spread the word that Dolores Claiborne cried for Joe after all.

In the film, Dolores is not so well integrated into the small island community. In fact, much like the town witch or hag of colonial times, she lives on the margins, frequently an object of ridicule and harassment. This much is clear early on in the film when a young boy on a bicycle taunts Dolores as she leaves the police station with Salena—a tamer version of the threatening drive-by confrontations and the obscene phone calls we witness later.

"Hey Ms. Claiborne! Kill anyone else today?" the young boys yell at her.

"Not just yet," Dolores replies dryly. "When I change my mind I know exactly where I'm going to start."

This response is typical for Dolores, whose sharp tongue and caustic wit continually violate the expectations of those around her about how a woman suspected of murder (for the second time) ought to behave. When Frank tells Salena that her mother must remain on the island until the hearing takes place, Dolores cuts him off, "If I decide to make my grand escape to South America, I'll be sure to let you know first." Similarly, when Frank and Mackey show up at Dolores's house the next morning to find Dolores and Salena arguing outside, Dolores responds to Frank's greeting ("Hello, ladies, little mornin' walk?") with "Nope, just packin' up the speedboat so's I can make my big escape."

Frequently, her retorts draw attention to her marginal status as an "unfeminine" working-class woman. In the scene mentioned above, Mackey and Frank have to come for a sample of Dolores's hair, as they're "running some tests." Salena flatly refuses to comply ("I think we'll take a pass on that"), but Dolores looks Mackey straight in the eye and says, "Go on, take what you want. I ain't doin' any beauty pageants this week." Even Dolores's protestations of innocence are brusque and sarcastic: "I didn't kill [Vera]," she insists as she and Salena drive home from the station. "I didn't push her down that friggin' staircase. That's what you want to know, ain't it? I'm tellin' ya, I did not murder that bitch any more than I'm wearin' a diamond tiara."

Salena, teeth clenched on a cigarette, doesn't find this convincing, nor does the spectator at this early stage. For if we compare the two scenes of Vera's death, we see that the first is shot in such a way as to make Dolores's guilt not only possible but probable. In the opening sequence, immediately before Vera tumbles down the stairs, we see only two shadows on the wall, struggling, one towering menacingly over the other, and Vera gasping, "No Dolores, leave me be! Noooo . . . noooo Dolores! Let me go!" After she falls, the camera tilts upward to reveal Dolores's looming shadow (the music rising dramatically), then Dolores herself at the top of the stairs looking down at Vera's inert body. But Vera is still alive, and the next shot is of Dolores in the kitchen rummaging frantically for something to help finish her off. The mailman arrives just in time to find Dolores standing over Vera wielding a rolling pin. This is our introduction to Dolores, and it's a decidedly unflattering one—designed primarily to maximize suspense by suggesting Dolores's guilt, but also to foreground the woman's monstrous and violent potential.

By contrast, the later flashback in which Dolores finally tells Salena what really happened to Vera is shot primarily from Dolores's point of view, and shows that Dolores's struggle with Vera at the top of the stairs was an attempt to prevent rather than ensure the old woman's fall. We also learn that Dolores grabbed the rolling pin to finish Vera off, but at Vera's own request: Vera wants to die, and as she lies on the landing gasping for help, she begs Dolores to kill her not save her.

"Why?" Dolores asks, her voice breaking. "Why'd you do this, Vera, why?"

"Because I hate the smell of being old," Vera whispers. "I'm tired and I want to be done. Will you help me, Dolores? Will you please help me die? Don't let me die in some hospital! Kill me now."

The request horrifies Dolores, but she understands it. Vera suffers the indignities of a series of strokes, including mental failures and incontinence; her suicide occurs during one of her rare lucid moments and amounts to her final, defiant act of self-determination. Thus, one cannot understand the meaning of Vera's death, and Dolores's role in it, out of context, just as the real meaning of violence (for example, a wife's murder of her husband) lies in the conditions and circumstances that prompt it. The film withholds this knowledge early on and so frames Dolores as "bad" until the end. As we have seen, a shared history and understanding of women's violence binds Dolores and Vera together. "Necessary" or "justifiable" are matters of debate; both women have killed their husbands, and neither murder meets legal standards of self-defense. This is precisely what makes Dolores and Vera a couple of high-riding bitches and allows them to survive with dignity.

Interestingly, Vera's death parallels Joe's in significant ways. Both Joe and Vera fall from great heights after struggles with Dolores. Joe is drunk, while Vera has just awakened from one of her "spells." Neither one dies right away, however; both experience fleeting moments of lucidity and recognition where they understand what is happening and beg Dolores for help (Joe wants life, Vera death). In both cases Dolores is frightened and upset but ultimately follows her own moral convictions. The key difference is that Dolores deliberately takes Joe's life, whereas Vera takes her own. Yet the formal codes of the film refuse to frame Joe's murder as either evil or tragic. In fact, they do quite the reverse, expressing through aspects of soundtrack and mise-en-scène the joy and relief that Dolores herself cannot adequately articulate.

Like all Dolores's accounts of the past, the story of the murder unfolds primarily through flashback. Having been relieved of her duties at Vera's, Dolores goes home and plies Joe with whiskey and food. Time passes. Shots of the two of them alternate with shots of sleek white sailboats gathered in the harbor under a deepening sky. Brilliant orange and blue clouds race overhead. The music rises ominously; the earth's shadow has begun to cross the sun. When Dolores confronts Joe about the stolen money and his abuse of Salena, he lashes out and they struggle; twice Dolores falls to the ground before breaking free and running across the fields, Joe in dogged pursuit. She leaps across the camouflaged well. He falls in with a splintering crash, but catches himself on the edge and struggles to survive. Eventually he falls to the bottom with a scream, as hundreds of boats in the harbor blast their horns and shoot flares, celebrating his demise along with the eclipse, the background colors intense and surreal. The music signals a new day dawning even as the sky grows suddenly black. And then, in a point-of-view shot from the bottom of the well, we see the sun slowly reemerge. It suffuses the scene with a warm golden glow, suggesting rebirth, renewal, and conversion. Indeed, the murder sequence more than any other flashback illustrates an important feature of melodrama noted by Nowell-Smith: that the undischarged or repressed emotion that cannot be accommodated within the action finds expression through music and elements of the mise-en-scène. Formal elements not only heighten the emotion of a scene, but also to some degree substitute for it.[16]

Dolores doesn't tell her story at the inquest as she had planned, for Salena has undergone a conversion of her own and returns in time to stop the hearing. Thus, Dolores is never officially held to account for killing Joe, although she does not go unpunished. The fact that she kills and walks "free" makes the film interesting, especially in relation to other Hollywood films featuring violent women. As feminist scholars have pointed out, aggressive, murderous, or monstrous women are old fodder in Hollywood, and the dangerous predatory female is a popular trope.[17] But aggression is no guarantee of iconoclasm, and Hollywood continually finds new ways to arm women without upsetting more fundamental gender images.[18] Moreover, women in film often pay for the use of violence with their lives. In most film noir, for example, the "testing" of patriarchal law (both legal and familial) through criminal action (e.g., killing the father-patriarch) ends in disaster for all concerned. Classic noir suggests that for men and women to assume their "rightful" place in the symbolic order, they must renounce their transgressive desires and identify with/submit to patriarchal authority.[19]

Dolores Claiborne, along with some other contemporary film bitches, refuses to do this. She challenges the masculine regime and gets away with it. In this limited sense *Dolores Claiborne* stands as a kind of feminist corrective to *Chinatown,* in which the femme fatale is an incest victim shot dead at the end of the film as her tormentor makes off with her child. Dolores is successful in her challenge in part because she acts out of maternal desire, one of the few if not the only culturally sanctioned spaces for the exercise of female violence. But Dolores also succeeds because, as in *Chinatown,* the regime is so obviously corrupt. This is why Vera dismisses Dolores's scheme of running away with Salena. In the murder sequence when Dolores confronts Joe over abusing the girl, she brings his rage to a boiling point by telling him, "The only thing you're gonna get is a long stretch in Shawshank prison for child molesting!" The threat is hollow, however, for at this point Dolores has already decided on another course of action, having seen the writing on the wall (recall the word "bitch" scrawled on her front door). The solution, like the problem itself, must remain all in the family. Hence Dolores takes her private revenge outside the bounds of official discourse.

In this key sense Dolores Claiborne has much in common with Jennifer, the heroine of the rape-revenge film *I Spit on Your Grave,* or the title characters of the more highbrow *Thelma and Louise.* These women circumvent the law and play according to the rules of a higher justice because they understand the law has never been particularly friendly to women in matters of sexual assault. One difference noted by Carol Clover between the rape-revenge films of the 1970s and more contemporary versions such as *Thelma and Louise* or *The Accused* is that the earlier lowbrow films do not even bother giving the legal system a role, even a negative one. In her comparison of *I Spit on Your Grave* and *The Accused,* Clover notes that by eschewing engagement with the law, the former film keeps at center stage what the latter film tends to lose sight of: the wronged woman herself. Of *The Accused,* she writes, "[T]here is a sense in which the third party, the legal system, becomes the hero of the piece: focus has in any case shifted from the victim to her lawyer; from questions of why men rape and how victims feel to questions of what constitutes evidence; from bedroom (or wherever) as the site of confrontation to courthouse."[20] As Clover points out, the final shots of the two films are illustrative of the difference: *I Spit on Your Grave* shows Jennifer, smiling, speeding along in a motorboat (having single-handedly vanquished all four of her tormentors); *The Accused,* by contrast, shows an aerial view of the courthouse.

Dolores Claiborne does give the legal system a role, but only to reveal its biases, flaws, and inadequacies, and in this regard it is not unlike *Thelma and Louise.* Like Louise, Dolores has come to learn that "we don't live in that kind of a world," meaning a world in which a woman could go to the police, report a sexual assault, be taken seriously, and be treated fairly. Thus, Dolores, like Louise, is suspicious of the law (Dolores will not even look at the list of lawyers Salena compiles for her), even though both films take pains to provide us with good as well as bad representatives of the legal system (Frank and Mackey, respectively, in *Dolores Claiborne;* Slocombe versus the other cops in *Thelma and Louise*). In both films women rely on each other instead of the law, and here, too, the final shots of the films are illustrative: Thelma and Louise together in the car suspended over the Grand Canyon; Dolores and Salena saying good-bye at the ferry, having reached a tentative but hopeful alliance.

Both films thus emphasize the enmeshment of the personal and familial with larger institutional mechanisms, and the importance of homosocial female bonding to women's survival in a hostile environment. In *Dolores Claiborne*, the interdependence of the two levels—the familial and the sociopolitical—is symbolized by the two men with whom Dolores does battle. Once the husband is gone, the detective surfaces to take his place as the chief obstacle to both her own personal freedom and any possible reconciliation with Salena. In each case, Dolores requires the collaboration of another woman to "win": Vera helps her get rid of Joe, Salena herself helps defeat Mackey—who is pursuing Dolores as much for personal vengeance as legal justice, again proving that the two are very much intertwined.

The antagonism between Dolores and Mackey is clear (and clearly gendered) from the beginning, when Mackey calls Dolores "Mrs. St. George" and she snaps back at him, "the name is Claiborne. I changed it back after Joe died, and you know it." When he feigns an apology she gives him a disgusted look and says, "You sorry, are ya? I bet the last time you were sorry was when you needed to use the pay toilet and the string on your pet dime broke." There are countless such verbal exchanges between the two characters, signifying a long-standing and ongoing conflict; mid-way through the film when Salena admonishes her mother for deliberately making an enemy of Mackey, Dolores retorts, "I ain't making one, I'm keeping one." It is at this point that we get a flashback of the inquest following Joe's murder, in which Mackey is shown to be vicious and unscrupulous in his preliminary questioning of young Salena. Dolores intervenes and attempts to shield her daughter—a reversal of the hearing following Vera's death in which Salena is the one to protect Dolores.

To some extent, both hearings show the public as masculine and the private as feminine, and pit one against the other: Mackey, Frank, and the Judge versus Dolores and Salena. In the second hearing especially, the "old boys' network" aspect of the law is clearly foregrounded when the Judge repeatedly calls Mackey by his first name ("John, this is your ball game"). At the same time, Salena, as a successful, high-profile journalist, is also of the public sphere. Moreover, her job as investigative reporter makes her the perfect feminine counterpart to Mackey and ideally suited to challenge his authority, since journalists are supposed to play watchdog to the state. Initially, Salena's investigation is aimed at Dolores and is prosecutorial in nature, thus paralleling rather than contradicting Mackey's own. At one point in the film Mackey even tells Salena, "You know, we're probably more alike than you care to believe." Eventually, however, the daughter's investigative efforts are turned inward, and as she comes to learn the truth about the past, she begins to believe in, and defend, her mother.

In the end, Salena must defend Dolores because Dolores refuses to defend herself. Tired, hurt, and at the end of her rope, Dolores gives up fighting because the one person she loves, the one person whose opinion matters, still believes her guilty—or so Dolores thinks. The logic of the narrative also requires Salena to play the savior, the film's version of the knight in shining armor; Dolores once sacrificed everything to protect Salena from Joe, and now, for the mother-daughter dyad to work, there has to be reciprocity: Salena has to protect Dolores from Mackey, and thereby pay her mother back. Payback is a big theme in the film, and it too comes in both public and private forms. Joe gets his payback at home, Mackey gets his at work. Indeed, the highly charged scene where Salena makes a mockery of Mackey's "evidence" has the trappings of a classic courtroom drama. It is also fitting that she triumphs over Mackey by capitalizing on the education Dolores worked so hard to provide.

If the inquest is the public victory, the hug exchanged between Dolores and Salena at the ferry is the private one. "I don't know how to feel about what you did," Salena tells her mother. "But I know you did it for me." Their loving embrace is the counterpoint to the forced, awkward hug at the police station near the start of the film, when they meet for the first time in fifteen years as virtual strangers. The Salena-Dolores relationship thus picks up where the Dolores-Vera relationship leaves off. That relationship, too, was one of love, mutual dependence, and reciprocity. Dolores gave a lifetime of service to Vera; Vera in turn gave Dolores the solution to her problem with Joe, and ultimately left Dolores a million-dollar inheritance.

Conclusion

As Judith Halberstam notes in this volume, women in Western cultures have long identified as victims rather than perpetrators of violence; indeed, most people see femininity and aggression as mutually exclusive. In such a world, Halberstam argues, women have much to gain from new and different configurations of violence, what she calls "imagined violence." Films like *Thelma and Louise* or *Dolores Claiborne* suggest not that women pick up guns (or axes or sledgehammers or ice picks) but that women allow themselves to imagine the possibility of fighting violence with violence, of creating a new psychic landscape in which their rage and resistance is a plausible, even probable, response to gender injustice. Imagined violence is thus the violence of popular culture, "the fantasy of unsanctioned eruptions of aggression from the wrong people, of the wrong skin, the wrong sexuality, the wrong gender."[21]

As we have seen, *Dolores Claiborne* does not really celebrate the use of violence, even violence perpetrated to avenge a terrible injustice. Rather, it shows how violent law demands violent resistance and, even more importantly, how the effects of this cycle are no less real or shocking for being ghostly and invisible. It also shows how complicated the relation of women to violence often is (given the conflation of femininity with passivity) and the ways in which guilt and innocence are not always neatly separable, even in the case of battery and sexual abuse. At the same time, there is little doubt that the film sides with Dolores and justifies her actions: as in the rape-revenge films of the 1970s (but not classic noir), the woman who kills gets away with it in the end. Despite the attempts of the law (and its male representatives) to indict her, Dolores gets away with it because of the love, support, and intelligence of other women, each of whom, in their respective ways, has good reason to know that sometimes you have to be a high-riding bitch just to survive.

Notes

1. *Dolores Claiborne,* written by Tony Gilroy, directed by Taylor Hackford, produced by Taylor Hackford and Charles Mulvehill (Columbia, 1995).

2. See Diane Waldman, "'At Last I Can Tell It to Someone!': Feminine Point of View and Subjectivity in the Gothic Romance Film of the 1940s," *Cinema Journal* 23, no. 2 (winter 1983): 29–40; see also Andrea Walsh, *Women's Film and Female Experience, 1940–1950* (New York: Praeger, 1984), 1–22.

3. Walsh, *Women's Film and Female Experience,* 1–22.

4. Janet Walker, "Feminist Critical Practice: Female Discourse in *Mildred Pierce,*" *Film Reader* Issue no. 5, 1982: 164–72.

5. E. Ann Kaplan, "Theories of Melodrama: A Feminist Perspective," *Women and Performance: A Journal of Feminist Theory* 1, no. 1 (spring/summer 1983): 40–48.

6. See Thomas Elseasser, "Vincente Minelle," in *Home Is Where the Heart Is: Studies in Melodrama and the Woman's Film,* ed. Christine Gledhill (London: BFI Publishing, 1987); Geoffrey

Nowell-Smith, "Minelli and Melodrama," in *Movies and Methods,* vol. 2, ed. Bill Nichols (Berkeley: University of California Press, 1985); Laura Mulvey, "Notes on Sirk and Melodrama," *Movie* 25 (winter 1977/78): 53–56; Christine Gledhill, "The Melodramatic Field: An Investigation," in *Home Is Where the Heart Is.*

7. In *Mildred Pierce,* the father abandons the family, forcing Mildred to find a job to support her two daughters, Veda and Kay. Thereafter, she devotes her life entirely to her children, and when Kay dies (thus fanning the intense, quasisexual relationship that already exists between Mildred and Veda), Mildred works slavishly to satisfy Veda's increasingly expensive tastes, even marrying her own business partner to augment the household income. Veda is not particularly grateful for the sacrifice, however, and in the end tries to seduce her stepfather before finally killing him.

8. Pam Cook, "Duplicity in *Mildred Pierce,*" in *Women in Film Noir,* ed. E. Ann Kaplan (London: BFI Publishing, 1980).

9. Gledhill, "The Melodramatic Field," 33.

10. Nowell-Smith, "Minelli and Melodrama," 192.

11. See Sylvia Harvey, "Woman's Place: The Absent Family of Film Noir," in *Women in Film Noir,* 22–34.

12. See Diana Russell, *The Secret Trauma: Incest in the Lives of Girls and Women* (New York: Basic Books, 1986); Ellen Bass and Laura Davis, *The Courage to Heal: A Guide for Women Survivors of Child Sexual Abuse* (New York: Harper and Row, 1988); Lenore Auerbach Walker, ed., *Handbook on Sexual Abuse of Children* (New York: Springer Publishing Company, 1988).

13. See Richard Cordova, "A Case of Mistaken Legitimacy," in *Home Is Where the Heart Is,* 255–67.

14. Gledhill, "The Melodramatic Field," 37.

15. See Barbara Welter, "The Cult of True Womanhood, 1820–1860," *American Quarterly* 18, no. 2 (1966): 151–74.

16. Nowell-Smith, "Minelli and Melodrama," 193.

17. See, for example, Molly Haskell, *From Reverence to Rape: The Treatment of Women in the Movies,* 2nd ed. (Chicago: University of Chicago Press, 1987); Camilla Griggers, "Phantom and Reel Projections: Lesbians and the (Serial) Killing Machine," in *Posthuman Bodies,* ed. Judith Halberstam and Ira Livingston (Bloomington: Indiana University Press, 1995), 162–76.

18. See Krin Gabbard and Glen Gabbard, "Phallic Women in the Contemporary Cinema," *American Imago* 50, no. 4 (1993): 421–39.

19. See Frank Krutnik, *In a Lonely Street: Film Noir, Genre, Masculinity* (New York: Routledge, 1991).

20. Carol J. Clover, "Getting Even," *Sight and Sound* 2, no. 1 (May 1992): 17.

21. Judith Halberstam, "Imagined Violence/Queer Violence," this volume.

Waiting to Set It Off

African American Women
and the Sapphire Fixation

Kimberly Springer

Writing about spectatorship and the image of African American[1] women on the Hollywood screen, hooks reports, "Most of the black women I talked with were adamant that they never went to the movies expecting to see compelling representations of black femaleness."[2] As evidenced by the excitement and media hype around the film adaptation of Terry McMillan's 1992 best-selling novel *Waiting to Exhale,* that expectation is changing.[3] African American women attended screenings of the film en masse, even going so far as to rent entire theaters.[4] The story of four middle- to upper-middle-class professionals, the film *Waiting to Exhale* (1995), audiences expected, would finally represent Black women as something other than Mamas 'n the 'hood or video 'ho'es.[5] Featuring a Black male director (Forest Whitaker) and four divas (Angela Bassett, Loretta Devine, Whitney Houston, and Lela Rochon), a predictable clamor ensued over the representation of African American *men* and whether the film participated in male-bashing. I use the word "predictable" because, though race, class, gender, and sexuality are inextricably linked in a film about Black women's lives, Black men often become the focus of conversation.[6] Underpinning accusations of Black male bashing is *Black women's behavior,* particularly their behavior toward Black men. Structural analyses of economic and social conditions influencing Black women's behavior fall by the wayside in favor of scapegoating representations of emasculating Black women.

Resistance to the hegemony of the dominant European American culture is found in the politics of feminism, antiracist work, work for the rights of the disabled, and the struggle against heterosexism. Granted, these are not mutually exclusive struggles, but the one outstanding trait they all have in common is that they observe culture, critique it, and at times revel in that critique. One of the goals of this volume on women's violence in film is to celebrate these women as we critique their actions. This critique of *Waiting to Exhale* and *Set It Off* is situated in a unique position that must be stated explicitly. In U.S. cinema, the violence of Black women always seems a result of their being Black, while the violence of white women is often celebrated as liberatory. The following examination of the violence of African American women attempts to break down the historical, social, and economic context of their violence. Understanding how Black women are defined in opposition to white women is key to understanding African American women's violence. Analyzing these two films without acknowledging the cultural and economic history of African American women in the United States is to allow stereotypes to remain hidden. These stereotypes, in turn, continue to influence the types of roles African American actors are permitted to play. Furthermore, as filmmaker Pratibha Parmar notes, "The deeply ideological nature of imagery determines not only how other people think about us [marginalized groups] but how we think about ourselves."[7] While I celebrate the new images of African American women on film I demand more from these images.

This essay explores the connections of race, class, gender, and sexuality in two films, *Waiting to Exhale* and F. Gary Gray's *Set It Off*, that purport to portray African American women in a more positive light than past Hollywood cinema.[8] At the same time, class dictates very different endings for the women involved. These endings depend on dominant stereotypes of African American female sexuality, the mediating influences of money and "good taste," and cautionary tales about mobility. In their own class-based ways, these two films move toward a redefinition of how African American women are portrayed, yet continue to uphold dominant stereotypes of them as prone to violence. While interpersonal issues are at the root of the problems of upwardly mobile women in *Waiting to Exhale*, the working-class African American women of *Set It Off* are pushed to extreme violence and tragic ends by outside social forces.

The remainder of this paper briefly reviews the iconography of African American women in the historical record of the United States as it relates to contemporary portrayals. I also establish the film and television context of the icon called "Sapphire," an icon that is gaining momentum in mainstream popular-culture production. Next, I describe the premises of the films *Waiting to Exhale* and *Set It Off* and examine specific characters in relation to the question, "What does the behavior of these particular representations of African American women say about violence and class among this group of women in the 1990s?" I conclude with a final comment on the guilty pleasures of watching African American women on the screen even if the representations are only a small step up from past stereotypical portrayals.

Which Sister Are You?

In discussing the representation of African American women in film it is important to recognize the always already constructed nature of Black womanhood in the United States. In popular culture and accepted historical iconography it would be redundant to speak of "African American women's violence" or the "violent African American woman." Black people, depending on the icons in current usage, are thought to be inherently violent.[9] I maintain that when it comes to women, race, and violence, white North American women are assumed to have been provoked to violence; they are not permitted violent impulses. Oppositionally, African Americans are thought to be always already violent due to their "savage" ancestry. Specific to this essay are definitions of Black and white womanhood and the historical resonance of the cult of true womanhood.[10]

Weigman observes, "[B]lack women have served primarily as white women's other, a dark continent of difference whose various lacks—of beauty, morality, and intelligence—subtend the cultural elevation and adornment of white womanhood."[11] Defined as everything that white women were not, Black women lived, in the nineteenth and early twentieth centuries, in the shadow of clichés: the Mammy, the Jezebel, and the Sapphire.[12] These icons represent the range of acceptable behaviors for African American women: passive and subservient or uncontrollable and rebellious. Their race defines African American women as outside of womanliness. After slavery, since the slave master's whip could not contain these women, they were mastered by definitions of Black womanhood.

The Mammy is a contested image, thought by some scholars to be a creation of the white, southern imagination, but nonetheless an image that haunts African American women today.[13] Constructed as a rotund, asexual, sometimes cantankerous, but often perennially happy servant, Mammy lingers in the memories of North Americans in films such as *Gone with the Wind* (1939) and Douglas Sirk's *Imitation of Life* (1959). And regardless of her 1980s makeover, she continues to adorn Aunt Jemima pancake boxes and syrup containers, reminding us of a model of Black womanhood who is only present to serve.

Conversely, Jezebel is present to serve the sexual needs of white slave owners. In her history of the lives of female slaves, Deborah Gray White describes the rationale for the creation Jezebel as intended to refute the fact that white men could rape Black women.[14] Jezebel is diametrically opposed to Mammy: "One was carnal, the other maternal. One was at heart a slut, the other was deeply religious."[15] In the parlance of Spike Lee's 1986 film, Jezebel's "gotta have it." Today, policymakers call upon the specter of the Jezebel as they discuss the alleged immorality of the "welfare queen." She also appears when Black male producers cast music videos with Black female body parts.

Finally, and most relevant to this examination, is the Sapphire. The Sapphire is an often cited but little documented icon of African American womanhood. Author bell hooks notes that "as Sapphires, black women were depicted as evil, treacherous, bitchy, stubborn, and hateful, in short all that the mammy figure was not."[16] Postslavery, the Sapphire image evolved as a devaluation of what little independence African American women had through their labor force participation, predominantly in domestic service. Most importantly, "the Sapphire image of African American womanhood, unlike other images that symbolize African American women, necessitates the presence of an African American male. When the Sapphire image is portrayed it is the African American male who represents the point of contention, in an ongoing verbal dual between Sapphire and the African American male."[17] Thus begins the scapegoating of the African American woman and her alleged advancements in the labor market as the crux of Black male-female relationship problems. Rather than examine structural impediments to the full employment of Black men since emancipation, social scientists cast African American women as matriarchs and deemed them castrating Sapphires.[18]

In their essay "Is the Black Male Castrated?" Bond and Peery describe Sapphire's entrance into popular culture as emerging in the 1930s and 1940s radio shows and films.[19] Black men and women were represented, respectively, as "simpering, ineffectual whipping boys" and as "iron-willed, effectual, treacherous toward and contemptuous of Black men."[20] Not only were radio and film availing themselves of this image, but television in the 1940s and 1950s also zeroed in on Sapphire as an adequate representation of Black women—when it was necessary to include them at all. CBS's *Amos 'n' Andy* (1935–51) was the first to openly utilize the Sapphire image by naming "the nagging, shrewish wife" of Amos and Andy's friend Kingfish after the icon.[21]

Sapphire's presence carried on past the demise of *Amos 'n' Andy* in the 1950s and on into late-twentieth-century television, perpetuating the "comedic" device of contemptuous Black female-male relationships. Norman Lear's comedy about a family living in the Chicago projects, *Good Times* (1974–79), showed the often adversarial, but loving relationship between sister Thelma and brother J.J. Florence the maid's verbal combat with her employer, George, in *The Jeffersons* (1975–85) reversed the image of the subservient African American domestic servant. Florence was often sitting in the kitchen avoiding work when she was not giving Mr. Jefferson a piece of her mind. In the 1990s, television brought us Sapphire in the character of Pam on the sitcom *Martin* (1992–97). Like her predecessors, Pam does not "take any stuff off" of Martin, though this does not stop him from viciously likening her appearance to a dog's. Clearly, Sapphire maintains her control as the predominant image of African American women on television and remains an embittered, single woman.

Though this essay is about representations of African American women's violence in film, given the dearth of representations of Black women in any medium, the boundaries between film and television are necessarily blurred. Images of African American women in one medium become representative of African American women on any sized screen and in real life: "Distinctions no longer exist between movies and news, television and real life. There is nowhere left to avert the gaze."[22] No matter how offensive the representation, African Americans must interrogate, in fact bear witness to, the images disseminated by Hollywood film producers for their stated purpose, as well as subsequent consequences. Sapphire leaps from silver screen to television screen and back again, retaining her fiery tongue that, while often witty, must be contained.

Historically, for African American girls and women, Sapphire is a dangerous model *not* to emulate because she has the potential to be violent. Sapphire is not afraid to be loud and to speak her mind. Her danger lies within her words and only *home training* constrains her violence. Most African Americans are familiar with the concept: "That girl ain't got no home training." A lack of home training marks a deficiency in breeding. Home training is about being well mannered in public, being a lady, and being middle class or working toward that class status. If one comes from a good home, one knows that talking back and running one's mouth are verboten activities.

Only through the whip and being in proximity to whiteness were Black people thought to have been "tamed" in slavery. Late-nineteenth- and early-twentieth-century African American intellectuals, such as Anna Julia Cooper, W. E. B. Du Bois, and Gertrude Mossell, espoused viewpoints that favored emulating white men and women in terms of family life, education, and upward mobility. Socioeconomic class replaced religion as the colonizing tool of whiteness that civilizes African Americans, particularly African American women. Hammonds observes that "some middle-class black women engaged in policing behavior of poor and working-class women and any who deviated from a Victorian norm in the name of protecting the 'race.'"[23] She notes that these reformers also did so to thwart the deployment of the Jezebel and Sapphire icons, which were used to justify violence against Black women.[24]

Similarly, Mossell, an influential journalist and women's rights crusader, wrote progressively for equality in marriage in 1894, but had this warning about Black women's roles in marriage:

The one remaining thought unmentioned is *temper*, the disposition to scold and nag. . . . It may be humanity or masculinity's total depravity, but I believe more men tire of sweet women than even of scolds, and yet I do not desire to encourage the growth of this obnoxious creature. The described partner for a successful, peaceful married life is a woman of well-balanced temperament, who is known among her associates as one not given to what is often called fits of temper, and yet withal possessing a mind of her own.[25]

Temper fits and nagging had no place in the new middle-class African American home, with the implication that these women, because of middle-class comforts, had no cause to be disgruntled. Middle-class decorum required a balance between speaking one's mind and being outspoken. Reformers believed that through proper home training and upward mobility resembling that of their white counterparts, African Americans would know no bounds to the uplift of their race.

The ideas of home training and mobility carried on into the late twentieth century and are seen in film representations of African American women. Sapphire is still present but she has some "class": she attained middle-class status and she must behave as if she has refinement and good taste. Money and mobility can help her quell "the beast within." Class is no more a topic of polite conversation in the African American community than it is in the rest of U.S. society, so cinema serves as an illuminating entrée into the nexus of race, gender, and class. Also revealing are what two recent films, *Waiting to Exhale* and *Set It Off,* tell us about violence that is supposedly inherent in African American women and what can be done to contain that violence.

Waiting to Set It Off: Exchanges of Race, Gender, Class, and Violence

Waiting to Exhale and *Set It Off* were both films featuring quartets of African American women living their lives bounded by class and circumstances often beyond their control. Another factor uniting these films was the level of anticipation among African Americans, particularly women. These women were starved for representations that were not hookers, Superbad Mamas of the Blaxploitation era, or castrating matriarchs who did not want their boyz 'n the 'hood to escape the confines of poverty. Rather, the emphasis for these New Jill Films would be Black women proceeding successfully down their chosen life paths.[26] Whether or not it is explicitly acknowledged, social structures and economics determined the lives and choices of these eight women.

Waiting to Exhale is the story of four African American women living in Phoenix, Arizona. Savannah (Houston), an up-and-coming television producer, moves to Phoenix upon the recommendation of her friend, Bernadine (Bassett). "Bernie" has an MBA, but she chose to stay home with her two children while her husband, John, runs the company she helped him build during their marriage. Bernie also introduces Savannah to her friends, Robin (Rochon) and Gloria (Devine). Robin, an insurance executive, is the youngest of the women and seems usually to have a trio of male lovers. Gloria is divorced from her husband, who later comes out as gay. She often appears insecure and, frankly, hard up for sex. Though Gloria runs a flourishing hair salon, her single status becomes even more acute as she deals with her son's graduation from high school and his departure from home. Each woman is preoccupied with finding a mate and relationships that can complement their successful careers and child rearing. They are the anti–*Feminine Mystique*. Unlike the white, suburban, college-educated women of Friedan's exposé of "the problem that has no name," these women, except for Bernie, have careers and now they want the stabilizing influence of home, hearth, and husbands.[27]

Audiences expected this film to show images of African American women contrary to previous Hollywood depictions of Foxy Brown, Cleopatra Jones, and Beulah. Opening number 1 at the box office and garnering $65 million from Black women who attended the film multiple times opening weekend, *Waiting to Exhale* was a renaissance in portrayals of African American women.[28] In the tradition of melodrama, the protagonists of *Waiting to Exhale* confront issues deemed universal to all women regardless of race, including love, happiness, and motherhood. Seeing representations of Black women on the silver screen as the tragic heroes of their own stories, which dealt with familial conflicts, failed romance, and the perils of rebuilding a life after disappointment, appealed to Black women. Previously on the sidelines or wholly invisible in melodramas starring actresses such as Joan Crawford, Bette Davis, Barbara Stanwyck, and Greta Garbo, contemporary African-American women lived these life-dramas vicariously through Bassett, Houston, Devine, and Rochon. *Waiting to Exhale* mirrored the turn in post-1930s melodramas where "protagonists in women's films would often overcome stereotypical gender roles, and the films would examine the strong achievements of these characters."[29] Excluded from stereotypical gender roles by historical iconography, the women of *Waiting to Exhale* and their audience made full use of melodramatic devices to include African American women in dominant concepts of womanhood.

Reviews, when not preoccupied with the portrayal of men in this Black chick flick, were mixed. Some women, many of whom attended the film in groups, appreciated the divergence from what was "once described by Sheryl Lee Ralph, a black actress, as 'the Fat Mama on the Couch syndrome or the Sassy Sister on the Corner syndrome.'"[30] Others scolded a Black writer and a Black director for bringing to the screen women who, "though educated and beautiful, are portrayed as clueless harlots whose worlds revolve negatively (and unrealistically) around men."[31] Or as one columnist complained, "Four-letter words are spewed from the mouths of the leading women frequently and loudly, and temper tantrums loom ominously nearby. . . . This vile profanity really degrades the supposedly educated and cultured black women."[32] This reaction and others like it echo Mossell's 1894 warning: a rise in social class and status requires certain rules of decorum.

Originally a "clichéd script about 'four bad bitches' . . . with a proclivity for sociopathic activities," *Set It Off* brings to the screen four working-poor African American women who are pushed to the edge.[33] Cleo (Queen Latifah), Tisean (Kimberly Elise), and Frankie (Vivica A. Fox) are friends who live in Acorn Street Development, an L.A. housing project. The main protagonist, Stony (Jada Pinkett), has known them all since childhood, but she lives in a house near Acorn with her younger brother since their parents died in a car accident.

The capitalist, white patriarchy provokes them to commit a bank robbery by pushing them over the edge of social disenfranchisement. Though they are bold, these four women will subsequently die for their actions because dreams of middle-class respectability failed to tame their Sapphiric violent tendencies. Stony sees her brother, Stevie, who is wrongly assumed to have been involved in an earlier bank robbery, murdered by the Los Angeles Police Department (L.A.P.D.). Having already traded her body to an older neighborhood businessman for cash to send her brother to college, Stony views robbing a bank as a strike against a system that has wrongly taken her brother's life and forced her to prostitute herself. Tisean needs money to prove that she is capable of raising her son. While at work with the foursome who clean office buildings, the toddler ingests poison. He is there because Tisean, as a working-poor, single mother, cannot afford childcare. Frankie, whose scene opens the film, has been fired from her job as a teller at a bank. She has failed to follow protocol in the aforementioned robbery and is also implicated as an accomplice because she knows one of the thieves from her housing development. As Frankie sits splattered with the blood of a woman who was killed during the robbery, her supervisor asks rhetorically, "What happens the next time one of your friends robs the bank?" Lastly, Cleo is depicted as inherently violent, with her lesbianism and transgression of gender boundaries serving as a contributing factor. Her motivations for robbing banks appear to be the thrill of it and for the sake of getting paid. A *Denver Post* film critic summarized the motivations of these four women when he stated, "Cleo . . . may have a natural penchant for rebellion and violence, but the other three want desperately to make it into middle-class comfort and respectability and have simply reached their limits of frustration."[34]

Set It Off traverses the border between the crime story and gangster film genres through its use of multiple characters. Dirk describes the crime story genre as celebrating the rise and fall of particular criminals as they enter power struggles with law-enforcement figures. Gangster films, as an extension of the crime story, are

morality tales, Horatio Alger success stories turned upside down in which criminals live in an inverted dream world of success and wealth. Although they are doomed to failure and inevitable death, criminals are portrayed as the victims of circumstance, because the stories are told from their point of view—all other "normal" avenues to the top are unavailable to them.[35]

Both celebrating the rise and fall of this girl gang as well as serving as a morality tale, the characters in *Set It Off* embody multiple characteristics of gangsters as alternately "materialistic, street-smart, immoral, meglo-maniacal [*sic*], and self-destructive . . . but underneath they can express sensitivity and gentleness."[36] Though critics did not recognize *Set It Off* as a modern-day gangster film, several tuned in to the multifaceted characteristics of the characters as they attempted to change the course of their fate as dictated by race, gender, sexuality, and class constraints.

More often than with films featuring white characters, journalists usually go directly to the source to find out what African Americans think about a so-called Black film, but here film critics served as a proxy for the white audience's reaction. Their responses to *Set It Off* were more focused on the race and class aspects than cinematic constructs of a well-written script or dynamic acting. For example, some were surprisingly compassionate and laudatory of the film's ability to make the audiences care about the characters and their plight:

The movie is more aware of the economic struggles of its characters than most American films allow themselves to be. . . . There's a wonderfully written scene where the women sit on a rooftop, smoking pot, looking at a factory and observing wistfully, "Before they started laying people off, they were paying $15 an hour at that place."[37]

According to Ebert, poverty and racism are approved rationales in film for committing crimes against an uncaring capitalist system and, indirectly, the state. By robbing banks and, most importantly, getting away with it, the four women of *Set It Off* engage in a form of revolutionary expropriation: they steal what has already been stolen. Frankie uses this logic in trying to convince the other women, "Look, we're just taking away from the System that's fucking us all anyway, you know?"

Of course, there are those who wish that Tisean, Stony, Cleo, and Frankie had stopped at one bank robbery. For some reason, robbing one bank is understandable, but

[t]he women grow increasingly comfortable with violence, which adds to the tension and makes you worry that the four will be completely lost to decency and peace. . . . The mix of thrill and fear turns slowly darker. The voices of the women grow more arrogant and threatening; their talk starts to sound like real gangsters. The fun vanishes. The movie shows how easy it is for people barely out of poverty to fall back into it. And what gives the film its grit is its understanding that the women are not heroic for losing that fight, no matter how much we care for them.[38]

Clearly, "gritty realism" and "*Waiting to Exhale* meets *Thelma and Louise*" has its moment, but a quick jab at power structures is enough for this particular critic. The film implicitly demonstrates how easy it is for the icon of Sapphire to come out and assert her true colors, nineties-style.

Unlike the women of *Waiting to Exhale,* the women of *Set It Off* cannot keep Sapphire in check. To paraphrase a popular essentialist saying: "You can take a Negro out of the ghetto, but you can't take the ghetto out of the Negro." In the 1990s, socioeconomic class mediates Sapphire's violence. Gloria and Bernie demonstrate the extremes of a continuum of violence of upwardly mobile African American women while Stony and Cleo represent working-poor women. For the remainder of this essay I analyze these characters in turn and discuss how their violence comes to seem either provoked or inherent. Sexuality and class combine with historical images to mitigate the violence of these modern-day Sapphires.

Sapphire in the 'Burbs

It is tempting to pigeonhole the character Gloria as the "Mammy" of the four women in *Waiting to Exhale*. But it is not only insulting to Loretta Devine, who is radiant as Gloria, but too easy. Gloria is nurturing of her friends, she offers to cook for her attractive new neighbor, and she has an ever-present shy smile. Yet, it would be a betrayal of these qualities to deem them subservient and Mammy-like. Also, unlike the Mammy icon in past films, Gloria is not asexual by her own choice. The only thing constraining Gloria is her weight, or rather her self-consciousness about it, which by the end of the film is not a hindrance to her finding a loving, sexual relationship.

Most notable about the convergence of the image of Mammy and violence is that Gloria cannot seem to act when she is truly angry. In one scene, Gloria's search for her son, Tarik, leads her to her pool house where she interrupts a white teenage girl performing fellatio on her son. The girl runs out and her son, zipping up his pants, follows her to the house apologizing profusely but hardly repentant.

I recall audience members collectively groaning, "Uh-oh," and one member yelling out to the screen, "Slap him upside his head!" However, this violent reaction does not come. Instead, Gloria tells Tarik ominously, "Get out of my face." This phrase, in African American vernacular, is the final warning before violence erupts. When Gloria issues this command, and has to tell Tarik a second time, those familiar with this phrase know the implicit ending, ". . . or I swear to God I will kill you!"

Tarik also just learned that his father is gay and jumps around shouting, "My daddy's queer! My daddy is a fucking queer!" Gloria reprimands him and tells him not to use that word, but also they are outside by their pool and he is causing a scene. The icon of the Mammy joins with economic class to silence Tarik's homophobic outburst, but also to stop Gloria from stepping over the line into violence. Mammy is allowed to be cantankerous. Her physical violence is restrained in the public view of her middle-class neighbors, and the active violence in *Waiting to Exhale* is left for Bernie.

Promotional trailers highlighted the scene featuring Bernie setting fire to her husband's car. From watching these previews the viewer perceived that in order to set fire to expensive things this sister sure must be pissed. The film tells us early on what has brought out the Sapphire in Bernie: her husband John's infidelity with a white woman. Sapphire has new challenges to deal with in the 1990s. Wealth, upper-middle-class life, and an MBA cannot protect her from the perils of African American men's freedom to assert their masculinity in ways that mimic the status of white patriarchy.

As Bernie prepares for a New Year's Eve party, John confesses to Bernie that he is taking his mistress, Kathleen, who also happens to be the bookkeeper for their company, instead of her. Bernie's anger, emphasized by Bassett's razor-sharp features, is palpable by the time John gets around to saying that he wants a divorce.

BERNIE: You're telling me that you're leaving me for a white woman?

JOHN: Would it be better if she were Black?

BERNIE: No, it'd be better if *you* were Black!

Bernie's anger, and violent reaction, is multiplied by the nature of the betrayal. Sapphire of the forties and fifties never faced this type of infidelity because, presumably, few Black men then had the money or power to be desirable to white women.[39] But in the 1990s African American men can have everything that Sapphires and Black matriarchs allegedly kept from them for all these years. In this scene, Bernie accuses John of losing his "Blackness" to power and prestige. Being part of the upper middle class has brought havoc into her life; therefore, Bernie begins to exact her revenge on the accoutrements of fine living.

After wallowing in depression for several days, including the class trespass of shopping at the Circle K convenience store with rollers in her hair and wearing a bathrobe, Bernie suddenly comes to her senses. Or perhaps, Sapphire takes over. She kicks open the door of the walk-in closet. The camera zooms in on her eyes, which are bloodshot from crying. In a series of quick cuts the camera zooms from her eyes to John's watches, back to Bernie's eyes, over to his suits, and then to his shoes, which are carefully lined up. Bernie's destruction of her husband's status symbols is, simultaneously, irrational and methodical. As she grabs armfuls of clothing and accessories and marches them out to the garage, she mutters the following soliloquy for cheated wives everywhere:

Yeah, a white woman is probably the only one who will tolerate your smug ass. Yeah, I was your white woman for eleven years. You couldn't have started that damned company without me. Hell, I worked my ass off. I mean, I've got a Master's degree in business and there I was his secretary, his office manager, and his computer.

[Bernie brings a child's red wagon into the house to expedite the house cleaning.] No, Bernadine, you can't start your catering business this year. Why don't you wait a few years, huh? Yeah, don't start it right now. Wait one, two, three years. I need you to be a fucking background to my foreground. . . .

But the worst, the fucking worst is making my kids go to a school where there are only two other Black children because you don't want them to be "improperly

influenced." Well, guess what, John?!? You're the motherfucking improper influence!

[Cramming John's clothes into the sunroof of his car] Get your shit, get your shit and get out!

At the end of her tirade, all of John's belongings are in his BMW. She backs the car out of the garage and into the driveway. Getting out, she douses the car and its contents with gasoline, lights a cigarette and throws the match in the sunroof. The car is quickly engulfed in vengeful flames. The dowdy bathrobe that Bernie has been wearing since New Year's Eve swings open to reveal that she is still wearing the sexy, black bustier and diamond necklace for the party. With a renewed confidence she turns and strides back into the house still smoking her cigarette.

Everything that was supposed to make Bernie's life perfect turned out to be wrong. The attractive husband is now a cheat. The money to buy her children the best education possible isolated them from other African Americans. John used Bernie's MBA and skills against her to build a business that is now solely in his name.

FIGURE 16. Bernie gets "ghetto" in the suburbs. Swaggering vandalism marks a proud movement from faithful wife to dangerous woman in *Waiting to Exhale*.

But if Bernie is not mindful of how wrong her life has gone, a white male firefighter appears at her door to speak to proper etiquette for the newly mon-eyed African American woman:

FIREFIGHTER: Ma'am, are you aware that your car was on fire?

BERNIE: Yes.

FIREFIGHTER: Did you start this fire, ma'am?

BERNIE: [Takes drag off her cigarette but remains silent.]

FIGHTFIGHTER: It's against the law to burn anything except trash in your own yard, ma'am.

BERNIE: It *is* trash.

FIGHTFIGHTER: This is a nice area. Luckily a neighbor cared enough. The next time you want to burn something . . .

BERNIE: It won't happen again.

Bernie slams the door in the firefighter's face and is almost serene. Recognizing that money cannot buy everything, Bernie considers her husband's belongings and her marriage trash. The rationales behind her actions are lost on the firefighter who is concerned about the law, but also propriety. He serves to re-mind Bernie, and the viewer, that she has ascended into a better kind of neigh-borhood and this (ghetto) behavior will not be tolerated. Bernie's comment ("It won't happen again") refers to starting the fire, but also to her life with John and her gullibility in their marriage.

Bernie's second incident of violence is still provoked by John's interracial infidelity, but this time it is directed against Kathleen, who is also a symbol of John's upward mobility. The scene opens with Bernie storming into a meeting at John's office: "Would you mind terribly if I had a few words with my hus-band?" Kathleen opens her mouth to respond but Bernie slaps her across the face, a blow that causes Kathleen's blond hair to whip around and knocks her to the floor. She gets up and runs from the room with the rest of the staff. While the violence of women against men, particularly those guilty of misogyny, is often cheered on, violence against other women is rarely explored. In the con-text of African American women's feeling of betrayal and anger over interracial dating, Bernie's striking out at Kathleen elicited a cathartic cheer from most Black women who went to see *Waiting to Exhale*. Frustrations over always being placed as inferior to white women in beauty standards and demoted as the love interests of some Black men made this moment of African American women's violence a welcome version of the Sapphire role.

However, the additional reasons for Bernie's violence become clear when we learn that John has cleaned out their bank account, leaving Bernie nothing to pay the mortgage on the house. Finding herself unable to provide for her children brings out her maternal instincts. As she had earlier said to Savannah, "It's amazing what can happen when you give a man control over your life." While white women discovered this pitfall of marriage long ago and perhaps counted on remarriage for renewed financial stability, African American women were not guaranteed this safeguard. Bernie violated an age-old dictum that African American mothers dispensed for years: "Don't depend on no man for nothin.'" Bernie had the education and the business sense to start her own independent company, but she lapsed and allowed John control of their finances.

Waiting to Exhale serves as a cautionary tale for upwardly mobile African American women in two ways. First, Bernie made the mistake of thinking that her money, her home, the expensive school to which she sent her children, or her beauty would keep her husband from being lured by the ultimate prize: a white woman. Second, Bernie failed to realize that she could not find safety in her upper-middle-class lifestyle. In addition to disrupting her ideal family, John forced her to get "Black" on him. In other words, Bernie was driven to let the Sapphire within her loose. Sapphire, as the bitter, vengeful "Black bitch," destroys all that she had thought would bring security and respect.

Bitches with Guns

Most of the women of *Set It Off* are provoked to violence by their economic situation, believing that robbing banks is their only recourse. As previously noted, Stony, Tisean, and Frankie were all abused by the judicial and law-enforcement systems. They see money as their way out of poverty and into middle-class respectability. Cleo, on the other hand, is never given a motive for her violence and therefore is depicted as a stereotypical "bulldagger" with violent tendencies. While Stony acts as the moral conscience of this group of women, Cleo has the dubious privilege of being all "id" and aggression.

Cleo initially suggests robbing a bank, but Stony scoffs: "Too bad we ain't some hard-up crackhead motherfuckers like Larenz and them. Then sure we could do some suicidal shit like rob a bank. But we ain't crazy so we can't." After the police kill her brother and she has prostituted herself, Stony is convinced by Frankie's logic that they need to exact revenge on a system that continues to oppress them. Tisean is the one holdout who reluctantly agrees to rob a bank because she cannot think of any other way to prove that she can support her son financially.

The scene that best illuminates their individual leanings toward violence shows Stony, Cleo, Frankie, and Tisean going to a neighborhood friend, Black Sam (Dr. Dre), for weapons. Through character development, this scene establishes who will be tough, who will live, and foreshadows who will die. Tisean is hopeless. She fires one bullet and squeamishly drops her gun. Frankie fires several rounds with such concentration and zeal that the paper target of a man in a suit is riddled with each shot fired. It seems as though she is aiming her weapon at the bank supervisor who chose not to recognize the exceptional work she performed in his service. Stony is a competent shooter, but shows no real love of handling a weapon. Finally, there is Cleo. Cleo fires two-fisted and demands higher-caliber weapons, saying to Black Sam, "We ain't robbin' stagecoaches. I need something I can set it off with."

Halberstam rightly observes that the female masculinity of Black lesbians is circumscribed by race, but at the same time aspects of Latifah's portrayal of Cleo are played as a one-dimensional stereotype of the big, tough bulldagger.[40] Cleo spends most of the film in overalls, often letting them sag around her waist. She loves cars and is a competent mechanic. Though her lover (Ursula) is a tall, beautiful femme to Cleo's rough-and-ready butch, she never speaks. It is fair to make the argument that there are lesbians who embody Cleo's brand of female masculinity, but that does not necessitate the latent homophobia that emanates from women who are supposed to be Cleo's best friends and from the audience response. When Ursula comes around, the other three women usually avert their eyes. Tisean, Stony, and Frankie's silence around Cleo's lesbianism are indicative of the workings of homophobia and silence in the African American community. Aside from name-calling by their employer, Luther, Cleo's lesbianism is met with typical silence; but this does not necessarily connote acceptance. In fact, such silences are complicit in maintaining the idea that, "Okay, you be like that, but just don't bring it over here." One could make the case that no one discusses heterosexuality either, but such a point ignores the dynamics of compulsory heterosexuality.[41] Though Stony prostitutes herself for money to pay for her brother's first semester of college, she redeems herself and heterosexuality when she tears up the check and pursues her romance with a Buppie (Black urban professional) banker.[42]

In a *Village Voice* article Queen Latifah notes the lack of motivation for Cleo's violence in the script: "I definitely drew on people I knew from the streets when I had to have a reason for Cleo's behavior."[43] More specifically, lesbianism reinforces the idea that this particular poor African American woman is violent. In the character of Cleo we have a fascinating convergence of class, race, and lesbianism. Cleo is given stereotypical attributes of what someone wrongly thought a Black lesbian would want to be: a man. According to Omosupe a bulldagger can be described as "capable of beating up your daddy if it was necessary. In other words, lesbians were constructed as aberrant women who wanted to be men, and so, they acted more like men than the 'real' men acted: the only thing missing was the penis."[44] The writers of *Set It Off* and Latifah in her portrayal conflate female masculinity into the category lesbian, making explanations for Cleo's violence simplistic and overdetermined.

The icon of the bulldagger is used in *Set It Off*, but it harks back to definitions of the Sapphire as the bitter adversary of Black men. According to this particular incarnation, Sapphire is not bitter because she cannot get a man, but because she cannot be a man. Cleo has no illusions about her chances for mobility, and the film's implicit message is that homosexuality or inappropriate masculinity will not get you where you need to go in a society that emphasizes heterosexuality or femininity for biological women. It is most definitely not conducive to finding Mr. Right and escaping from the ghetto. Cleo even admits, in a conversation with Stony, the allegedly innate limits that her class and sexuality circumscribe for her: "Stony, you can go to suburbia and start a new life; but we ain't nothin' but 'hood rats. Now I can live with that. You can't. The 'hood is where I belong. . . . I'm not thinking about five years from now. I'm trying to get through the day." Not only is Cleo resigned to a life in the housing projects, but the film's writers would also have us believe that she has given in to a "deviant" lifestyle. Cleo's unwillingness to give up those things that, presumably, make her violent foreshadows her demise and depicts a pedestrian view of African American lesbians. Rather than a nuanced view, the idea of the disenfranchised young Black male is superimposed onto the character of Cleo.

The film spends more time with Stony, who sacrificed her body and even her baby brother to an uncaring system of economics and class. Stony serves as

Cleo's counterpoint: she agrees to participate in one bank robbery but finds committing another one excessive. When Frankie and Cleo attempt to bully Stony into committing another robbery, Stony remarks, "All right, Louise. You take Thelma over there and y'all go rob another bank, if you all that." The tension quickly escalates when Cleo then pulls a gun and holds it to Stony's face. When Cleo calms down and removes the gun, Stony slaps her and warns her not to ever do that again. It is here that the buddy system and bonds of outlaw friendship break down, signaling a breakdown in the fragile honor among thieves that Cleo, Stony, Tisean, and Frankie established through their first successful heist.

In addition to firing a gun, slapping Cleo is Stony's most violent act precipitated by the betrayal of her friendship with Cleo, which is the oldest bond in the group. Stony, with the potential for upward mobility, is trying to control her Sapphire within. At Stevie's graduation party she continually emphasizes, "We got into UCLA!" Stony sees her brother's chance to leave poverty behind them as her own success. Unlike the other main characters of *Set It Off*, Stony and Stevie live in a house and not the projects. She provided for them both to the best of her abilities, and this is *their* chance to be successful. They are on the road to being middle class, but this dream is endangered by Stevie's death.

Stony's last chance for upward mobility is through a (superfluous) romance with Keith, the Buppie banker. Keith serves to remind the audience that Stony is different from her friends. She is a sensitive soul of whom Keith finds it "hard to believe that you're this hard when you're so beautiful." Keith pushes Stony to think about the future and expanding her horizons through his upwardly mobile lifestyle: a tastefully decorated Afrocentric home, international theme dinners, and probing questions. He asks Stony the question she later poses to Cleo: "Where do you see yourself five years from now?" Stony cannot answer this question. She responds with a question of her own for Keith, "Do you feel free? I don't feel free. I feel very much caged."

Significantly, Stony is the least caged of the four women, and this is proved when the other three women commit a murder. Stony's absence, combined with her chances for mobility, saves her life. Tisean, Frankie, and Cleo discovered that their boss, Luther, stole the money they hid from the second bank robbery. Ironically, the same factors that provoked Bernie to violence in *Waiting to Exhale* lead to Luther's death: the misappropriation of money and a white woman. Luther, who has spent his brief screen time calling the women who work for him

FIGURE 17. Robbing banks is not where Stony sees herself in five years, but in *Set It Off* she assumes the violent woman's expression and stance.

"bitches," and Cleo a "gentleman," found their money and spent it on his own upward mobility. The signifiers of Luther's wealth are offensively stereotypical of what the film's writers assume a working-class Black man would buy to signify his own upward mobility: a Cadillac, a perm for his hair, gold jewelry, and a white prostitute.[45] These markers are not very different from John's in *Waiting to Exhale* but are considered to be in poor taste, a sign of "new money." Nonetheless, Luther's abandonment of Black women will earn him the wrath of Sapphire. In a heated exchange with Cleo, Luther pulls a gun on her and is shot by Tisean. This turn of events is unexpected given Tisean's squeamishness at the gun range and her flight from the first bank robbery. Luther's murder is the point of no return for the women in *Set It Off.* They must now rob another bank and flee the city, including Stony who was not even present for the murder.

Rather than wearing the black wigs, which made them resemble a 1950s singing group and connoted the exhilaration of the initial robberies, the women don plastic masks that distort their features for their final robbery attempt. The camera, which framed the women straight on during the other bank robberies is now tilted as they plan their final heist. Clearly, this is the robbery that will not succeed and the police interrupt it. Tisean, who commits the only murder in the film by one of the four leading women, is shot by a security guard as she and

Stony are about to surrender. Cleo and Stony shoot their way out of the bank, but Tisean subsequently dies from her wounds in the getaway car.

Cleo's death scene, reminiscent of heroic last stands in gangster films and Westerns, is brash and startling. As one journalist noted, "those lame 'black Thelma and Louise' comparisons need to be scrapped. If we must go Hollywood, yo, let's throw up honorifics like 'the Afro-Amazonian James Cagney.'"[46] Cleo, Frankie, and Stony are trapped in a tunnel with the L.A.P.D. at one end and a police helicopter at the other. Cleo orders the other two women out of the car, promising to meet up with them later. Cleo guns the engine and plays chicken with the helicopter, forcing the police to blink first. Though she won this round, police cars soon surround Cleo. She calmly lights a cigarette and attempts to plow through the police blockade. Her newly refurbished muscle car is riddled with a hail of bullets from the L.A.P.D. As it creeps to a stop, Cleo slumps over the steering wheel and friends from the neighborhood, who are watching the action live on television, are stunned. Suddenly, Cleo jumps out of the car and begins firing her semiautomatic weapon at the police. Her body,

FIGURE 18. The Black butch, like the Black man, goes out in a blaze of rebellious glory in *Set It Off*. The bullet-riddled body and car mark hers as a hero's death.

buffeted by the gunfire of the L.A.P.D., falls to the ground where she dies in a classic blaze of glory.

Cleo's death is shocking because of its brutality, but also because the audience grew to care for Cleo *in spite of* her rough manner, her pot smoking, and her lesbianism. Queen Latifah says of her character: "I wanted Cleo to be so real to you, the viewer. My challenge in playing Cleo was to make you like her. To make you not be disgusted by her lifestyle or her mouth or her never being calm or civil."[47] In my opinion, Cleo dies twice, and suffers the most violent death, because she is a woman who transgressed gender, race, and heterosexual norms *unrepentantly.* Unlike Stony, Cleo is killed in part because she had no aspirations to be anything but a 'hood rat and was open about her lesbianism.[48]

Stony, on the other hand, survives this misstep in the game of structural inequality. After Frankie and Stony split up, Stony makes it to a tour bus heading across the border into Mexico. While on the bus, she and the other passengers witness Frankie attempting to run from the police. Frankie knows that she will not make an escape, but she turns and runs anyway. Frankie is shot in the back and killed.

As in *Thelma and Louise,* the women of *Set It Off* are pursued by a white male police officer, Detective Strode. The difference is that this man was responsible for Stevie's death and, yet, has no sympathy for the women's plight. As Detective Strode kneels over Frankie's dead body, he looks up at the passing tour bus and meets Stony's eyes. He opens his mouth to speak, but instead he lets her escape. The implication is that Detective Strode feels bad about killing her brother because he believes previous information that Stevie was college bound. Stevie's murder and "good-kid" status translates into Stony's redemption for her part in the violence that ensued.

Later, in a Mexican motel room, Stony cries over the money scattered across the bed and remembers the good times she had with Cleo, Tisean, and Frankie, now dead. After these memories, Stony cuts off the short braids she wore throughout the film and then calls Keith. After a long silence she says, "Thank you." Stony is grateful for Keith's influence and belief that she is capable of being something more than who she is at the moment. The film closes with Stony driving a red jeep into the mountains of Mexico. The degree of her freedom is debatable, much of the debate revolving around how one views Stony's freedom that will be lived in exile without family, friends, and lover.

The women of *Set It Off* demonstrate the dangers of Sapphire in the 'hood.

Given the lack of material goods and possibilities of upward mobility, they had nothing to rely on to keep their "inner bitch" in check. Frankie saw that working for The Man in his bank will get you nowhere because you are still guilty by association. Is Tisean the first to die because she is a *Black single mother?* Is Cleo, as a Hollywood idea of a Black lesbian (read: like Black men), killed for her knowledge of the ways the System works to disenfranchise young African Americans? Do Stony's hopes for middle-class mobility, and heterosexual alliance, save her? Perhaps as demonstrated by her desire to send Stevie to college and her adoption of Keith's rhetorical question ("Where do you see yourself in five years?"), Stony is worth saving because she aspires to be more than a 'hood rat. As Cleo noted, Stony cannot accept that fate, and her denial of poverty turns out to be the key to her cage.

Exploring the Possibilities of the Reclamation of Sapphire

Given the two very different endings of *Waiting to Exhale* and *Set It Off,* I believe that a celebration of violent African American women on-screen is contingent upon the outcome of that violence. Women empowering themselves by fighting back, physically and psychically, against systems of patriarchy can be liberating to watch. Yet we need to examine how race, class, gender, and sexuality interact with women's empowerment through violence. My lengthy critique of *Waiting to Exhale* and *Set It Off* in this essay does not mean that, as an African American woman, I did not find the mere presence of eight Black women on the cinema screen exhilarating and a cause for celebration. Both films challenge my enjoyment and spectatorship.

In *Waiting to Exhale* Bernie and Gloria are driven to threatened or actual violence by clearly perceivable actions (e.g., teen sex, a philandering husband). Though they are confined by the rules of class and upward mobility, their violence is comprehensible. In fact, the role of the Sapphire becomes a contradiction: Bernie's class position required that she not show her anger, but what African American audience would have respected the character had she continued to wallow in self-pity and visit the local convenience store looking dejected?

Set It Off is a more complex film to embrace, but it is not impossible to do so. Through the closing montage sequence, the audience remembers with Stony the laughter and camaraderie of Tisean, Cleo, and Frankie. This sequence makes it difficult to find cause for celebration when three young, vibrant African American women died. It is rare to have leading African American women alive on the screen much less in a prominent role. These women sacrificed their lives in an effort to advance despite a system of economic exploitation and social structures designed to work against them. The challenge with this film, and with future films, is to find a middle ground between cinematic enjoyment and cultural critique. Part of that middle ground includes knowing the historical context of representations of African American women and all marginalized groups in the United States. The question is then whether to reclaim those representations or strive to create new images.

The Sapphire icon and its implications for representations of African Americans spill off the Hollywood screen and into the lives of Black women. When it comes to images of people of color and other marginalized groups in the United States, interrogating popular culture representations and demanding better roles are positive interactions with mainstream Hollywood film. As the press for the video release of *Set It Off* noted, "It's about crime. It's about payback. It's about survival." Now that the dominant culture is finally beginning to understand that Aunt Jemima representations are racist and sexist, Sapphire could easily take over as a "natural" depiction of Black women.

As the following article excerpt demonstrates, at this historical moment we need to be vigilant for the image of the Sapphire, which could easily take over as the reigning icon of African American womanhood. We must also acknowledge our own complicity in the manufacturing of this image. Take, for example, the following *Detroit News* excerpt on life imitating art:

Rene Bradley, 18, told police she was at a beauty shop getting her hair done Jan. 15 when she found out her boyfriend was two-timing her. Bradley said her boyfriend's name came up during a conversation among the patrons, when another woman said that she, too, was going out with him.

Angered by her boyfriend's philandering, Bradley told police she thought of the movie's showstopping scene in which the character Bernadine, played by Angela Bassett, sets fire to her rich husband's BMW and Armani suits after he announces that he is leaving her for another woman.

Bradley told police she left the beauty shop, drove to the 7700 block of St. Mary's and set fire to his late-model silver Chevrolet Monte Carlo.

In the movie, the vengeful wife didn't even get a ticket. Bradley, however, was arraigned and jailed in lieu of a $3,500 bond. She could face up to five years in prison.

Capt. Jon Bozich of the Detroit Fire Arson Unit said women and men often act out what they see on the movie screen.[49]

Rene Bradley may have confused her boyfriend's Monte Carlo for a BMW, but the implicit tone of this news article was that this was a ridiculous mistake. Not only was she not Angela Bassett, but also Bradley did not go unpunished. The only thing Bradley had in common with her on-screen counterpart is that a firefighter serves as the sentinel at the gate of good taste and, most importantly, good sense. The *Detroit News* reporter uses Captain Bozich's statement as expert testimony on the delusional violence of this Black woman, but then he refers to the movie as if it were fact, not fiction. Rather than belaboring the issue of whether Bradley or the *Detroit News* is more deluded, the point is that a dearth of factual representations of Black women leaves us relying on Hollywood film for genuine representations of them.

Though *Waiting to Exhale* and *Set It Off* relied on stereotypical icons of African American women, they were a move in a more positive direction compared to past depictions. African American women have been confined long enough to maid, sensitive nanny, prostitute, and the "best-friend-who-is-murdered-before-she-can-warn-the-white-protagonist" roles. As demonstrated by actresses such as Angela Bassett, Queen Latifah, and Jada Pinkett, African American actresses can make the most of the few roles they are allowed even if they are cast in timeworn molds. The task before us, as a critical audience, is to tease apart the contradictory messages that are delivered for what they say about African American women.

The balances of power are as slow to shift in Hollywood as they are in other U.S. institutions. It is way past time for Black audiences, with their increased spending power, to demand more accountability for portrayals of the Black community. "It is only as we collectively change the way we look at ourselves and the world that we can change how we are seen. . . . [W]e seek to create a world where everyone can look at blackness, and black people, with new eyes."[50] To paraphrase Cleo, continuing to talk back to films can give us, the audience, something we can set it off with.

Notes

1. I use *Black* and *African American* interchangeably throughout this chapter. These terms, as opposed to "Negro" and "Colored," specify the political and nationalist impulses in my analysis. I do not capitalize "white" because, until recently, whiteness was unrecognized as marked and political, except in the context of white supremacist writings.

2. bell hooks, *Black Looks* (Boston: South End Press, 1992), 119.

3. Terry McMillan, *Waiting to Exhale* (New York: Viking Books, 1992).

4. Karen DeWitt, "For Black Women, a Movie Stirs Breathless Excitement," *New York Times,* 31 December 1995, 1.

5. *Waiting to Exhale,* written by Terry McMillan and Ronald Bass, directed by Forest Whitaker, produced by Deborah Schindler and Ezra Swerdlow (20th Century Fox, 1995).

6. Gregory Freeman, "After 'Exhaling' I Feel Much Better about the Plot," *St. Louis Post-Dispatch,* 6 February 1996; Salimah Nemoy, "'Exhale' Doesn't Represent Black Women," *New York Times,* 8 January 1996.

7. hooks, 5.

8. *Set It Off,* written by Takashi Bufford and Kate Lanier, directed by F. Gary Gray, produced by Oren Koules and Dale Pollock (New Line, 1996).

9. For example, the emphasis of "Black-on-Black" crime connotes an inherent, irrational violence in African Americans, while few people cite "white-on-white" crime. This has been noted by Angela Davis, "Reflections on the Black Woman's Role in the Community of Slaves," in *Words of Fire: An Anthology of African-American Feminist Thought,* ed. Beverly Guy-Sheftall (New York: The New Press, 1995).

10. Hazel Carby, "Slave and Mistress: Ideologies of Womanhood under Slavery," in *Reconstructing Womanhood: The Emergence of the Afro-American Woman Novelist* (New York: Oxford University Press, 1987); Barbara Welty, "The Cult of True Womanhood," in *Dimity Convictions: The American Woman in the Nineteenth Century* (Athens: Ohio University, 1976).

11. Robyn Weigman, "Black Bodies/American Commodities: Gender, Race, and the Bourgeois Ideal in Contemporary Film," in *Unspeakable Images: Ethnicity and the American Cinema,* ed. Lester Friedman (Urbana: University of Illinois Press, 1991), 313.

12. Davis, "The Black Woman's Role"; bell hooks, *Ain't I a Woman: Black Women and Feminism* (Boston: South End Press, 1981); Sue K. Jewell, *From Mammy to Miss America and Beyond* (London: Routledge, 1993); Deborah Gray White, *Ar'n't I a Woman? Female Slaves in the Plantation South* (New York: W. W. Norton, 1985).

13. Carby, "Slave and Mistress"; hooks, *Ain't I a Woman;* White, *Ar'n't I a Woman?*

14. White, *Ar'n't I a Woman?*

15. Ibid., 46.

16. hooks, *Ain't I a Woman,* 85.

17. Jewell, *From Mammy to Miss America,* 45.

18. E. Franklin Frazier, *The Negro Family in the United States* (Chicago: University of Chicago Press, 1939); Daniel Patrick Moynihan, *The Negro Family: The Case for National Action* (Washington: U.S. Department of Labor, 1965).

19. Jean Carey Bond and Pat Peery, "Is the Black Male Castrated?" in *The Black Woman,* ed. Toni Cade Bambara (New York: Penguin Books, 1970).

20. Ibid., 116.

21. hooks, *Ain't I a Woman,* 85–86.

22. Jacquie Jones, "The Accusatory Space," in *Black Popular Culture,* ed. Gina Dent and Michelle Wallace (Seattle: Bay Press, 1992), 97.

23. Evelynn Hammonds, "Black (W)holes and the Geometry of Black Female Sexuality," *differences* 6 (1994): 133.

24. Ibid., 132.

25. Gertrude Bustill Mossell, "The Opposite Point of View," in *Words of Fire: An Anthology of African-American Feminist Thought,* ed. Beverly Guy-Sheftall (New York: The New Press, 1995), 59.

26. "New Jill," as opposed to the late 1980s–early 1990s designation of Black urban gangster films as "New Jack," based on the precedent set by Mario Van Peebles's 1991 film *New Jack City.*

27. Betty Friedan, *The Feminine Mystique* (New York: Dell, [1963] 1984). Bernie is already married at the start of the film, but like her friends searches for a good man (better than her cheating husband).

28. Isabel Wilkerson, "Hollywood Shuffle: With White Men Calling the Shots, Black Women Have No Reel Power," *Essence,* March 1997, 71–72.

29. Tim Dirk, "Melodrama Films," on the Web site "The Greatest Films: Film Genres"; on-line: <http://www.filmsite.org/melodramafilms.html>.

30. DeWitt, "Movie Stirs Breathless Excitement," 1.

31. Nemoy, "'Exhale' Doesn't Represent Black Women," 26.

32. James E. Alsbrooks, "Use of Sex, Profanity Stain Movie Featuring Educated Black Women," *Los Angeles Sentinel,* 15 January 1996, A7.

33. Rebecca Ascher-Walsh, "Stealing Booty," *Entertainment Weekly,* 15 November 1996, 38.

34. Howie Movshovitz, "Wronged Bank Robbers Likable but Not Heroic: *Set It Off* Foursome Slides into Violence," *Denver Post,* 6 November 1996, G10.

35. Tim Dirk, "Crime and Gangster Films," on the Web site, "The Greatest Films: Film Genres," on-line: <http://www.filmsite.org/crimefilms.html>.

36. Ibid.

37. Roger Ebert, "Sharp-Edged Reality: *Set it Off* Offers People, Not Caricatures," *Chicago Sun-Times,* 6 November 1996, final edition, 51.

38. Movshovitz, "Wronged Bank Robbers," G10.

39. Or perhaps the taboos around representing Black male/white female relationships on the screen have lost some of their power. From Sidney Poitier's platonic friendship with a young white girl in *A Patch of Blue* (1965) to Spike Lee's *Jungle Fever* (1991), opportunities to portray interracial relationships have arisen and been underutilized. See Judith Halberstam, *Female Masculinity* (Durham: Duke University Press, 1998).

40. Ibid. I concur with Halberstam's assessment of Cleo's Black female masculinity as informed by her life in the 'hood, as much as it is by her lesbianism. However, I put the icon of the Sapphire and its historical resonance in conversation with this idea of Black female masculinity, concluding that Cleo's lesbianism outplays her poverty on-screen.

41. For a fuller explanation of the dynamics of "compulsory heterosexuality," see Adrienne Rich, "Compulsory Heterosexuality and Lesbian Existence," in *Feminism in Our Time: The Essential Writings, World War II to the Present,* ed. Miriam Schneir (New York: Vintage Books, [1975] 1994).

42. Stony tears up the check because it turns out that Stevie was hiding the fact that he was not

accepted to UCLA. He and Stony then have an argument and he leaves the house. He goes to visit one of the men who robbed Frankie's bank and, through a case of mistaken identity, is killed by the police.

43. Greg Tate, "Waiting to Explode: As Cleo the Carjacking, Glock-Orgasmic Gangsta Dyke, Queen Latifah Tears Up the Screen in Her Big-Screen Debut," *Village Voice,* 19 November 1996, 49.

44. Ekua Omosupe, "Black/Lesbian/Bulldagger," *differences* 3 (1991): 102–3.

45. Luther fails in his mobility because he chooses "B-grade" objects, in contrast to John in *Waiting to Exhale.* The business he owns, a janitorial service, cleans office buildings such as the one where John's offices are located. His white woman is a hooker, rather than a working professional like Kathleen (the police certainly treat her like a prostitute when they ask her to pick out Luther's murderer in a lineup); he buys the "luxury car" assumed to be preferred by African American men and often the car of pimps in Hollywood film; and he uses a relaxer on his hair, a sign that he is effeminate regardless of his braggadocio.

46. Tate, "Waiting to Explode," 49.

47. Ibid.

48. Perhaps it comes too close to valorizing and essentializing identity, but I question the ability of a script rewritten by a white female writer, produced by two white male producers, and directed by a Black male to reflect authentically the life of a working-poor, African American lesbian. See Ascher-Walsh, "Stealing Booty."

49. David G. Grant, "'Exhale' antic lands jilted woman in city jail," *Detroit News,* 26 January 1996, A1.

50. hooks, *Black Looks,* 6.

The Gun-in-the-Handbag, a Critical Controversy, and a Primal Scene

Barbara L. Miller

If you think about it, you notice that after a certain situation posed at the start as a problem or as an enigma, the film gradually leads to a final solution which allows the more or less conflicting terms posed at the beginning to be resolved, and which in the majority of cases takes the form of a *marriage.* I've gradually come to think that *this pattern organizes—indeed, constitutes—*the classical American cinema as a whole, but I first became aware of it through the western, where one might have thought a priori that it played a less determining role. (emphasis added) [1]

RAYMOND BELLOUR

In the opening section of *Thelma and Louise* (1991), Louise (Susan Sarandon) works hard to serve breakfast in a diner. She takes a quick break to call Thelma (Geena Davis). Thelma, a working-class housewife in the process of cleaning up the morning's dishes, answers the phone. In a voice that reveals her anticipation, Louise asks Thelma if she is ready to leave for their "girls only" weekend in the mountains. Sheepishly, Thelma admits that she has yet to ask her husband for permission to go. After promising to call her back in a few minutes, Thelma hangs up the phone and calls out to Darryl (Christopher McDonald).

Even before he enters the kitchen, Darryl begins scolding Thelma, as though she were his child. As he primps his hair and finishes getting ready for work, he directs a continuous barrage of verbal abuse at his wife.

A few minutes later, after Darryl storms out, still dressed in her bathrobe and still looking as though she could use a shower, Thelma calls Louise back. Even though she knows that Darryl expects her home that evening, she tells Louise that she can go. With schoolgirl innocence, Thelma excitedly asks Louise what she should pack: "Oh, I don't know," says Louise, "it's the mountains . . . it gets cold at night. . . . *I am just going to bring everything.*"

The scene then cuts to the two women, in their separate apartments, packing their clothes. Contrary to what she says, Louise neatly folds a few sweaters and meticulously wraps her sneakers in plastic. She then carefully places these few items in a single overnight bag. Meanwhile, Thelma virtually empties her closets and drawers. She randomly tosses everything into several open cases and bags. Besides filling two large suitcases, a small suitcase, a makeup case, and a tote bag, Thelma also takes along a cooler, two fishing poles, a fishing net, and a lantern. At the end of her packing frenzy, Thelma—almost as an afterthought—pulls a handgun from the nightstand drawer. Using only her forefinger and thumb, she tosses it into her gaping *handbag*.

In the late 1980s and early 1990s, Hollywood released a number of movies in which women carry guns and shoot high-powered weapons. These films fall into two general categories. The first includes such titles as *Aliens* (1986), *Desperate Hours* (1990), *License to Kill* (1989), and *Terminator 2* (1991). Here, female leads

FIGURE 19. Housewife Thelma drops her gun into her handbag, preparing for the outlaw journey ahead (*Thelma and Louise*).

suggestively strap guns to their inner thighs and brazenly sling high-powered weapons over their shoulders. Even though these characters look as though they break from historical precedents, the hard-bodied and at times flipped-out maternal figures are not new. They are updated versions of the antiheroine types found in such exploitation or "gangster" movies as *Crazy Mama* (1975), *Bloody Mama* (1969), and *Big Bad Mama* (1974).[2] Surprisingly, it is the uninflated figures in the second group of women-and-gun films that open up a new area for female characters.

In contrast to the higher-caliber "Mama," the female leads in such films as *The Silence of the Lambs* (1991), *Blue Steel* (1990), *Love Crimes* (1991), and the made-for-cable movie *The Killing Mind* (1991) have few if any historical models.[3] In this set of films, they are physically unassuming, nonsexualized novice detectives whose main lines of defense are neither their weapons, which for the most part remain out of sight (often in their purses), nor their academy-trained investigative techniques. Instead, they rely on beginner's luck. With chance on their side and helpful hints from more seasoned partners, they solve the crimes.

Within this second set of women-and-gun films, we find a small group of unassuming female leads in such theater releases as *Thelma and Louise* and *The Gun in Betty Lou's Handbag* (1991) as well as a few made-for-cable movies like *My New Gun* (1992) and *Guncrazy* (1992).[4] These films actually challenge both categories of women-and-gun films: the female leads in these movies are neither, at least initially, "lethal" women nor, to any believable extent, even "novice" detectives. They are innocent feminine stereotypes—isolated housewives or withdrawn high school students—whose opening scene aversions to deadly weapons and unsophisticated knowledge of sexual affairs seem obvious to all.

In *Thelma and Louise,* for instance, Detective Hal Slocombe (Harvey Keitel) questions the Silver Bullet Bar's waitress about the murder in the parking lot. When he suggests that the two women might have been involved, the waitress swears that neither Thelma nor Louise is the murdering type. Likewise in *The Gun in Betty Lou's Handbag,* when the police captain suggests that Betty Lou (Penelope Ann Miller) might have murdered a lover, Betty Lou's sister immediately blurts out that Betty Lou "wouldn't hurt a bug." No sooner does each film stress the lead's naïveté than it contradicts that very portrayal.

Even though the female lead in this set of renegade films initially refuses to touch the "thing," she hastily learns how to hold and shoot a gun. Armed with this new skill, she goes against her "essential" feminine character. She, for reasons beyond her control, leaves her domestic sphere and inadvertently involves herself in a crime scene. At this point these films break with Hollywood murder-mystery conventions: although their alleged crimes vary from murder to robbery to impersonation, these films concentrate not on the crimes committed, but on the circumstances surrounding the transformation of characters. By the film's end, the fugitive housewife no longer passively accepts her fate. Instead, she overtly flaunts what many in the popular press today refers to as a Thelma and Louise–style female empowerment.

In this essay, I look at this small group of renegade films that, for the purposes of my argument, I call the "gun-in-the-handbag" films. Most critics summarily dismissed the group; but *Thelma and Louise* is not an isolated feature, as many would have it. It belongs to a set of films that suddenly appeared and then quickly disappeared in the early 1990s. Unlike the first two categories of women-and-gun movies,[5] the gun-in-the-handbag film had a rather short Hollywood life span. These narrative types existed only from about 1991 to 1992.[6] Looking back from the end of the decade, I now see that Hollywood and B-budget directors and writers portrayed a type of female empowerment that was possible only then. This type of empowerment simultaneously speaks to the limits of Hollywood conventions and the changing political and social attitudes of the early 1990s.

To build my case, I begin with a discussion of the critical response that arose around the release of *Thelma and Louise*. I consider the timeliness of the film and the extent to which the popular appeal of the characters played a role in a variety of cultural events. As a 1991 cover of *Time* suggested, *Thelma and Louise* struck a nerve to such a degree that some writers erroneously began to refer to the film as though it were a docudrama.[7] Some went so far as to compare the fictional characters directly to real-life serial killer Aileen Wuornos and her lover Tyria Moore.[8] These responses were often divided along gender lines and closely mirrored the internal problem represented in these films: the conflict between the sexes.

In the second part of this essay, I concentrate on the gun-in-the-handbag narrative. In contrast to Raymond Bellour's observation of Westerns, marriage does not help resolve the conflict posed at the beginning of each film. Instead, it exacerbates it. In these films, a Hollywood romance is not an option. Likewise, any decision to remain within a melodramatic, claustrophobic, and potentially threatening domestic sphere is also not a choice. In gun-in-the-handbag films, the female lead leaves her domestic sphere and enters the space at the margins of the social order. There she discovers or becomes part of a scene in which two characters are involved in a sexual encounter. Her discovery of or participation in this event becomes the film's primal crime scene. In each of these films, a Thelma and Louise–style empowerment ensues only if the female lead replays this scene as though she were the figure who controls the action—the one of whom everyone in the film sits up and takes notice.

The Critical Controversy

For the most part, the critical reaction to *Thelma and Louise* split along gender lines. Writing at the time of the film's release, several male critics denounced the film as providing for women dangerous role models who simply mimicked outdated, masculine Hollywood clichés. Many argued that this inversion added nothing to current debates but merely re-created gender differences, albeit in inverted terms.[9] More virulent writers went so far as to label *Thelma and Louise* fascist and compared the film to Mussolini's infamous exploits.[10] Alluding to similar sentiments, others called the characters "feminist," declaring the film a "male-bashing prototype." As one writer had it, the antics of these out-for-revenge feminists were far more disturbing than the out-for-blood male and female characters in such spine-chilling and body-ripping films as *Death Wish* (1974), *Friday the 13th* (1980), and *I Spit on Your Grave* (1978).[11]

In contrast to these male writers' responses, female critics writing at the same time generally praised the movie, arguing that the film offered positive role models for women. Despite the characters' questionable escapades, many authors pointed out that Thelma and Louise took control of their situations and talked back to their male oppressors. They pay for their insubordination with their lives; but despite the duo's suicide, many still declared the film a feminist landmark.

In retrospect, the debate that arose in critical circles and the popular press touched as much on the social context of the film's release as on the actions of the characters. Even though *Thelma and Louise* featured far less violence than *Terminator 2* (also released the same summer), it "plugged into," as Sharon Willis argues, "ambient anxieties about sexual difference."[12] These anxieties influenced many writers' interpretations of the film, becoming an undercurrent that fueled the division in the ensuing critical dispute.

Cognizant of this undercurrent, Manohla Dargis explains the source of these anxieties. In "Guns 'n' Poses," Dargis points out that *Thelma and Louise* opened on the very day that the Supreme Court's gag rule on abortion information and family birth-control counseling hit the headlines.[13] The film's "complex and contradictory messages about women, violence and power," she states, could not have been more on cue. Dargis argues that Thelma and Louise's suicide is not "a punishment from patriarchy, a nihilistic gesture, or an affirmation of female powerlessness." Instead, she interprets their defiant stance as a salute to those women and men fighting against the Supreme Court's gag rule; their "*clasped hands and a last, tender kiss* strike hard as a powerful, even radical, salute. Surely some things—such as freedom and subjectivity—are worth dying for, even for women" (emphasis added).[14] More recently, writers have begun to offer different spins to the characters' defiant stance.

For example, in a 1998 article posted on the Hotwired Web site Jon Katz looks at the historical significance of the film. He argues that "the roar of women (and a few men) cheering in movie theaters all across the country when Thelma and her buddy blew up the lughead's oil truck was unforgettable, and helped punctuate a defining moment in our shared popular and political culture."[15] For Katz, the image stood as an important cultural signpost that coincidentally set the stage for the most important domestic event of the early 1990s, the Anita Hill and Clarence Thomas Senate hearings. Because politicians did not consider the popular appeal of the scene, as Katz argues, they mishandled the media coverage of the Senate hearings. They did not seriously consider the effects within popular culture of a lone woman—Anita Hill—standing up to a group of mostly male interrogators. Politicians did not see how clearly Hill's image—despite the obvious race and class differences—resonated with the fictional portrayal of Thelma and Louise.[16]

Like Dargis, Katz points to the public response that arose around the film. Similarly, he suggests that the "*Thelma and Louise* discourse"—not the film itself—played and continues to play an important role in the political mobilization of women. While Dargis's and Katz's arguments could be dismissed as wishful thinking, both point to the fact that since 1991, women's issues have played a larger role in politics. Campaign strategists increasingly target women, gender voting gaps have grown, politicians overtly include domestic policies in their platforms in an attempt to capture the "women's vote."

Unsurprisingly, the portrayal of female defiance and empowerment reflected in this newfound political voice has become part of popular culture. To a greater degree than any other Hollywood-spawned female fictional duo, Thelma and Louise have entered the popular imagination. On Web sites, individuals describe their fantasies of "female empowerment" through Thelma and Louise–style getaways.[17] In TV sitcoms, writers poke fun at the duo. Comedic skits of "on-the-run" couples have appeared on a variety of shows, from *Saturday Night Live* to *The Simpsons* to *Designing Women*.[18] The film's signature images have become so familiar that sitcoms need only include simple gestures to make their point.

For example, in its final season *Seinfeld* aired an episode on 12 March 1998 in which Kramer goes to a car dealer and takes a vehicle out for a spin. While out on the freeway, he makes a pact with the salesman: they decide to see if they can bring the car back "bone dry." Once the gas gauge hits empty, he and the salesman head back to the dealership. At the last minute, however, they decide to miss their exit. Holding up their tightly clasped hands—in an overt reference to the final scene in *Thelma and Louise,* though curiously missing the tender kiss —Kramer and the salesman speed down the highway. Unable to make it to a ravine, their car rolls to a rather unheroic stop on the median.

The fantasy of Thelma and Louise–style defiance also figures in a disturbing murder case. The release of *Thelma and Louise* came on the heels of a breaking news report; late in 1990, police pursued a "pistol-packing" pair of highway-traveling women. Police soon identified the pair as Aileen Wuornos and her lover, Tyria Moore. In early January 1991, agents arrested Wuornos. She promptly confessed to killing several men to protect Moore, who subsequently became a witness for the state.

Some tabloid writers and news reporters found the details of this case—a disreputable bar, a gun in the handbag, two working-class women driving down the highway, a car crash, a questionable act of self-defense, and allusions to lesbian sexuality—strikingly similar to the story line in *Thelma and Louise*. One writer, obviously capitalizing on the film's popularity, blatantly compared the two in his headline, "Kiss and Kill: Out of Florida's Recent Wave of Horrific Crimes Comes a Dark Version of *Thelma and Louise* in a Rare Case of a Female Serial Killer."[19] Such comparisons, however, are not uncommon: while Jeffrey Dahmer stood trial, newspapers evoked similar film characters such as Hannibal Lecter in *The Silence of the Lambs.* This collapse between fictional characters and real-life figures speaks less to the social issues raised in the cases than to the significance ascribed to the characters' ability to capture the popular imagination. In this case, however, the allusion to *Thelma and Louise* does not just address the characters' popularity but points to an unusually telling turn of events that are atypical even for Hollywood.

Hollywood films often heighten the appeal of fictional story lines by incorporating references to real-life case histories. Of these, *Psycho* (1960) and *The Silence of the Lambs* (1991) are probably the most notable. Each uses details from the famed 1950s killer, Ed Gein, to intensify their horrifying effects. *The Silence of the Lambs* goes one step further and includes references to FBI profilers, real-life modern-day investigative experts trained at such facilities as the Behavioral Sciences Center at Quantico, Virginia. In contrast, gun-in-the-handbag films arose independent of any actual case history. Scriptwriters, upon learning of the Florida "couple," did not suddenly decide to capitalize on the event and incorporate details of the crime into their scripts. The police only realized that they had a possible serial killer, and that the killer was most likely a woman, late in the summer of 1990. By that time, production on many of these films was well under way.[20] Hence, these films do not allude to the actions of a real-life figure. Their portrayals of empowered women evoke no actual personae, but mythical manifestations, more threatening than any incarcerated individuals.

In addition, female empowerment occurs not as something consciously earned and sought after but as something individually acquired. Her revised sexual identity occurs in response to a particular fictional sequence: a female character stumbles across a scene in which a sex crime has been or will soon be committed. Gun-in-the-handbag films stage similar foundational sequences through which the female leads become empowered. These scenes loosely interpret what psychoanalysts call the "primal scene": a child, whether in reality or fantasy, observes the parents having sex and interprets this as an act of violence by the father.[21] This scene pictures or sets the stage for "the origin of the individual."[22] It establishes roles for the sexes.

Gun-in-the-handbag films rewrite this primal scene as a crime scene: in *Thelma and Louise* it takes place in a bar's parking lot, and in *The Gun in Betty Lou's Handbag* it occurs in a sleazy motel room. In doing so, these films decenter the family myth that organizes fantasy life. Rather than being safely tucked away in the domestic sphere, it occurs at the outskirts of town on the other side of the law. Instead of setting the stage for a male or a female sexual identity to emerge and to lead to a resolution, these films depict destabilized and decentered sexual identities. In doing so, they suggest that such organizational myths can become renegade fantasies, opening the door for women's violent transgressions.

The Primal-Crime Scene

After stowing her cases in the trunk of Louise's green Thunderbird convertible, the two women drive away from their small-town lives. No sooner do they hit the road than Thelma—again using only two fingers—pulls the gun from her bag. Unwilling to take charge of the weapon, she turns to Louise.

LOUISE: What in hell did you bring that for?

THELMA: Oh, come on—psycho killers, and bears, or snakes. I just don't know how to use it. Will you take care of it?

LOUISE: Would you put it away? Just—here, put it in my purse.

With the gun "safely" stowed in Louise's purse, the two women are now ready for the first stage of their journey. This initial phase begins with a traumatic event that occurs at the outskirts of town, when Thelma and Louise stop at the Silver Bullet Bar for a few drinks.

After drinking several cocktails quickly and dancing too vigorously, Thelma goes outside for some fresh air. Thelma's dance partner follows her out of the bar and attacks her in the parking lot. Louise, realizing that Thelma has left the bar, searches for her. She arrives just after Harlan (Timothy Carhart) has repeatedly struck Thelma and pinned her to the hood of a car.

In the film's portrayal, the scene resembles a primal scene: a voyeur watching a couple have sex. However, it presents the scenario as a crime scene and resituates the event outside the family home. The film's primal scene becomes a public display that sets the stage not for the origin of the individual's fantasy life, but for a series of actions and reactions that propels the remainder of the story line.

Spying Thelma and Harlan, Louise pulls the gun out of her purse and threatens to shoot. Harlan freezes, and Thelma escapes his grip. Although he stops his sexual assault, Harlan continues his abuse verbally. His derogatory comments send Louise over the edge. She raises the gun and shoots. After he falls to the ground, the women escape in Louise's green convertible.

Much of the criticism directed against the film centers on the shooting in the bar's parking lot. As Sharon Willis points out:

Louise shoots him, not in the heat of a rage when she intervenes to prevent the rape, but rather, in a calm pause afterwards, when he insists upon having the last word . . . 'Suck my cock!' She kills him, not for what he does, but for what he says, a far thinner pretext.[23]

The following scene at the railroad tracks fuels this controversy. The film suggests that Louise's thinner pretext has less to do with the male character's language than her "personal" history.

As they wait for a train to pass, Louise hands Thelma a map and tells her to find an alternate route to Mexico. When Thelma points out that the quickest way to Mexico from Oklahoma takes them through Texas, Louise refuses to set foot in that state. Despite Thelma's plea to make an exception—after all, they are running for their lives—Louise remains steadfast and offers only a cryptic comment:

LOUISE: Thelma, I am not going to talk about this. Now you either find another way, or give me the goddamn map and I will! Do you understand?

THELMA: No, Louise, I don't. Now, how come you never told me what happened to you there?

LOUISE: [*looking away to avoid the question*] Look, you shoot off a guy's head with his pants down—believe me, Texas is not the place you want to get caught. Now trust me. Now I told you I am not going to talk about this anymore.

The intensity of her verbal outburst and the strength of her resolve not to enter the state that would ensure their quick getaway suggest that Louise has experienced some traumatic event in Texas, of which she refuses to give details. In juxtaposing these two scenes, the film roots Louise's use of force in the Silver Bullet Bar's parking lot in an unspecified Texas scenario. Critics such as Alice Cross argue that this event, rather than the parking lot scene, drives the film. Because Louise does not explain the event, it becomes a hole or blank in the film: "Everything that happens in the movie," she states, "is a consequence of [Louise's] earlier experience."[24] While I agree that this event becomes a blank or hole that disallows sympathetic identifications, I disagree that it drives the plot. Rather, it brings Louise's story to a halt. At this point, the film jumps tracks and begins to focus less on Louise's history than Thelma's reactions to the scene outside the Silver Bullet Bar. Thelma—the flaky character who whines about her life—initiates the sequence that leads to female empowerment. By demanding an answer from Louise, she sets in motion a series of events in which she shifts from a passive housewife to a take-charge character, enabling the film's legacy—the Thelma and Louise–style female empowerment.

After the fight in the Silver Bullet Bar parking lot, Thelma and Louise spend the night at a sleazy motel. As Louise ponders their options, Thelma undergoes a visual transformation. She tosses out her "excess baggage"—her bikini and form-fitting dresses, not to mention her husband's fishing pole and tackle box—in favor of T-shirts and blue jeans. Along with the wardrobe change, Thelma radically alters her gestures and poses. She is now ready not to be "chosen," with or without her consent, but to choose a sexual partner.

Along the way, Thelma and Louise pick up a young hitchhiker, J.D. (Brad Pitt). That evening, he talks his way into Thelma's motel room. Rather than immediately hopping into bed, J.D. (whose initials suggest both James Dean and juvenile delinquent) curiously interrupts the scene: before the couple have sex, he performs an odd striptease. Instead of disrobing and exposing his genitals, he remains partially clothed and pulls Thelma's hairdryer from his pants. The hairdryer stands not for his penis, though that organ is not far away, but for his unholstered gun. With the piece in hand, he recites his "holdup script": when committing a robbery, he uses an adulterated version of "Simon Says." After J.D. completes his performance, the couple have sex. J.D.'s performance and holdup script become the sexual foreplay that enables Thelma to have her first orgasm.

The next morning, Thelma leaves the room and recounts the previous night's escapades to Louise. While she is gone, J.D. steals their money. Thelma, taking responsibility for having left the money in the room with a known stickup man, tells Louise that she will make good their loss; she will get them some cash. The women then leave the motel and drive to a small town. With the car idling, Thelma disappears into a grocery store. A few minutes later she comes flying out of the store and tells Louise to hit the gas. As they speed away, she shows Louise the money.

LOUISE: What happened? . . . You robbed a store?

THELMA: . . . We needed the money, and now we have it.

LOUISE: Oh shit! . . . Well, how—What did you say?

Thelma then continues with her version of the holdup: "Well, I just waltzed in there and I said . . ." But before she continues, the film cuts to video footage from the in-store surveillance cameras. In the following sequence, this footage becomes not a mere replay of Thelma's actions but the vehicle through which the film represents female empowerment.

After a few seconds of video footage, the visual sequence shifts from grainy to smooth film stock. In the process, it performs a second alteration. Rather than cut back and forth between the grocery store and the two women in their getaway convertible, the image oscillates between Thelma facing the camera and a group of men sitting around an interrogation table. Through this visual distortion, the men appear as if they watch the event from a surveillance booth in the back of the store and Thelma appears to be speaking directly to them. Even though Darryl has told the police that Thelma would never touch a gun, he faces her video incarnation and plainly sees that Thelma not only touches the "*thing*" but recites a holdup dialogue. He hears Thelma say: "Good morning, ladies and gentlemen. This is a robbery." With the gun in full view and with her open bag dangling at her hip, she continues her borrowed text: "Now if nobody loses their head, nobody'll lose their head."

On the surface, the sequence portrays an illegal act: Thelma robs a store. However, it also operates at the phantasmic level of the film's story line. In her grocery store holdup, Thelma brings together the parking lot scene and hairdryer encounter. In doing so, she links her act of violence with sexual foreplay. As she commands, "Simon says, You all lie down on the floor please. . . . You're going to have an amazing story to tell all your friends. If not, you'll have a tag on your toe," the detectives and her husband become speechless and stiff as corpses. They—as if reduced to physical appendages—sit up and finally listen to Thelma. She, transformed from an infantilized housewife to a violent woman who holds her "muscle," now controls the action. The action, however, does not follow traditional Hollywood dictum.

In the process of repeating her outlaw script, Thelma shifts from what Fredric Jameson calls a modernist's notion of a centered subject to a postmodernist's sense of multiple personalities. In "Postmodernism, or The Cultural Logic of Late Capitalism," Jameson proposes that postmodernist texts stress a type of modern-day condition, what he calls a "schizophrenic" subject.[25] To clarify his position, he argues that this post-1960s form of subjectivity has less to do with a mass pathology than a structural change that has infiltrated all forms of culture and products of society. In particular, he sees not necessarily an interpretation of psychoanalysis along the lines of Deleuze and Guattari,[26] but a movement instigated by the development of multinational capitalism. Using the term schizophrenia as metaphor, Jameson argues that an older notion of subjectivity associated with capitalist societies has given way to an idea of split personalities allied with multicapitalist strategies. While many argue that Jameson exaggerates the influence of modern-day economies on subjectivity—we have not suddenly all become schizophrenic—his analysis helps us understand many forms of visual art, film, and literature of the seventies, eighties, and nineties.

Postmodern texts of these decades sideline their protagonists along with traditional notions of "realism" in character. Instead of featuring lone heroes who save the day, these movies offer different characters, each telling his or her story, which may or may not further the plot.[27] In postmodern narratives, plots do not unfold and characters do not grow in linear fashion. Instead, they accumulate through the layering of differing stories and multiple points of view through the "movement from signifier to signifier" or, in the case of *Thelma and Louise*, the shift from housewife to outlaw.[28]

In *Thelma and Louise*, once the characters leave their domestic spheres they become outlaws, randomly passing renegade fantasies between themselves. Their stories become, in Jameson's terms, "neither personal in the modernist sense, nor depersonalized in the pathological sense of the schizophrenic text."[29] The characters shift identities, from male to female, housewife to criminal. They recite these stories not to confess crimes, but to demonstrate transgressions. "[T]he stories you tell [and the confessions you make]," argues Jameson, "as an individual subject don't belong to you since you don't control them the way the master subject of modernism would. But you don't just suffer them in the schizophrenic isolation of the first-world subject of today."[30] In *Thelma and Louise*, the characters act out their social transgressions not in isolation, but in front of an audience.

Thelma and Louise does not uphold Hollywood conventions in which characters follow discrete lines and perform separate actions. Instead, the character holding the gun tells the story. He or she repeats the dialogue of another, but adds his or her own intonation. In addition to a fluidity between characters, the character him- or herself shifts between "persons." For instance, in the grocery store holdup, Thelma swings from first person—"Well, I just waltzed in there"—to third person—"Simon says, you all lie down"—and back again. At this point the story not only becomes fragmented, but is quite literally "held up." As such, the film shifts from the modernist's notion of a centered subject to the postmodernist's sense of fractured stories, fragmented surfaces, and multiple identities. As a result, the film moves in a circular fashion and takes on a life of its own apart from any effect that any character's action might "realistically" produce. As a result, a device such as the grocery store surveillance video does not lead to Thelma's apprehension (the standard function of video surveillance cameras). Even though Detective Hal—the would-be modernist hero attempting to save the women—has all the facts, he does not control the plot. It unfolds out of his control. In the final scene, he stands helplessly as the two characters drive to their deaths into the Grand Canyon.

The loss of a controlling voice and the characters' ability to shed and adopt identities amount to the most subversive aspect of the film.[31] To expand this notion and demonstrate the significance of the primal-crime scene, I now turn to the less sophisticated *Gun in Betty Lou's Handbag.*

In *The Gun in Betty Lou's Handbag,* Betty Lou's (Penelope Ann Miller) detective-husband (Eric Thal) stands her up on their anniversary. After being jilted, she and her faithful dog, Scarlet, go on an ice cream–eating binge. They drive through the streets of their small town in her white Volvo. Along the way, Betty Lou spots her husband's car parked in a motel lot. Fearing the worst, she peers through the crack in the door. Instead of her husband having sex with another woman, Betty Lou sees two men—her husband and his partner—standing in the middle of a motel room. They are discussing the details of the murder that occurred there. A man has been shot to death, and Betty Lou's husband and his partner have been assigned to the case. In short, she stumbles across a primal-crime scene, the details of which govern her subsequent transformation.

The next day, again with Scarlet's help, Betty Lou finds a gun on the shore of a canal, not too far from the crime scene. In a flash, she understands its significance—she has found the murder weapon. Showing her aversion to touching the piece, Betty Lou holds the gun upside down, between her forefinger and thumb—reminiscent of the sequence early in *Thelma and Louise.* As she opens her purse, the screen suddenly goes dark. The blackout represents a shift from outside to inside the handbag. As the gun falls into the sack, the camera looks up through the dark and sees a hole at the top of the opening handbag.

With the weapon tucked in her purse, Betty Lou tries to report it to her cop-husband. He assumes she has called about a domestic matter and, given the importance of his investigation, hangs up the phone. This second rejection sends Betty Lou over the edge. She leaves the phone booth and runs into a public washroom. In the mirrored section of the powder room, she pulls the gun from her purse and shoots her reflection. The bang of the bullet and the shattering of glass prompt an older woman to burst from her stall. With her underwear around her knees, the woman screams as she hobbles out the door.

The shattered mirror provides a key element in Betty Lou's transformation. She has fractured her image and visually become a multiple personality, able to slide in and out of several bit-part identities at will. At the police station, Betty Lou recounts the details she overheard at the motel. Her knowledge of its specifics convinces the captain that she is what everyone insists that she is not—the murderess who, in a fit of jealous passion, killed her lover in a motel room. She becomes, in a male fantasy, an unfaithful wife, a passionate lover, and a hired killer.

By the time of her courtroom arraignment, Betty Lou's gestures, pose, and wardrobe have changed. In contrast to Thelma's blue-jean and comfortable-boot transformation, Betty Lou trades her floral print dresses and fussy shoes for a more hard-edge feminine type: she dons a bright red leather jacket and miniskirt. She changes from an infantile housewife who works at the local library to someone whom everyone notices. In jail, she talks with local prostitutes, and while out on bail, with local TV reporters. She teams up with a new partner; she and her lawyer Ann Arkin (Alfre Woodard) drive away from the courthouse in the murdered man's shiny red Cadillac convertible. Meanwhile, because he cannot control his wife or his investigation, her husband loses the case and his job.

In the final sequence Betty Lou discovers the murderer, who captures Betty Lou and her lawyer. The now estranged cop-husband comes to their rescue and the couple makes up. Betty Lou returns to her domestic sphere. In contrast to the mousy housewife of the opening sequences, she is now a vibrant, exciting character whom everyone wants to know. The film ends with the couple sandwiched between two rows of library shelves, locked in a passionate embrace. Although they resolve their opening scene conflict, the marital bedroom does not return to its proper place. Left outside the domestic sphere, it compares to the opening motel sequence and becomes a modified primal-crime scene.

This pattern with which Hollywood presented female empowerment in the early 1990s emanates not from real-life case histories, but from the popular attitudes toward real-life situations. The female empowerment in these early 1990s films addresses growing awareness of isolated housewives; their separation from their family, economic aid, educational services, and legal agencies. In the previous decade, TV movies such as *The Burning Bed* (1984) showed how women learn not to trust their partners and not to request outside help. In cases where emotional and physical abuse occur, they cannot protect themselves and their children and escape life-threatening situations. A handful of these women find themselves in a position of kill or be killed. In self-defense, some battered women murder their battering spouses.[32]

In the early 1990s, gun-in-the-handbag films emerged and for a brief moment parodied this real-life situation. Thelma's and Betty Lou's opening-scene isolation suggests that these films tap into growing awareness of battered and verbally abused women rather than the possibility of serial killers. As much as humor can open lines of communication, the controversy around *Thelma and Louise* shows that people can reentrench such fact/fantasy divisions as well. In the end, the isolation of the female characters in these films affirms long-standing Hollywood paradigms.

From horror to slasher to murder-mystery, Hollywood narratives typically isolate female characters. Dario Argento, Brian de Palma, and Alfred Hitchcock have all made comments to this effect. Most specifically de Palma states, "Women in peril work better in the suspense genre. . . . If you have a haunted house and you have a woman walking around with a candelabrum [isolated and helpless], you fear more for her than you would for a husky man."[33] In *Thelma and Louise* and *The Gun in Betty Lou's Handbag,* female empowerment comes into view only through the figure at the margins: the unfaithful wife or the outlaw on the run. Female empowerment occurs in isolation. Thelma and Louise die at the outskirts of the social order. They never cross back into the domestic sphere, threatening to overturn domestic order and the identity of the sexes. Similarly, Betty Lou returns to her domestic duties. Despite her spiced-up sex life, the film's ending suggests no further changes in her marriage. However, these films did, if only inadvertently, push one Hollywood convention.

What is so potentially threatening about these films is the correspondence between the crime scene and the act that occurs in the marital bedroom. Each film, including *My New Gun* and *Guncrazy,* rewrites the scene that occurs in the culturally sanctioned private bedroom as a primal-crime scene. The scene that in psychoanalytic literature establishes the origin of the individual and the role of the sexes (Laplanche and Pontalis, *Formations,* 19), is not only out of place, but out of law. In doing so, the films destabilize the portrayal of sexual identity. Rather than resolution of the conflict between the sexes, the storylines in these films double back on themselves and characters slip and slide from one identity to another. As a result, each film's outcome is inconclusive. Hence, the representation of a primal-crime scene is the most controversial aspect of gun-in-the-handbag films. While demonstrating that female empowerment can occur through identity exchanges, role reversals, and sexual play, such a fluidity puts access to legal and social agencies in jeopardy. Without discussing the ways in which these films represent a more open-ended notion of identity and sexuality, *Thelma and Louise* itself will become, if it has not already, a blank or hole to which ideas of female empowerment return, but are never fully articulated, only continuously parodied. Its legacy, like that of other gun-in-the-handbag films, will add little or no insights to the complex and contradictory messages concerning violence, power, and pleasure in the early 1990s.

Notes

1. Janet Bergstrom, "Alternation, Segmentation, Hypnosis: An Interview with Raymond Bellour," in *Feminism and Film Theory,* ed. Constance Penley (New York: Routledge, 1988), 187.

2. The earlier films starred Angie Dickinson, Cloris Leachman, and Shelley Winters, respectively.

3. The only representation that comes close is the TV series "Police Woman," which also starred Angie Dickinson. It aired from 1974 to 1978.

4. Films such as *Mortal Thoughts* (1991), however, do not quite fit this category. In the gun-in-the-handbag film, the female lead leaves her domestic sphere and the main emphasis in the film is on her transformation, from housewife to outlaw. In contrast, *Mortal Thoughts* stresses the lead character's confession. In may ways, this film continues a line of representation that is central to such films as *Black Widow* (1987).

5. These character types resurface in such films as *The Matrix* (1999) and *Copycat* (1995).

6. It is not coincidental that gun-in-the-handbag films ceased to exist in 1992. For reasons discussed below, these films lost their public appeal around the time that *Overkill* (1992)—a collaborative piece that brought police investigators and Aileen Wuornos's former lover Tyria Moore, who turned state's evidence, together—and Nick Broomfield's *Aileen Wuornos: The Selling of a Serial*

Killer (1992) were respectively broadcast on television and released in theaters. Wuornos has the distinction of being the only female serial killer convicted in the United States. As of mid-2000, she still sits on death row.

7. Quoted in Manohla Dargis, "Guns 'n' Poses," *Village Voice,* 16 July 16 1991, 22.

8. Legal and feminist scholars debate Wuornos's status as a serial killer. Many argue that she merely defended herself from violent customers. For an opinion to the contrary, see Candice Skrapec, "The Female Serial Killer: An Evolving Criminality," in *Moving Targets: Women, Murder, and Representation,* ed. Helen Birch (Berkeley: University of California Press, 1994).

9. Sharon Willis argues these critics paint the film as "wrong-headed because it invites women to take on wholesale the tired old clichés of Hollywood masculinity and male bonding that prevail in the history of Westerns, road movies, and action films. For women to embrace and celebrate feminine versions of these clichés, the very clichés that men increasingly reject, such readings argue, advances nothing and merely inverts the current gender imbalance in representation. But this argument skips over the process by which the film parades the takeover of clichés, a process that foregrounds the posturing involved." See Sharon Willis, "Hardware and Hardbodies, What Do Women Want? A Reading of *Thelma and Louise,*" in *Film Theory Goes to the Movies,* ed. Jim Collins, Hilary Radner, and Ava Preacher Collins (New York: Routledge, 1993), 124–25. See also Cynthia Fuchs, "The Buddy Politic," in *Screening the Male: Exploring Masculinities in Hollywood Cinema,* ed. Steven Cohan and Ina Rae Hark (New York: Routledge, 1993).

10. In her synopsis of male critical responses, Manohla Dargis points out: "Shrill dissenters fear the 'bad' role models, nail its 'gender quisling' director (*People*'s Ralph Novak), cry foul about 'male bashing.' Particularly noxious is *U.S. News and World Report* columnist John Leo, who's wormed his way into notoriety by labeling the film *toxic,* invoking fascism and Mussolini for comparison." "Guns 'n' Poses," 22.

11. Joe Bob Briggs lists this group of revenge/horror/slasher films in his essay; see "The Mutant Offspring of Thelma and Louise," *Playboy,* 41, no. 2 (February 1994): 35.

12. Willis, "Hardware and Hardbodies," 120.

13. On 23 May 1991, the Supreme Court handed down its decision in *Rust* v. *Sullivan.* The results of the case effectively banned Planned Parenthood from any form of abortion counseling.

14. Dargis, "Guns 'n' Poses," 22.

15. Jon Katz, "The Gender Chasm: Media Rant," on-line: <http://www.hotwired.com/netizen/96/19/katz3a.html> (posted 1 February 1998).

16. Ibid. Katz argues that many analysts "believed [that] the political spectacle of the hearings helped defeat George Bush in 1992."

17. For example, in "Canada—Cruisin' Canada," Nancy Vaughan recounts her "Thelma and Louise–style" cross-country trip. She and a friend traveled from Toronto to Vancouver in a Mustang convertible. On-line: <http://www.tntmag.co.uk/travel/c/can_cruisin.html>.

18. Thank you to Robert Cagle for bringing these to my attention.

19. Mark MacNamara, "Kiss and Kill: Out of Florida's Recent Wave of Horrific Crimes Comes a Dark Version of *Thelma and Louise* in a Rare Case of a Female Serial Killer," *Vanity Fair,* September 1991, 91–106.

20. Wuornos is not the first female serial killer. However, she is the first woman to leave the domestic sphere, roam the countryside and murder men. Unlike their male counterparts, female serial killers usually operated within either the domestic space or its institutional manifestations, such as

children's hospitals and homes for the elderly. Wuornos's actions suggest that women are becoming more at ease outside the domestic sphere and some may begin to kill in ways that have historically been the province of the male serial killer. Again, see Candice Skrapec's analysis of this case. For a broader study of the history of female serial killers, see Michael D. Kelleher and C. L. Kelleher, *Murder Most Rare* (New York: Dell, 1998).

21. Laplanche and Pontalis state that there are four typical fantasy structures: intrauterine existence, primal scene, castration and seduction. These primal fantasies are "responsible for the organisation of phantasy life. . . . Like collective myths, they claim to provide a representation of and a 'solution' to whatever constitutes a major enigma" for the subject. Jean Laplanche and Jean-Bertrand Pontalis, *The Language of Psychoanalysis,* trans. Donald Nicholson-Smith (New York: W. W. Norton, 1973), 331–33.

22. See Jean Laplanche and Jean-Bertrand Pontalis, "Fantasy and the Origins of Sexuality," in *Formations of Fantasy,* ed. Victor Burgin, James Donald, and Cora Kaplan (New York: Routledge, 1988), 19.

23. Willis, "Hardware and Hardbodies," 123.

24. Alice Cross, "The Bimbo and the Mystery Woman: Should We Go Along for the Ride? A Critical Symposium on Thelma and Louise," *Cineste* 18, no. 4 (1991): 33.

25. Fredric Jameson, "Postmodernism, or The Cultural Logic of Late Capitalism," *New Left Review* 146 (July–August 1984): 71–72.

26. See Gilles Deleuze and Felix Guattari, *Anti-Oedipus: Capitalism and Schizophrenia,* trans. Robert Hurley, Mark Seem, and Helen R. Lane (Minneapolis: University of Minnesota Press, 1983).

27. Many argued that the loss of the protagonist accompanied "the death of the author" or artist. Besides Roland Barthes's and Michel Foucault's writings, see Craig Owens's "Honor, Power, and the Love of Women" for discussions on this topic, in *Beyond Recognition: Representation, Power, and Culture,* ed. Scott Bryson, Barbara Kruger, and Jane Weinstock (Berkeley: University of California Press, 1992).

28. Jameson, "Postmodernism," 72.

29. Fredric Jameson, interview by Anders Stephanson, in *Flash Art: Two Decades of History,* ed. Giancarlo Politi and Helena Kontova (Milan, 1989), 159.

30. Ibid., 131.

31. The point here is not that these women take on a male subject position or that the female viewers engage in what Laura Mulvey and Mary Ann Doane call transvestism. Rather, the characters adopt a renegade script irrespective of their gender and class positions. See Mulvey, *Narrative and Other Pleasures* (Bloomington: Indiana University Press, 1989), and Doane, *The Desire to Desire* (Bloomington: Indiana University Press, 1987).

32. Christine Holmlund states that "psychologists and criminologists generally agree today that abuse plays a key role in triggering female homicide. . . . In the 1970s and 1980s, thanks to feminist pressure on the legal system, social services and mass media, they [wives who kill their husbands] were more likely to be seen as victims . . . terrorized by repeated beatings into . . . 'learned helplessness' . . . Today battery, like rape, is commonly discussed in terms of power, not sexuality." "A Decade of Deadly Dolls," in *Moving Targets,* ed. Birch, 132.

33. See Carol J. Clover, *Men, Women, and Chain Saws: Gender in the Modern Horror Film* (Princeton: Princeton University Press, 1992), 42.

Action Heroines and Female Viewers

What Women Have to Say

Tiina Vares

In the 1990s women have been increasingly represented as violent protagonists. Films, television, magazines, popular books, advertisements, and comic strips have participated in the proliferation of images of gun-toting and physically aggressive women. This construction of women challenges their status as "victims" in both popular and feminist literature. Although there is a lot of "noise" about women as perpetrators of violence in popular culture, there is a relative "silence" in feminist writing on this subject, noticeable particularly in light of the extensive description of women's experiences as victims of rape, domestic violence, and sexual abuse as children.[1]

Movies have become the focus of heated debates that capture both the cultural fascination and horror surrounding those who are sometimes referred to as "killer women."[2] Women employ physical feats usually reserved for male heroes, they get even in the face of victimization and oppression, and act autonomously on their own and other women's behalf. Violent action and physical display, although offensive to some female viewers, appear to tap into others' fantasies of power.[3]

Despite the focus on gun-toting women in the 1990s, movies of women as violent protagonists are not a new phenomenon. Women feature as violent protagonists in film noir in the 1940s, as well as in the slasher and rape-revenge subgenres of the 1970s and 1980s. While these latter genres were criticized by feminists for their violence against women, Clover, Lehman, and others have demonstrated that women in these movies were more often protagonists of violence than victims.[4] They perpetrated horrific violent acts of revenge—quite frequently cutting off, or shooting, the genitals of rapists. Clover argues that films in the 1980s and 1990s with women as violent protagonists bring these earlier B-grade scenarios to the mainstream.[5] I think there are also important differences between slasher films and the "killer women" films of the nineties, such as female road movies like *Thelma and Louise*. The crucial difference for this research relates to the gendered "pleasures" of viewer response. The slasher and rape-revenge films drew predominantly male audiences who responded pleasurably to the spectacle of a woman wreaking havoc on a male body.[6] Feminist critics have found these films very hard to watch.[7] The films of the nineties, however, have elicited very different reactions. *Thelma and Louise,* for example, has sometimes provoked cheering by female viewers when Louise pulls the trigger on the would-be rapist.[8] Male critics have often been extremely critical of this violence.[9]

A number of analyses of films with action heroines[10] do not include actual spectators' responses to these representations, except in anecdotal accounts.[11] As textually based studies they can only theorize the pleasures available to viewers. Although it has been acknowledged that we need to move toward studies of film that look at both the text and its reception, such studies are not common. That few film theorists have engaged in reception research, Stacey suggests, is "quite incredible" given that the subject of female spectatorship (by which Stacey means "members of the cinema audience") has dominated the agenda of feminist film criticism for two decades.[12] This study works toward filling the gap in our knowledge about viewers' responses to film texts, particularly those that include representations of violence (as have some other recent studies).[13] In this article I discuss the ways in which different groups of women responded to *Thelma and Louise* and other films featuring women engaged in violent actions.

The pleasures of experiencing women as powerful and dangerous have been identified as the source of the popularity of *Thelma and Louise, Terminator 2, Aliens,* and *Blue Steel.*[14] Lentz has argued that these movies appeal to a popular feminist discourse that provides a "justification" for female violence:

[W]e can happily come away from the imaginary revolution staged in these texts with a newly earned status as dangerous women, a status which we can appropriate, manipulate, revise and define any way we choose. As empowering fantasies which engage an emergent, popular, feminist sensibility, these embattled texts thus carve out new possibilities for female subjectivity.[15]

In a similar vein, Ehrenreich suggests that many women cannot get enough of the "warrior women flicks," many are rushing out to buy the magazine *Women and Guns* (and guns themselves), and are sporting the old finger peace symbol "V" as snipping scissors (presumably on a penis).[16] She concludes:

Personally, I'm for both feminism and non-violence. I admire the male body and prefer to find the penis attached to it rather than having to root around in lots with plastic bag in hand, as did the police for John Bobbitt's. But I'm not willing to wait another decade or two for gender peace to prevail. And if a fellow insists on using his penis as a weapon, I say that one way or another he ought to be swiftly disarmed.[17]

My research into women's responses to violent female protagonists was prompted by reflection on the contradiction between many feminists' embrace of nonviolence and pacifism, and feminists' pleasure and satisfaction with representations of women as physically violent, in particular, acts of revenge against violent male protagonists. Commentaries on these films have tended to homogenize women's reactions to action heroines. I was interested in developing research strategies that facilitated the documentation of a more complex analysis of women's responses to these film texts, one that attended to differences among women and the ways in which interpretations are constructed actively in social situations.

To find possible differences in women's talk about movies like *Thelma and Louise*, I recorded five focus-group discussions, each with a group of women who might be expected to respond somewhat differently to these films. The five groups involved women who participate in martial arts (M), film buffs who watch a large number of films (F), university students interested in gender and representation (U), women who belong to a peace group (P), and women involved in a battered women's refuge collective (R).[18] My interest was not in representativeness, nor research that would be the basis for claims about women in general. The focus was on the potential variety of "pleasure(s)" that some women might experience when viewing these films, and the ways their talk about women as violent subjects might relate to other discourses that make "pleasure" problematic for women. The participants were all given the film *Thelma and Louise* to view at their leisure and then met to discuss their responses to this and other films in which women engaged in violent actions. Discussion of *Thelma and Louise* acted as a catalyst for wide-ranging talk about women and violence. While some writing in this field has assumed women's "pleasure" in these images of women's violence,[19] the conversations with the particular women who participated in this study suggested that, although some women talked about their positive reactions, many women do not respond pleasurably to these representations. This indicates the inadequacy of both textually and anecdotally based assumptions about women's responses to films that feature action heroines.

"Audiencing Violence": Complicating Definitions of "Violence"

Fiske and Dawson use the term "audiencing violence" in their discussion of homeless men's responses to the movie *Die Hard*.[20] I use the term, as they do, to refer to the process through which audiences selectively produce meanings and pleasures from texts.[21] I illustrate that research participants' understandings and assessments of representations of violence are highly contextualized. "Violence," therefore, cannot be understood either as a homogeneous or a static concept. We need to look at the resources viewers bring to their film viewing and the context of the group discussion. The participants' talk in this section also demonstrates some of the ways in which the meaning of violence shifts with subsequent viewings and as viewers interact with each other, that is, as responses are formulated relationally. This draws attention to the ways in which the research participants construct particular individual and/or collective identities through their talk on their understandings of, and emotional reactions to, violent images and/or films.

Focus-group discussions produced a variety of understandings of a "violent" act or film. Discussion in some groups related closely to the politics of the group activities in which they were involved. The women who belonged to the peace group, for example, considered that aggressive and violent behavior included actions in which no physical harm occurred:

AMANDA (P): For me I notice that women are taking the role of men—like smoking and drinking—things that before you couldn't see in the movies so much. . . . I think that now aggression is portrayed through the movies in lots of different ways, not just holding guns, [also with] smoking and the clothing.

EMMA (P): Transgressive language too and that's something in that particular video [*Thelma and Louise*] too. There's a lot of violent language as well, and it's not the "I'm going to stab you" type of violent language, it's the—what's some of it?—"fucked-up idea of fun," and things like that. Throwing words at you that once again have some sort of implication of violence, and that was just before she shot the guy.

AMANDA (P): I didn't like it because I associated Louise . . . with a very male attitude, because she is constantly smoking and delivering orders. She shouts . . . so many times at Thelma and manipulates her to some extent. It's like Thelma left a very oppressive relationship [with her husband] just to be in another.

JANET (P): I enjoy women being heroines—I think that's quite important—but I don't agree that women have to imitate male standards of force.

The women in the P group code particular behaviors as "violent" or "aggressive," drawing on discourses from the peace movement and radical feminist understandings that frame "violence" as "masculine." Thus, when women adopt these behaviors they are not behaving as "women." The idea that violent behaviors include, for example, language and dress concurs with Ramazanoglu's argument that violent behaviors are associated with "any action or structure that diminishes another human being."[22] Morrison and MacGregor also found that some viewers considered swearing violent.[23] Furthermore, as Potter and Warren point out, the broader the definitions of violence, the greater the number of behaviors will be regarded as violent.[24] Thus, with a broad definition of violence, the women in this group are more likely to frame a film/action as "violent" than are other groups in which "violence" is defined only as a physical action against another human being.

The fact that members of the P group choose not to watch "violent" films, as a political statement, goes some way toward explaining why I had difficulty getting women involved in peace activism to participate in the research. They considered *Thelma and Louise* a "violent" and "offensive" film. In addition to being critical of the "masculine" behaviors of the women's smoking, drinking, and cursing, they also considered the following scenes violent: the sexual assault of Thelma and shooting of Harlan; Thelma robbing the supermarket; locking the patrolman in the truck; and blowing up the truck. The final scene of the movie, in which Thelma and Louise drive off the cliff, was interpreted as "self-inflicted [violence] when they actually destroy themselves" (Emma). The peace group participants were remarkably unified in their personal responses to the film and their general textual definitions of violence.

In contrast, the members of the film buffs group did not frame *Thelma and Louise* as violent. The following comment from Claire came in response to a male reviewer of *Thelma and Louise* who called it "violent":

CLAIRE (F): Has this guy ever watched a spy movie or a Jean-Claude [Van Damme]? I mean, hello! There's a lot more fucking violence there.

NICKY (F): I don't even consider it a violent film.

Like the film buffs group the martial arts group also defined violence in relation to other acts of filmic violence and film culture in general.

SHARON (M): It wasn't really violent. It wasn't violent because I didn't see someone's head splattered half way across the pavement or someone's guts ripped out.

JANE (M): But they killed [Harlan], though, and they did blow up that truck.

SHARON (M): I suppose it was violent in what they actually destroyed, but I mean if you look at film culture that's nothing, that's soft.

Sharon draws on two different understandings about violence. The first concerns the degree of injury represented. Harlan's death by a bullet wound does not count as violence, whereas the representation of "blood and guts" does. In her second comment Sharon redefines "violence" in response to Jane's state-

FIGURE 20. Violence? Heroes of *Thelma and Louise* take aim at a harasser and blow up his oil rig. The familiar image—gun raised and angry expression—marks a challenge to feminist definitions of bad behavior.

ment that *Thelma and Louise* did, in fact, kill someone and blow up a tanker truck. Her definition of violence shifts to include damage to property and acknowledges that the film could have been called violent. However, in terms of her viewing habits and understandings of film culture, this movie is still "soft" since it portrays violent acts and their consequences less explicitly than some other movies.

The women in groups M and F watch many films, including "violent films." Thus, they tend to contextualize filmic violence in relation to other films and film culture. The peace group members, on the other hand, watch fewer films and avoid "violent" films. Their interpretations, therefore, focus more on the specific film context and draw on political discourses to frame violence as embracing a range of behaviors that potentially diminish the power of others.

Like the participants in the peace group, some women in other focus groups also choose not to view "violent" films. For Diane, a member of the university students group, the coding of particular actions, and hence films, as violent is an important aspect of her film selection process:

DIANE (U): Talking about *Pulp Fiction,* **I don't go to see violent films. In the beginning when** *Thelma and Louise* **came out I heard that it was about two women who murdered a man, so I didn't go and see it, because nobody explained the circumstances. . . . I just happened to see it because I was at a friend's one night and they got the video out. So I never actually saw it on purpose. So I didn't go and see that for the same reason I wouldn't go and see** *Pulp Fiction* **or** *Reservoir Dogs* **or** *Trainspotting.* **. . .**

TIINA: How would you describe a violent film?

DIANE (U): Anything at all with torture I simply cannot bear. Like I've heard about this ear scene in *Reservoir Dogs,* **and that sort of thing just horrifies me. I just can't stand it. So I don't mind so much if there's a bit of a shoot-up, but nothing to do with torture.**

TIINA: Does it make a difference if the protagonist of the violence is male or female?

DIANE (U): No.

HELEN (U): It makes a difference to me. Like, I'd never bother to go and see *Reservoir Dogs*—**it just never interested me—even though it was a film festival**

film. If that had one or two or three female characters in it, I'd think twice—so when I hear of something like *Thelma and Louise*, I immediately think, oh great, I'll go and see it.

Diane bases avoidance of films on a particular classification of violence. The fact that "two women murdered a man" was enough to put Diane off viewing *Thelma and Louise*. In the latter part of her comment she is more specific in defining what constitutes filmic violence: a bit of a shoot-out is bearable, but nothing with torture. Yet Diane's categorization of films as violent seems to be based on a single decontextualized image or scene. This assessment of films, based on reviews and what others say of them, enables Diane to avoid films with material she feels she will be unable to cope with. Buckingham refers to this as a way of regulating one's own viewing and emotional responses.[25] At times, however, Diane reflects on how her coding of films by decontextualized violent action is not always an adequate gauge of the film, as was the case with *Thelma and Louise*.

Helen, in contrast to Diane, comments that the gender of the violent protagonist makes a significant difference in her selection of films, particularly "violent" films. She elaborates on this later in the university-student group's discussion:

HELEN (U): Basically I would say that I don't enjoy violent movies unless I know there's a woman there, and then I watch it out of interest. . . . I'm always looking for a lesbian subtext, so if I saw a write-up in the paper, I'd immediately think, oh, two women on the rampage. I'm always looking and wanting to actively read into things. I'd go.

Whatling argues that popular films have always been a source of pleasure for individual lesbians who have become skilled at challenging dominant images of heterosexuality. Lesbians, she suggests, work to find ways to "read between the lines."[26] Helen is very explicit about bringing a lesbian agenda to her viewing of the text and therefore about possible pleasures that are not available to all viewers. Thus, in a context in which women are often defined as "victims," filmic violence with female participants has a political edge.

The contrasting positions between university students Diane and Helen, who both identify themselves as lesbian, illustrate the importance of looking at differences within the focus groups, in addition to between groups. The differing reading positions and interpretations offered by the two women also indicate the need to challenge any notion of a unitary lesbian subject and to pay attention to the context in which these readings occur.

Multiple Viewings and Shifting Readings

Responses change with subsequent viewings, and examining these "shifts" highlights complexity in viewers' definitions of "violence." Many of these participants acknowledged second and third viewings of some movies. The popularity of *Thelma and Louise* meant that most women had already seen it, and were thus reviewing it before the focus-group discussion. In the following excerpt Diane (of group U) reflected on her changing assessment of what constitutes "violence" in the scene in which Thelma and Louise are pulled over by a patrolman for speeding. When he attempts to use his radio to verify Louise's license, the women destroy his radio and lock him in the trunk (they do provide air holes by shooting into the car):

DIANE (U): [The violence] was reactive, it wasn't just violence out of nowhere. Like for one thing, what that cop was doing. I mean he was mind-fucking that woman: "Oh, come in and sit down, take off your eyewear"—just doing this huge power trip and trying to frighten her and all the rest of it. So he really got what was coming to him, and I change my mind about that every time I see it. The first time I saw it I thought—sticking the cop in the boot [trunk]—I thought that was a bit off, but the last time I didn't mind at all. . . . It's not as though they were beating and torturing people, they were just blowing up the boys' toys. Essentially that's what they were doing. I mean they shot the radio, they shot the car, and they blew the truck up, so I don't see how people can say they're [violent].

In her first viewing Diane reads the locking of the patrolman in the trunk as "a bit off." However, on her last viewing she "didn't mind at all." For Diane it was not so much a question of whether the act of locking up the patrolman was violent or not. She instead reflected on the level of violence, assessed the "appropriateness" of the act, and thus justifies the action by interpreting the patrolman's behavior as aggressive. She sees him as using his official power to intimidate and frighten the women. Diane's description of the patrolman's actions as "mind-fucking" can also be framed in terms of "psychological" or "institutional" violence.[27] She sees damage to property as more acceptable because "they were just blowing up the boys' toys." In other words, Diane takes account of the power relations between the patrolman and the women, and then locates these more specifically in gender terms. The "boys' toys" is a way of describing certain technologies as "masculine," and then undermining the "power" with which they are endowed. Framing these items as "boys' toys" further lessens the destructiveness of the heroines' actions.

Diane's shifting interpretations illustrate that "violence" is not simply a homogeneous category that can be read off filmic actions. As Morrison argues:

[I]n understanding how viewers define violence, we must understand how they define the acts they see: the definitions are created out of the viewers' interpretation of events and the moral judgements they make on their interpretations. . . . [I]n judging something to be violent [or not], viewers [bring] into the definitional frame ideas of the rightness or justice of the acts. . . .[28]

Diane's increasing acceptance of what might be interpreted as "violent behavior" can be contrasted with a comment by Marie, a member of the battered women's refuge activists group, in which she relates how her response to *Thelma and Louise* became more analytic and less pleasurable with subsequent viewings:

M A R I E (R): When I watched it the other day I just felt intensely sad all through it and I just thought—oh God—and it was quite depressing for me. The more times I watch it, there's more analysis, more things come through and after I'd watched it I just thought—oh God—and it's just the sort of things that happen to women in real life—that disempowerment, the constant energy drain in reacting to men's violence and as [Julia] said, they knew it. One of the women said, "They'd never believe us" after the rape—even though they were reacting in self-defense. It was just an innate thing that you know—she knew—that it's useless going to the law when you're a woman in that context.

Marie suggests that her reading of this film has "shifted" with subsequent viewings. She employs what Tannen calls a "film-viewer frame" in which one's experience as a viewer is part of one's story.[29] In Tannen's words, "[H]er inclusion of this internal process of interpretation reflects her telling not only the story of the film, but the story of her experience watching it."[30] Marie also rereads this film in terms of its "emotional truth," with the focus on the connection to women as real-life victims of male violence. In other words, what happens to

Thelma and Louise is "recognizable" to Marie in terms of women's experiences of abuse and a critical analysis of the ways in which women typically are treated by the law in cases of rape and self-defense. Furthermore, Marie's reassessment frames *Thelma and Louise* more as a film about male violence toward women than a film about women as the "subjects" of violence.

Diane's and Marie's responses to *Thelma and Louise* indicate that we need to pay more attention to what Christie has referred to as the "process of interpretation" and the different interpretive strategies that viewers employ in particular contexts.[31]

"Fantasy" and "Reality": Negotiating the Potential Pleasures of Action Heroines

A great deal of film theorizing has focused on the pleasure(s) we take from our engagement with cinema without attending to what viewers specifically have to say about their responses to films. In this section I examine some of the pleasures articulated by the women who participated in this study. While some action heroines have been described as "rife with the potential of pleasurable, vicarious empowerment for women,"[32] many participants in this study took no satisfaction in women's violence. For others, their pleasures were muted, contradictory, resisted, and critiqued.

Women used notions of "fantasy" and "reality" as categories for defining film "violence," and to legitimate certain responses and disavow others. At some points women drew clear distinctions between fantasy and reality. At other times the boundary shifted, and was used strategically to distinguish between film "fantasy" and "reality," different films, and also moments within a particular film.

Kate (film buffs, group F) and Sharon (martial arts, group M), addressed contradictions between their positions on violence and their enjoyment of women's violence. Sharon opposes the "real" to the film "fantasy":

S H A R O N (M): I abhor violence, I really do hate unnecessary violence. I do! But then someone who's on the outside looking at me would say, well, that's a wee bit contradictory and you're telling fibs because you watch violent movies. . . . I watch violent movies but I honestly don't take them seriously. It's a movie for God's sake, it's not real.

Sharon acknowledges that one should not like or approve of "violence," but then excludes "necessary violence" from her definition and hence allows for the practice of martial arts as a form of self-defense.[33] She justifies her enjoyment of "violent" movies by drawing a clear distinction between "fantasy" violence (which is acceptable) and "unnecessary" "real" violence (which is not).

Kate, however, makes the divide between film and "real life" more slippery as she describes the contradictions she experiences. She finds her enjoyment of action heroines problematic in relation to her current position on violence:

KATE (F): I'm all for action heroines in films, but that doesn't mean that I support violence as an answer. . . . There's this split inside myself, like for example when I watched *Blue Steel* I totally loved it. From start to finish I just totally got into it, but at the same time I question myself as to why, why? . . . I don't want to kill anything, not an insect, I don't want to kill a thing. So why am I still getting that out of that film?

The pleasures Kate derived from viewing the action heroine in *Blue Steel* continue to highlight what she refers to as a "split inside" herself, which is the apparent contradiction between holding a nonviolent position and enjoying violence in which women refuse the position of "victim." At another point in the group discussion Kate talked of her experiences of male harassment. She can, therefore, identify with a fantasy situation in which a woman uses a gun to be in control. In other words, the personal feelings and dilemmas of the female protagonist in *Blue Steel* were "recognizable" to Kate in terms of her own experiences of harassment.[34] Kate does not confuse "fantasy" and "reality" but rather attempts to understand or "translate" the events in the film across to her own life.[35]

Other research participants connected *Thelma and Louise* to their own and/or other women's experiences of harassment and sexual assault. It is not simply the portrayal of a situation similar to one's own experiences that makes a film relevant, but the way in which it is represented. There has to be a "recognition of relevance" that relates to the text's degree of "realism."[36] These connections are often not a feature of film texts, but are rather determined in the "contextual intersection" between viewer and film in a social context.[37] Gillian in group R, for example, "recognizes" the "violence" enacted by Thelma and Louise as "real/relevant":

GILLIAN (R): It was a different kind of violence. I still really liked that, because it was real women's violence not just action violence. The women had reasons—how it came about.

For Gillian *Thelma and Louise* depicted "real women's violence," contrasted to filmic "action violence." By "real" violence Gillian refers to women's aggressive response to male aggression. Or as Robyn (also of the refuge activist group) said, "I think the difference between male and female violence is that few women would mindlessly use an act of violence. They do it as a last resort to an intolerable situation that they can't deal with in any other way." In making this distinction between different kinds of filmic violence and employing specific notions of masculinity-as-action, femininity, and the "real," Gillian legitimates her enjoyment of the film and the film itself. *Thelma and Louise* is enjoyable and "relevant" because it makes the oppressiveness of particular gendered social relations highly visible and highly charged.[38] The appeal of the film is located in its representations of "masculine" and "feminine" violence that correspond to Gillian's and Robyn's understandings and/or experiences of "male" violence.

Women also used notions of "fantasy" and "reality" to distinguish violent actions both within a film and between films, to both accept and resist the potential pleasures of viewing violent women. While all groups had viewed *Thelma and Louise*, each group discussed it in relation to a specific set of other films that individuals had viewed in the last few years. The group of refuge workers extended the discussion of *Thelma and Louise* to include the Dutch film *A Question of Silence*. This film tells the story of three women who kill a male dress-shop owner and their subsequent trial.[39] Some of the women in the group recalled the film and responses to it:

JULIA (R): There was an all-woman audience and they all came out smiling.

MARIE (R): It was so wonderful.

[Laughter]

They [the three women characters] just decided they'd had enough and they were going to do something about this bastard, and they just looked at one another and [pause] it was incredible.

JULIA (R): It was so wonderful in court when they just laughed, and I think of the power of laughter that that film signifies. . . . I've used that since, and lifted it out

**of that film and laughed—at times in crisis—which actually takes people back—
totally—it does. They just can't cope.**

Women described the transgressiveness of this film, particularly the murder of a stranger by three women unknown to each other, as pleasurable for the "all-woman audience." Smelik observes that the film has become quite famous for its "empowering effect" on the women in the audience as they burst out laughing at the end of the film.[40] She suggests:

It is a liberating laugh which binds the women together. . . . The laughter breaks through the silence that has surrounded the women for so long. It also thwarts all male authority, turning the court case into the farce it has been from the start. Hence the laughter becomes a symbolic sign for women's resistance against the masculinist order.[41]

Smelik also comments that many female spectators probably remember their own laughter, as does Julia in the above extract. For Julia the pleasures of this film were connected to this totally unexpected response to "patriarchal" power. The laughter is remembered as powerful and as a "metaphor for the smothered anger and resistance of women."[42] Julia tells of the way in which she has since used such laughter in various situations as a signifier of power and resistance, as well as noticing its unsettling effect on others (as in the film). In this sense the laughter of the film was "empowering" for her.

Marie also recollects her pleasure at the wordless solidarity between the women during the murder scene. This scene represents a sense of communality of experience between all women, one that is based on women's experiences in a male-dominated world. It also evokes a deep sense of recognition for Marie and Julia and hence sympathy for the female protagonists, rather than for the male shopkeeper.

As the discussion progressed, Sarah made a connection between the killing of the shopkeeper in *A Question of Silence* and the killing of Harlan in *Thelma and Louise*. She drew a distinction between her responses to the two murders:

SARAH (R): I can't remember it. Has the guy been a pain in the butt and been rude to the women in the shop—that he represents something, or is it he personally who has the issue?

MARIE (R): What he represented.

SARAH (R): Personally I feel a bit uneasy about it. But in *Thelma and Louise* when they shot that man, I could just totally understand that happening because of what he had done to her. . . .

MARIE (R): But when you say he was just being rude or he was just something, that is a whole lived collective experience of those women, and all the times they've taken it and had been stripped of their power or abused or whatever and so something sort of ticked over.

SARAH (R): But if you'd been in a relationship and this person abused you day after day after day, then one more little thing and that was it. I can feel more comfortable with that, than one assistant in a shop, where really that could have been the only time in his whole life where he ever. . . .

[all talking]

JULIA (R): In *Thelma and Louise* what happened, to me, was part of reality and then it became fantasy. The other [the murder in *A Question of Silence*] was all fantasy, but what that said to me that he was symbolic of the systematic abuse that women were subjected to constantly and these three women saw that. . . . It was a symbolic action more than a real action in my opinion.

This discussion looks at two separate acts of violence by women in two different films. Sarah finds discomfort in the way other women enjoyed *A Question of Silence*. In reference to the murder of the salesman, she draws a distinction between "what he represented" and the individual himself. She found the idea that he was killed for enforcing the law of "patriarchy" (of which all women are "victims") problematic. The killing of Harlan in *Thelma and Louise* was more acceptable because he had sexually assaulted Thelma and we know something of his personality (for example, he is a "womanizer"). In *A Question of Silence* the murder of the salesman is "justified" by the fact that he was a man who attempts to assert his "patriarchal" authority over the women. We know nothing else about him. In a similar way to Sarah, feminist film critic Koenig Quart does not find it "so easy" to step around the violent act.[43] She, too, is unwilling to accept that the salesman "is culpable only because he is a man."[44] Although the narrative structure of the film gradually reveals (through a series of flashbacks) that the murder is the indirect outcome of years of the women's humiliation and objectification under patriarchy, for Sarah and for Koenig Quart this interpretation is problematic.

One could argue that both films frame the violence committed by women as a form of resistance to injustice, to men's abuse of power, and/or to men's sexual violence. Sarah, however, draws attention to the way in which *Thelma and Louise* provides a more concrete justification for its murder than does *A Question of Silence*. This connects with MacRory's argument that Hollywood films work hard to justify and/or excuse their representations of female violence.[45] With the European film, *A Question of Silence*, Sarah's unease can thus be understood in relation to the absence of a concrete motive, which the Hollywood film, *Thelma and Louise*, provides.

Julia employs notions of fantasy and reality to explain and legitimate her enjoyment of *A Question of Silence* and resist the potential pleasures of women's violent action in *Thelma and Louise*. Julia describes *A Question of Silence* as symbolic/fantasy violence, a feminist social statement, in line with Fiske's discussion of filmic violence as "symbolic":

Violence is performed through the clash of individual bodies, but in popular symbolic violence, heroes, villains and victims are incarnations of the social body, and the relations between them are consequently social.[46]

Julia is reading the killing of the shop owner as "symbolic" in Fiske's terms. The women in the film embody a particular set of social relations. Their violent action is a response to, and symbolic of, all "the systematic abuse women are subjected to constantly," which places this action in the context of "real" violence women experience every day. The paradox of the "pleasure" of this symbolic violence is that it uses socially unacceptable means to achieve socially legitimate ends,[47] as does the murder in *A Question of Silence*.

On another level Julia's comments potentially respond to the devices the film employs that contribute to its "symbolism." Smelik, for example, argues the murder is a "ritual" rather than a "real act."[48] This reading is encouraged by the camera work—for example, the way in which the murder is below the frame line and the use of a handheld camera that focuses on the faces of the women. We never see the body, only the objects the women use—a broken plastic coat hanger and a shattered glass shelf. The stylized mode of rendering the murder emphasizes its ritualistic nature.[49]

Julia indicates that *A Question of Silence* was "fantasy" while *Thelma and Louise* was both "reality" and "fantasy." Thus the fantasy/reality distinction is used not only to distinguish between the two films, but also to distinguish different parts of *Thelma and Louise*. Julia goes on to explain this in more detail:

JULIA (R): For me the first part of the film was reality and then from when she shot him, then the fantasy started. I felt that the shooting of the rapist was really real, but the blowing up of the petrol wagon for example, I thought was a wonderful fantasy scene.

Julia uses notions of "fantasy" and "reality" in different ways for different reasons. Harlan's murder could be seen as "real" because the film makes different readings difficult. It clearly depicts sexual assault, and subverts rape myths, as Louise says to Harlan, "When a woman's crying like that she isn't having any fun." Thelma's distress, confusion, and pain are as much the focus of the scene as Harlan's brutality and violence. (This scene was described by most of the participants as hard to watch.) The women of group R, who work with victims of rape and violence, described this scene as a representation of the "reality" of many women's lives. The incident in *A Question of Silence,* however, involves no physical assault on the women, and can therefore be seen as more "symbolic" than the sexual assault of Thelma. Julia's use of "fantasy" and "reality" resists the potential pleasures of Louise's violent action, whereas the construction of the latter scene as "symbolic" embraces them.

In contrast to the "reality" of the scene in which Harlan sexually assaults Thelma and is shot, Julia frames the rest of the film, particularly the scene in which the "petrol wagon" is blown up, as "fantasy." Violence in the film never results in death, only the destruction of property. The exploding oil rig, as a spectacular pyrotechnic special effect common to the action genre, reinforces reading it as "fantastical." By drawing this distinction in this way, Julia legitimates her pleasures in the latter scene.

Complicating "Pleasure(s)" in Representations of Action Heroines

The responses of the women in the focus groups to the representations of action heroines were not univocal. Rather, they responded with various combinations of pleasure and disgust, enthusiasm and suspicion.[50] Discussions for this study tended to focus less on the violent actions of heroines than on other aspects of their representation. So rather than there being an "overestimation of the film's few moments of violence," as many critics claimed,[51] the research participants focused on other filmic "moments." Thus, the pleasures derived from women's violent actions were frequently diffused with dissatisfaction, anger, and/or frustration at other representations in *Thelma and Louise*.

The film buffs group, for example, distinguished between "violent" and "intelligent" women:

CLAIRE (F): [The action heroine] needs to be an intelligent woman. Action is important, but action isn't necessarily violence.

KATE (F): Exactly.

PENNY (F): You can use your brain to be strong.

KATE (F): Yeah, that's what I think. . . .

CLAIRE (F): Hollywood is catching up with violent women, but not intelligent women.

NICKY (F): That's the point about a lot of the action heroines: they're not all that smart.

Participants enjoy representations of women exercising control through the use of their wits, action, and strength. However, they argue that the combination of intelligence and physical action are not attributes generally available to female characters in contemporary Hollywood cinema.

Some women in the peace group looked critically at the film's portrayal of Thelma as "not all that smart":

AMANDA (P): I also didn't like Thelma either because she was . . . very childish.

JANET (P): Yes, I agree. She annoyed me for that kind of girlishness about her.

EMMA (P): In just about every aspect of her life—when she was ripped off by the guy she picked up, and the mere fact that she got herself in the situation in the bar where she was all giggly and silly and ended up out in the car park. She just didn't take control over anything.

Janet also connected this critique of Thelma with the buddy pairing in the television program *Xena: Warrior Princess*:

JANET (P): It's interesting when you think about Xena and her sidekick, Gabrielle—it's actually quite similar to Thelma and Louise. . . . I mean Gabrielle is also ditzy and stupid and keeps getting herself into danger and she keeps getting herself told off by Xena and they never share anything personal.

Participants in the focus groups were critical of women being represented as "giggly," "ditzy," and lacking control. The talk in the groups moved easily between film and television to connect particular representations with specific ideas. The participants were acutely aware of how contemporary movies, and television programs, represent women's strength and vulnerability simultaneously. Discussion of this surfaced in group F in talk about *The Silence of the Lambs:*

CLAIRE (F): But she's [Agent Starling/Jodie Foster] still controlled by Hannibal the Cannibal and her boss. She's completely always manipulated by everyone . . . and he tells her all about herself and she doesn't even know herself until he tells her. It really gets my goat.

What Claire finds problematic is Foster's lack of "authority," particularly the way in which the men around her never listen to her or take her seriously.

This critique of, and frustration with, representations of women as lacking control also extended to the final scene in *Thelma and Louise.* Claire explains why her enjoyment of the earlier scenes (particularly blowing up the gasoline tanker) was "undermined by the ending":

CLAIRE (F): I was really disappointed. I really hated that ending. It was such a cop-out. It was either drive off the cliff or go to Daddy Harvey [Detective Slocombe]. . . .

NICKY (F): You think they should have done it like *Natural Born Killers,* maybe—driving off in a Winnebago with children—as lovers?

CLAIRE (F): Yeah. When I first heard that Oliver [Stone] had changed the ending from Quentin's [Tarantino] script I thought oh. But when I watched it I thought—of course they should have lived at the end. In *Thelma and Louise,* they had just begun this whole new thing, they've opened the book and—why did they bother?—why did they run away to jump off the cliff?

PENNY (F): I think they chose to remain victims rather than survivors.

CLAIRE (F): But I don't think their characters chose that. I didn't feel like Thelma and Louise wanted to jump off, I didn't feel like that. They wanted to fuck off to Mexico but the producer or the writer or whoever wanted them to jump off a cliff. That's what it felt like to me.

In referring to the "constructedness" of the scene, Claire suggests that a member of the production team "chose" this ending. In fact, she makes it quite clear that *Thelma and Louise* is not "reality" and therefore the heroines did not have to die. This reading strategy deals with her uneasiness with the ending and the alternative outcome of giving themselves up. Claire also argues that the two women "themselves" would not have driven off the canyon edge. At one level Thelma and Louise become characters who potentially transcend their own construction by producers, scriptwriters, and directors. On another level, however, they are still "controlled" by the production team. Claire's frustration and resentment at the film's narrative resolution appears to be directed at the way in which the "new" story line, of Thelma and Louise as agents of aggression (how they "had just begun this whole new thing"), does not displace the "older" story of women as victims.

These film buffs also locate *Thelma and Louise* within a broader knowledge of genres and evaluate the ways it plays with viewer expectations. Claire talks of being dismayed initially when she heard that Oliver Stone had reworked Quentin Tarantino's script of *Natural Born Killers* and broken with generic convention. On viewing the film, however, this disruption appealed to her, and in her critique of *Thelma and Louise,* she uses this as a springboard. For her, the ending of *Thelma and Louise* should subvert the generic expectation of the heroines' deaths.

Conclusion

While recognizing the small scale of this research, the preliminary analysis of five focus-group discussions has indicated the importance of examining viewer responses to particular representations and films. In this chapter I have highlighted differences in what behaviors are considered "violent" and what constitutes a "violent" movie. Some women frame violent actions, which include aggressive language, as "male." For others, films were considered "violent" in terms of their visual representation of "blood and guts" and/or in relation to film culture in general. Understandings of what constitutes "justified" violence also influenced viewers' assessments of particular actions as violent or not violent. The varied definitions of violent actions and/or films demonstrate that "violence" should not be treated as a singular category whose meaning can be taken for granted or read off the film text. The meanings of violence were highly contextualized and also shifted with the position from which they were being read. In other words, a violent action or film could be constituted as violent in one context, for example, through reading reviews and hearing about it, and then be read as "not violent" on viewing. Assessments of a film's "violence" can also shift with subsequent viewings and through talk with others.

The participants' definitions of "violence" influenced their responses to representations of women engaged in violent and aggressive actions. Thus, for the women in the peace group who defined violence as a "male" behavior that women should not imitate, the action heroine enabled few pleasures. One participant's idea that the action heroine is "really a man" represents an attempt to secure the logic of a gendered binary in which the terms "male," "masculine"/"female," "feminine" are locked together.[52] In this framework it is difficult to view the action heroine as a challenge to gender categories because when women assume "masculine" behaviors they are not seen as behaving like "women." While the refuge activists held similar understandings about gender and violence, their work with battered women facilitated some pleasures in the representation of women responding aggressively to male aggression. The actions of Thelma and Louise, for example, were framed as "real women's violence" rather than "action violence." For these women, there was a "recognition of relevance" in the representation of women as violent agents that was not present in many of the action-based genres that feature female protagonists. For other women, however, representations of action heroines or "women on the rampage" were framed as a challenge to more traditional representations of gender. For example, one university student's "resisting" of pleasures in women as violent subjects was explicitly connected to her viewing practices and strategies as a "lesbian spectator." While this viewer read the action heroine as transgressing gender codes because of her "violent" actions, members of the film buffs group also pointed to the ways in which action heroines affirmed these gender codes. In other words, the film buffs (members of group F), while taking some pleasures in action heroines, were nevertheless critical of these roles for not be-ing transgressive enough.

The notions of "fantasy" and "reality" were employed by some participants to reflect on their pleasures in action heroines in relation to their own positions on "violence." The refuge activists group also demonstrated the "slipperiness" of these notions as they used them to distinguish between women's violent ac-tions in different films and within one film. This strategic interpretive process served to legitimate certain pleasures in women's violent actions and disavow others.

This chapter illustrates that "pleasures," and the lack thereof, in action hero-ines cannot be "read" off film texts, but are the product of a contextual inter-section between viewers and films in a particular social and historical context. In attending to differences between groups, within groups, and over time, this study indicates the inadequacy of attempts to construct "women's" responses to films like *Thelma and Louise* through analysis of the film text alone. I would sug-gest a more fruitful avenue of investigation is looking at the range of possible pleasures and interpretive processes for different groups of female viewers. If we are indeed interested in female spectators and their responses to images of women who use weapons, disable attackers, and exert control, we should find out what female viewers have to say about them.

Notes

1. See, for example, Jalna Hanmer and Mary Maynard, eds., *Women, Violence, and Social Control* (London: Macmillan Press, 1987); Liz Kelly, *Surviving Sexual Violence* (Minneapolis: University of Minnesota Press, 1988); Jill Radford and Diana Russell, eds., *Femicide: The Politics of Woman Killing* (New York: Twayne, 1992); Kersti Yllo and Michelle Bograd, *Feminist Perspectives on Wife Abuse* (Newbury Park, Calif.: Sage Publications, 1988).

2. Julie Baumgold, "Killer Women: Here Come the Hardbodies," *New York,* 29 July 1991, 26.

3. Barbara Ehrenreich, "Feminism Confronts Bobbittry," *Time,* 24 January 1994, 62; Kirsten Marthe Lentz, "The Popular Pleasures of Female Revenge (or Rage Bursting in a Blaze of Gunfire)," *Cultural Studies* 7, no. 3 (1993): 374–404.

4. Carol J. Clover, *Men, Women, and Chain Saws: Gender in the Modern Horror Film* (London: British Film Institute, 1992); Peter Lehman, "'Don't Blame This on a Girl': Female Rape-Revenge Films," in *Screening the Male: Exploring Masculinities in Hollywood Cinema,* ed. Steven Cohan and Ina Rae Hark (New York: Routledge, 1993).

5. Carol J. Clover, "Getting Even," *Sight and Sound,* May 1992, 16–18.

6. Lehman, "Don't Blame This on a Girl,"; Clover, *Men, Women, and Chain Saws.*

7. Clover, *Men, Women, and Chain Saws.*

8. Ann Jones, "Living with Guns: Playing with Fire," *Ms.,* May–June 1994, 38–44.

9. For a discussion of some of these reviews, see Suzanna Danuta Walters, *Material Girls: Making Sense of Feminist Cultural Theory* (Berkeley: University of California Press, 1995), 6–7.

10. See, for example, Jeffrey A. Brown, "Gender and the Action Heroine: Hardbodies and the *Point of No Return," Cinema Journal* 35, no. 3 (1996): 52–70; Sherrie Inness, *Tough Girls: Women, Warriors and Wonder Women in Popular Culture* (Philadelphia: University of Pennsylvania Press, 1999); Lentz, "Popular Pleasures of Female Revenge."

11. Brown, "Gender and the Action Heroine."

12. Jackie Stacey, "Textual Obsessions: Methodology, History, and Researching Female Spectatorship," *Screen* 34, no. 3 (1993): 264.

13. For example: Philip Schlesinger, R. Emerson Dobash, Russell Dobash, and C. Kay Weaver, *Women Viewing Violence* (London: BFI Publishing, 1992); David Buckingham, *Moving Images: Understanding Children's Emotional Responses to Television* (Manchester: Manchester University Press, 1996); and Annette Hill, *Shocking Entertainment: Viewer Response to Violent Movies* (Luton, England: University of Luton Press, 1997).

14. Lentz, "Popular Pleasures of Female Revenge," 374.

15. Ibid., 398.

16. Ehrenreich, "Feminism Confronts Bobbittry," 62.

17. Ibid.

18. This study was conducted in Christchurch, New Zealand, in late 1996. Nineteen women participated in this research—aged between twenty-five and fifty-six, with the majority being in their late thirties. Half of the women (excluding the university students group) had tertiary qualifications (post–high school degrees). This is significantly higher than for the female population of New Zealand as a whole where only 16 percent of women over fifteen years of age hold tertiary qualifications (Statistics New Zealand 1998, *1996 Census of Populations and Dwellings, Education,* 24–25). The majority, but by no means all, were heterosexual. The groups had between three to six women each. With the exception of the university students group, the women all knew each other prior to the focus-group discussions. The women either worked together, as with the refuge workers and film buffs (who worked in a video outlet); belonged to a voluntary organization, as with those involved in a women's peace group; or participated in a sport together, as with the martial arts group. Most of the women in the university students group were known to each other with the exception of one woman. I approached the refuge, martial arts, film buff, and peace groups through a contact person. This individual in the group/organization gave out information sheets. Women who were interested in participating in the study returned these sheets to me. I contacted the women, discussed the study in more detail, and answered any questions; if they agreed to participate, I then organized the times for the group discussions and their access to a video copy of *Thelma and Louise.* The university students responded to the information sheet and/or verbal contact. The meetings were held as informally as possible in either my home or that of my research assistant.

19. Lentz, "Popular Pleasures of Female Revenge"; Ehrenreich, "Feminism Confronts Bobbittry."

20. John Fiske and Robert Dawson, "Audiencing Violence: Watching Homeless Men Watch *Die Hard,"* in *The Audience and Its Landscape,* ed. James Hay et al. (Boulder, Colo.: Westview Press, 1996).

21. Ibid., 297.

22. Caroline Ramazanoglu, "Sex and Violence in Academic Life, or You Can Keep a Good Woman Down," in *Women, Violence, and Social Control,* ed. Hanmer and Maynard, 64.

23. David Morrison and Brent MacGregor, with Andrew Thorpe, "Detailed Findings of the Editing Groups," in *Violence in Factual Television,* ed. Andrea Millwood Hargrave (London: John Libbey, 1993), 28.

24. James W. Potter and Ron Warren, "Considering Policies to Protect Children from TV Violence," *Journal of Communication* 46, no. 4 (1996): 120.

25. Buckingham, *Moving Images,* 130.

26. Clare Whatling, "Fostering the Illusion: Stepping Out with Jodie," in *The Good, the Bad, and the Gorgeous: Popular Culture's Romance with Lesbianism,* ed. Diane Hamer and Belinda Budge (London: Pandora, 1994).

27. David Buckingham, *Children Talking Television: The Making of Television Literacy* (London: Falmer Press, 1993), 12.

28. David Morrison, "The Idea of Violence," in *Violence in Factual Television,* ed. Hargrave, 125.

29. Deborah Tannen, ed., *Framing in Discourse* (New York: Oxford University Press, 1993), 29.

30. Ibid.

31. Chris Christie, "Theories of Textual Determination and Audience Agency: An Empirical Contribution to the Debate," in *Gendering the Reader,* ed. Sara Mills (New York: Harvester Wheatsheaf, 1994).

32. Brown, "Gender and the Action Heroine," 67.

33. David Gauntlett, *Moving Experiences: Understanding Television's Influences and Effects* (London: John Libbey, 1995), 4.

34. Buckingham, *Moving Images,* 157.

35. Ibid., 163.

36. John Tulloch, "But Why Is Doctor Who So Attractive? Negotiating Ideology and Pleasure," in *Science Fiction Audiences: Watching Dr Who and Star Trek,* ed. John Tulloch and Henry Jenkins (London: Routledge, 1995), 109.

37. Janet Staiger, *Interpreting Films: Studies in the Historical Reception of American Cinema* (Princeton: Princeton University Press, 1992), 35.

38. John Fiske, *Power Plays, Power Works* (London: Verso, 1993), 123.

39. *A Question of Silence* (1982) was the first film by Dutch feminist writer/director Marleen Gorris. It received much critical attention for its "brutal" murder of a salesman (in a women's clothing shop) by three women who, until that moment, were strangers to each other. The salesman had caught one of the women shoplifting. As he confronted her, two other women moved silently to her side and together beat him to death. The focus in this scene is on the solidarity between the three women, which is also extended to four other women in the shop who watch silently without interfering. As the women await trial the court assigns a female psychiatrist, Janine, to assess their mental health. The assumption is that the women will be declared "insane." Janine, however, discovers sexism not only in the defendants' lives but also in her own. The court is shocked when the psychiatrist declares the women "sane." The prosecutor then attacks Janine with the question "What if three men had killed a female shopkeeper?" and all the women—the accused, the witnesses (who had remained silent throughout the trial), and Janine—burst into laughter. A crucial aspect of the film is that the women who murder the salesman also never speak during or after the murder (although they do speak in the flashbacks to the period prior to the murder).

40. Anneke Smelik, *And the Mirror Cracked: Feminist Cinema and Film Theory* (Houndsmills, England: Macmillan Press, 1998), 105.

41. Ibid., 104.

42. Ibid., 105.

43. Barbara Koenig Quart, *Women Directors: The Emergence of a New Cinema* (New York: Praeger, 1988), 158.

44. Ibid., 159.

45. Pauline MacRory, "Excusing the Violence of Hollywood Women: Music in *Nikita* and *Point of No Return,*" *Screen* 40, no. 1 (1999).

46. Fiske, *Power Plays, Power Works,* 126.

47. Ibid.

48. Smelik, *And the Mirror Cracked,* 102.

49. Lucy Fischer, *Shot/Countershot: Film Tradition and Women's Cinema* (London: British Film Institute, 1989), 293.

50. Yvonne Tasker, *Spectacular Bodies: Gender, Genre, and the Action Cinema* (New York: Routledge, 1993), 135.

51. Sharon Willis, "Hardware and Hardbodies, What Do Women Want? A Reading of *Thelma and Louise,*" in *Film Theory Goes to the Movies,* ed. Jim Collins, Hilary Radner, and Ava Preacher Collins (New York: Routledge, 1993), 121.

52. Tasker, *Spectacular Bodies,* 132.

Imagined Violence/Queer Violence

Representations of Rage and Resistance

Judith Halberstam

Fear is the most elegant weapon

. . .

It will be demonstrated that nothing is safe,

Sacred or sane. There is no respite

From Horror. Absolutes are

Quicksilver. Results are spectacular.

JENNY HOLZER

. . . and there's religious leaders and health-care officials that had better get bigger fucking dogs and higher fucking fences and more complex security alarms for their homes and queer-bashers better start doing their work from inside howitzer tanks because the thin line between the inside and the outside is beginning to erode and at the moment I'm a thirty-seven-foot-tall one-thousand-one-hundred-and-seventy-two-pound man inside this six-foot body and all I can feel is the pressure all I can feel is the pressure and the need for release.

DAVID WOJNAROWICZ

An earlier version of this essay appeared as "Imagined Violence/Queer Violence: Representation, Rage, and Resistance," *Social Text* 37 (winter 1993): 187–202. Copyright © 1994 Duke University Press. All rights reserved. Reprinted with permission.

Preface

I thank the editors for deciding to republish this essay which was written as a polemical piece at a particular moment in time. It originally responded to a climate of unacceptable complacency in the wake of the L.A. rebellion following the Rodney King beating, and it attempted to link kamikaze AIDS terrorism to other forms of political rage. In this piece I am trying to ask questions about the different stakes different people might have in rhetorics of retaliation, revenge, and violent response. While mainstream feminism (with the notable exception of Valerie Solanis) has never been too interested in the tactics of threat or revenge, *Thelma and Louise* showed the power of deploying images of women fighting back.[1] Black violence, on the other hand, is most often represented as *the* standard narrative of black political response and is expected and feared. Here I attempt to line up black, queer, and female violence (as both separate and overlapping modalities) in order to shift the experience of fear from the marginalized body to the white male body. My point here is that debates about reality and representation would look very different if white male subjects were the subjects most regularly represented in mainstream culture as the objects of the gaze, both an erotic and a violent gaze.

If I was writing this piece now, obviously, there is much I would change. In fact, since 1992, the debate over violence and the representation of violence has

FIGURE 21. Louise responds to Thelma's rapist, shooting him after he no longer poses an immediate threat. *Thelma and Louise* challenges a feminist refusal to engage in violence except when clearly "innocent."

only intensified. In the wake of schoolyard killings in Jonesboro, Arkansas, and Columbine, various politicians and parents have tried to identify violent TV shows and video games as the source of the bad seeds who take guns and shoot at will in America's high schools. Shockingly, very little of the debate notes the remarkable uniformity of the young teen killers—all are white boys who feel disaffected in various ways and who blame women and minorities for those feelings. For the killers in Arkansas, a perceived humiliation at the hands of a female classmate was all that was needed to prompt an organized target practice in the playground. For the Columbine shooters, a variety of reasons were given for the two boys' feelings of exclusion. The important ingredient here, however, seems to be white masculinity and the power to which young white men feel entitled. Their "possessive investment" in whiteness and maleness, to quote George Lipsitz's formulation, leads to a sudden sense of disinheritance when young white men feel that their investments seem not to be paying off.[2] When these same young white men begin taking guns to school to shoot girls and minorities, it seems to me, it is time either to arm the girls and children of color or else to acknowledge publicly that there are some structural problems with the ways we raise, teach, and empower white boys.

This chapter has been modified from its original form. I have added a section on a powerful video documentary on AIDS called *Silverlake Life: The View from Here,* and I have moved my discussion of *Basic Instinct* from the conclusion to the first half of the essay. While the controversy around this film was potent and meaningful in 1992, the film itself has not maintained a central position in debates over lesbian and gay representation. I still believe in the power of representation not simply to effect change but to offer a potent challenge to the order of things. I also still believe with David Wojnarowicz that "one of the last frontiers left for the radical gesture is the imagination." And I still believe that "it is by imagining violence that we can harness the force of fantasy and transform it into productive fear."

1. "A Place of Rage"

In "Do Not Doubt the Dangerousness of the 12-Inch Politician," David Wojnarowicz asks, "Should people pick up guns to stop the casual murder of other people?"[3] In *Thelma and Louise,* a woman responds to a rapist who tells her to "suck my dick" by blowing him away and raises the question of what happens when rape victims retaliate. In "Poem about Police Violence," June Jordan asks, "[W]hat you think would happen if/everytime they kill a black boy/then we kill a cop?"[4] These questions are all rhetorical, hypothetical, and unanswerable. They are powerful rhetorical strategies, however, because they present possibilities and they trouble the fine line that divides nonviolent resistance from rage and rage from expression and expression from violent political response. This essay does not advocate violence in any simple sense; but it does advocate an imagined violence, the violence that is native to what June Jordan calls, in a film of the same name by Prathiba Parmar, "a place of rage."

What is the exact location of "a place of rage"? I will argue that rage is a political space opened up by the representation in art, in poetry, in narrative, in popular film of unsanctioned violences committed by subordinate groups upon powerful white men. The relationship between imagined violence and "real" violence is unclear, contested, negotiable, unstable, and radically unpredictable; and yet, imagined and real violence is not simply a binary formulation. Precisely because we cannot predict what action representations will give rise to, it is impossible to describe the boundary that divides imagined violence from real violence in any detail. Jordan's "place of rage" is a strange and wonderful terrain, it is a location between and beyond thought, action, response, activism, protest, anger, terror, murder, and detestation. Jordan's "place of rage" is ground for resistance.

A major controversy over the fragile line between the imagined and the real emerged in 1992 in the uproar over rap singer Ice-T's song "Cop Killer." In an election year and in the wake of the L.A. "insurrection," Ice-T's song created a consensus between liberals and conservatives about the limits of representation and what constituted their violation. People who would otherwise be defending free speech demanded that Ice-T not perform the song live and that the tape/CD be pulled from the shelves. Ice-T, well aware of the line he had crossed, had this to say to the question, "Why do you think people take your song so literally?":

Lots of reasons. Politics mostly. People trying to get elected and all that. There's people out there with nuclear bombs and yet we've got all these politicians trying to make a political platform based on a record. Isn't it ridiculous?[5]

He also points out that the media attention has focused upon the song as part of a problem genre: rap. But, he points out, the song is not even a rap song, it is a hard rock song. The significance of this error is glaring: any record by a black man is rap and rap music is a genre of music that must be contained. Genre, like racial categorizations, is supposed to essentialize and stabilize the form and content of Ice-T's cultural production. His protest, however, that the song is a hard rock song and that it should be heard as a fiction rather than as a direct provocation emphasizes the ways in which censors refuse to grant the song any moral or narrative complexity. The song is taken at its word as a call to arms.

Ice-T's song "Cop Killer" is a violent and rageful intervention into a stymied discussion about police brutality directed at minorities and especially at African American young men. While the debate surrounding "Cop Killer" centered upon whether or not Ice-T advocated violence against cops, Ice-T himself understood very well the power of representation. In response to the question, "Do you advocate the murder of law enforcement officials in your song 'Cop Killer'?" Ice-T responds: "No way . . . what I'm trying to tell people is that police brutality in the 'hood is nothing new. And the thing is that whether this guy, the cop killer in my song, is real or not, believe it, there are people at that point, OK?" [6] Later in the interview Ice-T suggests that cops should be scared by the song and he hopes that their fear will prevent further brutality. This is a complicated argument about the uses of fear, about the selective deployment of terror, and about the relation of threat to change.

The Ice-T controversy revealed a crisis in the politics of representation: the censorship activity directed at "Cop Killer" made visible the space of the permissible. It also marked racial violence as a one-way street in America: white violence is not only permitted but legally condoned while the mere representation of black-on-white violence leads to censorship and a paranoid retreat to a literal relation between representation and reality. While a white jury blurred the line between representation and reality in the case of the video of police brutalizing Rodney King, a white media jury established the stability of this relation in the case of Ice-T. Obviously, the interpretation of the literal is an ideologically valenced act, and in this instance, literality is a traditional political streamlining of complex material.

The eruption of rebellion in the streets of L.A. and its representations in hiphop culture indicate that violent law demands violent resistance. Tactics of nonviolence seem to have become dangerously hegemonic rather than disruptive. In political demonstrations, indeed, outrage often takes a back seat to organized, formal, and decorous shows of disapproval. In San Diego, for example, shortly after the L.A. uprising of spring 1992 in the wake of the Rodney King decision, people filled the streets to sing, give speeches, and march on the police station. What might have been an outpouring of rage and anger and frustration directed at the racist, violent tactics of the local police turned into a passive and indifferent meeting. The group of "protesters" followed a route laid out for them by a police escort and arrived at a deserted police building. Some chanting and shouting went on and then the crowd dispersed. Local newspapers reported that, in the case of San Diego, the city remained calm in the aftermath of the King verdict.[7] The failure of nonviolent resistance to register anything but the most polite disapproval, I suggest, is the effect of a glaring lack of imagination on the part of political organizers, and an overemphasis upon "organization" itself that often produces determined efforts to eradicate expressions of rage or anger from political protest. Such expressions, after all, might lead to something spontaneous, something that spills across the carefully drawn police lines, something threatening.

When and why and how did rage disappear from the vocabulary of organized political activism? In what follows, I will not attempt a historical or ethnographic answer to this question; rather, I take literary and cinematic examples of imagined violence and articulated rage and I elaborate a theory of the production of counterrealities as a powerful strategy of revolt emanating from an increasingly queer postmodern political culture. I use the word "queer" here to denote a postmodern postidentity politics focused on but not limited to sexual minorities.[8]

Postmodernism has been accused of not being political enough, but in fact it is political activism that often fails to be postmodern in America in the 1990s. Power and conflict no longer only spring from the domain of politics, and resistance has become as much an effect of popular culture—of videos, films, and novels—as of direct action groups. Postmodernism invites new and different conceptions of violent resistance and its representations. As Michael Taussig writes, we live in a "nervous system," a system characterized as "illusions of order congealed by fear."[9] The fear, the order, the nerves are all produced precisely as illusions, fantasies that govern and discipline the self. However, it is also in the realm of fantasy and representation that we make the system nervous, and that we can control and use our illusions. Imagination, in other words, goes both (or many) ways. So, what if we imagine a new violence with a different object; a postmodern terror represented by another "monster" with quite other "victims" in mind? "What if" denotes a potentiality, a possible reality that may only ever exist in the realm of representation, but one that creates an imagined violence with real consequences and which corresponds only roughly to real violence and its imagined consequences.

In the early nineties, queer activism revived an emphasis on loud and threatening political demonstration; groups like Queer Nation and ACT UP regularly created havoc with their particular brand of postmodern terror tactics. ACT UP demonstrations, furthermore, regularly marshaled renegade art forms to produce protest as an aesthetic object. As Douglas Crimp writes in *AIDS Demo Graphics:* AIDS activist art is grounded in the accumulated knowledge and political analysis of the AIDS crisis produced collectively by the entire movement. The graphics not only reflect that knowledge but actively contribute to its articulation as well.[10] Protest in the age of AIDS, in other words, is not separate from representation; and "die-ins," "kiss-ins," posters, slogans, graphics, and queer propaganda create a new form of political response that is sensitive to and exploitative of the blurred boundaries between representations and realities.

Meanwhile in the arena of popular representation, in popular film and video, the lines between representation and reality continue to be starkly drawn. Although liberals continue to complain about the violent subject matter that especially kids are exposed to on TV and in cinemas, I suggest that represented violence takes many forms and some still have the power to produce change. Conventional TV and movie violence, of course, consists of violence perpetrated by powerful white men often against women or people of color. Such violence is a standard feature of the action genre, of the rock video, of almost every popular form of entertainment, and to a degree it is so expected that audiences may even be immune to it.

On the other hand, violence against white men perpetrated by women or people of color disrupts the logic of represented violence so thoroughly that (at least for a while) the emergence of such unsanctioned violence has an unpredictable power. In recent years, popular texts that prominently feature violence against white men have been thoroughly analyzed by the popular media. So, for example, Ridley Scott's *Thelma and Louise* created an unprecedented wave of discussions around the issue of violence and women.[11] Suddenly, violence, and particularly female revenge fantasy violence, was tagged as "immoral," "extravagant," "excessive," or simply "toxic feminism."[12] Debates raged about whether we really want to condone a kind of role reversal that now pits female aggressors against male victims. But role reversal never simply replicates the terms of an equation. The depiction of women committing acts of violence against men does not simply use "male" tactics of aggression for other ends; in fact, female violence transforms the symbolic function of the feminine within popular narratives and simultaneously challenges the hegemonic insistence upon the linking of might and right under the sign of masculinity. Women with guns confronting rapists has the potential to intervene in popular imaginings of violence and gender by resisting the (liberal) moral imperative to not fight violence with violence. Films like *Thelma and Louise* suggest, therefore, not that we all pick up guns, but that we allow ourselves to imagine the possibilities of fighting violence with violence.

Women, in other words, long identified as victims rather than perpetrators of violence, have much to gain from new and different configurations of violence, terror, and fantasy. Within the "nervous system" women are taught to fear certain spaces and certain individuals because they threaten rape: how do we produce a fear of retaliation in the rapist? *Thelma and Louise* is an example of imagined violence that produces or may produce an unrealistic (given how few women carry and use guns) fear in potential rapists that their victims are armed and dangerous. Of course, there is no direct and simple relationship between imagined violence and real effects: just as it is impossible to judge the ways in which pornographic representation interacts with male sexual violence, it would only restabilize the relationship between the imagined and the real to claim that representing female violence quells male attacks.

The "place of rage" where expression threatens to become action is of course that tightly patrolled and highly ambiguous space that we call "fantasy." The power of fantasy in the realm of erotic desire has been theorized variously by feminist, psychoanalytic, and postmodern critics. In feminist theory, for example, fantasy constitutes a problematic site for various contests over representation and politics—the pornography debates have posed the question of whether rape and violence against women are in part produced by the objectifying dynamics of pornographic fantasy. Such questions about the relationship between desire and representation have proven to be unanswerable since this relationship is constantly being refigured. In an essay titled "The Force of Fantasy," however, Judith Butler proposes that we rethink the relationship between the "real" and fantasy by refusing to grant the "real" an a priori stability. She suggests that the "real" is "a variable construction which is always and only determined in relation to its constitutive outside: fantasy, the unthinkable, the unreal."[13]

What happens when we make imagined violence the object of critical scrutiny as opposed to erotic fantasy? What is at stake in this question is the way that sexual fantasies might or might not intersect with violent fantasies to force into visibility the constructed nature of the real. If imagining violent women does nothing else, for example, it might shift the responsibility for articulating the relationship between fantasy and reality from women to men. In other words, power lies in the luxury of not needing to know in advance what the relationship is between representations of violence or sexuality and acted violence or sexuality. The burden of stabilizing this relationship in the arena of sexuality has, of course, for too long fallen to women and to feminism and has produced unproductive alliances between antipornography feminists and the Religious Right. Texts like *Thelma and Louise* create anxiety about fantasy and reality in a very different group of spectators.

2. Female, Violent, and Queer

"Imagined violence" here is an adaptation of Benedict Anderson's conception of the nation as "an imagined political community."[14] Anderson explains that "communities are to be distinguished, not by their falsity/genuineness, but by the style in which they are imagined." While nationalism and national identity is one of the most powerful effects of imagining community, there are many other identities that are mobilized by the power of fantasy. Furthermore, imagined communities allow for powerful interventions: they allow for the transformation of imagined fear into imagined violence. One example of such a transformation is the Queer Nation/Pink Panthers slogan "Bash Back." In response to homophobic violence this group mobilized around the menace of retaliation. In an essay on "Queer Nationality," Lauren Berlant and Elizabeth Freeman explain the affectivity of this strategy:

"Bash Back" simply intends to mobilize the threat gay bashers use so effectively— strength not in numbers but in the presence of a few bodies who represent the potential for widespread violence—against the bashers themselves. In this way, the slogan turns the bodies of the Pink Panthers into a psychic counter threat, expanding their protective shield beyond the confines of their physical "beat."[15]

The power of the slogan, in other words, is its ability to represent a violence that need not ever be actualized. There is no "real" violence necessary here, only the threat of real violence.

The violence of the queer in this example is the moment when what Foucault calls the "reverse discourse" becomes something else, something more than simply "homosexuality beginning to talk on its own behalf."[16] The reverse discourse gathers steam, acquires density until it exceeds the category it purports to articulate. The excess is the disruption of identity and the violence of power and the power of representation; it is *disintegrational;* the excess is *queer.*

As the distinctions between the real and fantasy collapse upon each other, as representation seems already saturated with realism, as reality is reconstituted by acts of imagination, the effect, I have suggested, is a crisis of spectatorship. We simply do not know how to read imagined violences: all too often representations of the pernicious effects of homophobia, racism, and sexism are collapsed by the viewer into homophobia, racism, and sexism themselves. So, for example, a film about a racist white character might be interpreted as a racist film that produces racial hatred. Or a film about a sexist and homophobic police department challenged by outlaw lesbians might be interpreted as a homophobic film about murderous dykes. The plot of 1991's controversial film *Basic Instinct* actually foregrounded the relationship between reality and representation, imagined violence and the maintenance of law and order as major themes.[17] Disagreements about *Basic Instinct* tore through queer communities. While the film seemed to some people to move female heroism and cinematic lesbianism to a new and exciting place, others viewed *Basic Instinct* as a dangerous vision of lesbianism as a network of lesbian murderers. The film therefore drew outraged responses from some members of the gay community who read it as homophobic and as part of a general smear campaign that Hollywood has long maintained against queers.[18]

Basic Instinct weaves a tale of desire and destruction around a web of lesbian killers but may still not be a homophobic film. It became clear rather quickly in the debates around *Basic Instinct* that not everyone had the same stakes in attacking the film. The protests were led by gay men, for example, and many lesbians involved in the protests changed their minds after actually viewing the film. Many of the gay protesters of *Basic Instinct* assumed that homophobia infected all depictions of gays and lesbians as killers. The psychopathic queer, they claimed, was a homophobic standby in Hollywood cinema; and they tried to repress the film by "giving away" its ending by distributing "Catherine Did It" buttons.

The "Catherine Did It" buttons, however, underlined the miserable failure of this traditional civil disobedience. Viewers of the film know that there is no ending to give away, the film's conclusion is precisely a question—a question about homophobia, heterosexism, and a question about the possibility that female violence will disrupt once and for all any compulsory heterosexual resolution of narrative. The ending, moreover, mirrors the film's beginning scene, which opens with a shot of a couple having sex on a bed as seen in the mirror over the bed. The camera slowly pans down to fix upon the actual instead of the mirrored scene, and as we enter the filmic "real" the sex play turns to murder, the female partner stabbing her lover repeatedly with an ice pick as he climaxes. This intricate scene introduces the viewer to both the vexed relationship between fantasy, image, and reality and to the narrative trajectory of the film: what begins in bed will end in bed and what begins in compulsory heterosexuality ends in murder.

The beginning of the film gives away the ending, but in case there is any doubt Catherine herself destroys all narrative suspense. She writes novels that mirror perfectly her life and its violences. Her first book, *The First Time,* tells of a young boy who murders his parents by rigging a boating accident. Catherine's parents were killed in a boating accident. Her second book, *Love Hurts,* tells of an aging rock-and-roll star who is ice-picked to death by his mistress. The book that she is writing when she meets Michael Douglas's character, Nick, is called "Shooter" (Nick's nickname; although the pun tempts us to read Shooter as the "real" name and Nick as the nickname) and tells of a cop who falls for the wrong woman. "How does it end?" asks Douglas nervously. "She kills him," answers Catherine. Catherine, indeed, did it, but to give away that fact about the film is to give away nothing because narrative resolution is not the film's point. Like any good detective mystery, this movie plays with interpretation and the twists and turns of the relationship between crime and punishment, criminal and detective, violence and order. The evidence, in this film, is always textual evidence—Catherine's writing—and the work of detection is always the sorting of fact from fiction and the inevitable blurring of the two.

The gay protesters with their "Catherine Did It" buttons obviously failed to incorporate the kind of postmodern readings of culture that have invigorated many queer protests. As C. Carr wrote in the *Village Voice:*

Gay or straight, the critics were amazingly dense about the film. They saw date rape where there was mutual, exciting, rough sex. They saw "senseless thrill killings" triggered by lesbian sex when, in fact, the murder of a lover, husband, brother or father is always overdetermined.[19]

Indeed, murder was no accidental or gratuitous subplot in this film; murder was central not only to the action but also to the character identifications. Every main character in the film is a murderer, and murder comes to define relations between the characters and their jobs, their families, their lovers. The movie does, however, differentiate its murderers by gender: the men in the film who kill do so professionally or in the line of duty; theirs are sanctioned murders. The women—Catherine, her lover Roxie, her ambiguous friend Hazel, the psychiatrist Beth—all kill husbands, lovers, brothers, or fathers. These women have kept their killing in the family, disowning their families in violent outbursts.

Roxie killed her brothers, Hazel her whole family, and the police are stumped as to why they would have done so. The inability of the police to find motives for female murder corresponds to their inability to figure out the relation between Catherine's fiction and her life. Female aggression becomes unreadable, irrational, insane, motiveless, but the basis of a kind of sorority of empathy. They can read each other's murders, and chances are that at least female audiences will fill in the blanks when it comes to establishing a motive for the murder of brothers or husbands. But Catherine also understands the relationship between novels and reality—ambiguous, undecidable, negotiable.

The very fact that *Basic Instinct* plays with the relationship between representation and reality should defend against linear readings of the film when it comes to the characters' sexuality or their criminality. The movie emphasizes mirroring relationships throughout the film—female characters mistaken for each other, one dressing up and personating another, one killed when Nick confuses her with another. Also, Nick works as a distorted mirror image of Catherine: he slides ever more clearly into a criminal relation to the law, and she masters and manipulates his movements as if he were simply a character in a scene she has scripted.

Catherine calls attempts to collapse life into art and art into life "stupid." She knows the difference but is not beyond manipulating the blurred line between them for her own freedom of movement. Similarly, the critics of *Basic Instinct* who read it as homophobic and misogynist fall victim to the kind of facile reading of right and wrong, real and imagined to which, in this film, only the police are prone. Collapsing real and imagined totalizes narrative, refuses to read difference, refuses the interpretability of any given text, and freezes meaning within a static dynamic of true or false. This, of course, is not to say that texts may never be read as sexist or racist or homophobic—of course they are and can be, but to read homophobia where homophobia and sexism are the targets of an elaborate and prolonged critique misreads the power of an imagined violence and the violence of imagined power.

3. Disintegration: The View from Here

Imagined violence disintegrates the power of what Audre Lorde calls "the mythic norm"[20] and what David Wojnarowicz describes as the "ONE TRIBE NATION." It challenges, in other words, hegemonic definition and even the definition of hegemony itself. In *Close to the Knives: A Memoir of Disintegration* Wojnarowicz writes about being queer in the age of AIDS: "We're supposed to quietly and politely make house in this killing machine called america and pay taxes to support our own slow murder and I'm amazed that we're not running amok in the streets."[21] Wojnarowicz writes of murderous desires and desires for murder; he calls for bloody and violent change and he does so in what he calls "the language of disintegration." Language itself, for Wojnarowicz, becomes a weapon, a tool, and a technology and the act of imagination becomes a violent act. In Wojnarowicz's essays, he imagines a violence generated by HIV-positive bodies and transforms the AIDS-stricken body into a symbol of postmodern politics. The Person With AIDS, the junky, the homeless person, the queer in America have the power, as Wojnarowicz says, to "wake you up and welcome you to your bad dream,"[22] or the power to completely and utterly alter the contours of the real and to reshape them into realized nightmares.

Wojnarowicz's "memoir of disintegration" counters the slow decline of the body with speed—physical and mental speed. Life speeds up as time winds down, and the car traveling across an open landscape becomes a symbol for Wojnarowicz of desire without an object and of a kind of masturbatory pleasure in self-propulsion or auto-mobility. The automobile here signifies precisely the movement of the self, the multiplicity of the self as it disintegrates within the realm of the bodily and proliferates in the realm of fantasy. Fantasy, the safest sex of all, avoids physical contamination but it contaminates nonetheless. It contaminates by making information viral; information, in other words, is transmitted via images that enter language and mutate.

"Americans can't deal with death unless they own it," writes Wojnarowicz in reference to a museum of the atomic bomb.[23] Death, in this memoir, is stasis, the banality of arriving at one's destination; it is a full stop, an end to language and speed. Wojnarowicz's heroes with AIDS attempt therefore to stave off death with technology, writing, or photography. In one scene, the hero films his friend's dead body—here the video camera, like the King tape, like the Ice-T song, records a dangerous technovision of reality in the making. The "real" now is precisely a reel of tape, a memory that can be cut, edited, replayed, rewound, paused, or fast-forwarded. "There is no enlarged or glittering new view of the nature of things or existence," writes Wojnarowicz. "No god or angels brushing my eyelids with their wings. Hell is a place on earth. Heaven is a place in your head."[24]

In a documentary film that could have been lifted from the dark recesses of Wojnarowicz's imagination, two gay filmmakers with AIDS record their deaths from the disease as if to force a confrontation between the disintegrating self in the tape and the coherent self who watches. In this tape, *Silverlake Life: The View from Here,* violence is part of the documentary method in the sense that the filmmakers refuse to shield or protect the viewer from the horrors that visit the body with AIDS.[25] This work is an intensely painful record of the AIDS related deaths of two gay men, Tom Joslin and Mark Massi, who have been lovers for twenty years. Since both men die during the course of the video, the footage finally has to be organized by their good friend and Tom's student, Peter Friedman. The record of the daily lives and ultimate deaths of the two men is spliced with footage from an earlier documentary of Joslin's life called *Blackstar.* This earlier footage reinforces the overwhelming sense of disintegration that affects the entire tape by providing the viewer with a kind of "before and after" analysis of Silverlake life. Before AIDS, Joslin's documentary was an adept but slightly self-indulgent record of coming out. But this naive earlier work is shocking when placed in the middle of the later work on living with AIDS. In the "present" tense of the video, we find ourselves in a nightmare that is decidedly *not* the future imagined for Tom and Mark by the earlier work.

This sense of a past in which our subjects become violently severed from an imagined future becomes the apocalyptic present in *Silverlake Life,* and it gives the tape a temporal depth unusual to video work. If film has the ability to confer depth and richness of form and aesthetic complexity upon the image, video has the ability to go where cameras should not and reveal what film might blur. Video, we could argue, was invented to record the immediate or the unscripted; video finds its most compelling application in documenting crisis. In an essay on "AIDS-related documentary practices," Bill Horrigan suggests forcefully that

AIDS challenges documentary practices—calls for their refinement, perhaps, or exposes some unspoken assumptions regulating the relationship between who is viewer and who is viewed—in the sense that it has made comparable demands with respect to the myriad workings of the social order in general.[26]

I am particularly interested here in the claim that AIDS challenges or exposes "the relationship between who is viewer and who is viewed," and I take Horrigan to mean that AIDS or the threat of HIV infection erases the possibility of distance between the teller and the tale. Earlier in the essay he writes: "Here we are in the midst of the AIDS crisis. Yes, you are. Picture it."[27] Yes, you are. Horrigan articulates forcefully the exact strategy of alternative video documentary practice in the age of AIDS—the involvement of the spectator in the gradual erosion of boundaries between me, you, and them; between director, subject, and viewer; between positive, negative, and immunity. *Silverlake Life: The View from Here* willfully implicates the spectator in the unraveling crisis.

Silverlake Life records a holocaust and in doing so it refuses to respect some tacit agreement between viewer and artist over the boundaries of the watchable. This video also refuses homilies and comfort and moves inexorably toward wrongful death. In an essay on queer AIDS documentary, Gregg Bordowitz argues: "There are countercultural strategies that belong specifically to queers. A queer structure of feeling shapes cultural work produced by queers." He continues: "A queer structure of feeling is a set of cultural strategies of survival for queers. It is marked by an appreciation for the ridiculous, and it values masquerade."[28] Bordowitz's formulation of how certain crises and experiences structure the artwork and produce "cultural strategies of survival" clearly resonates with the Silverlake project. Joslin self-consciously constructs a video that responds specifically and queerly to the logic of the AIDS virus, and his recording of "Silverlake life" and Silverlake death takes a cultural strategy of survival to its absolute limit. Obviously, Joslin's video does not save his own life, but it does register the awful banality of the struggle not simply against sickness and despair but against an inactive government and a generalized political indifference.

The strategies deployed in *Silverlake Life* recall Wojnarowicz's language of disintegration and his efforts to rewind or fast-forward the real in order to destroy the America he calls the "ONE TRIBE NATION" in order to transform it into the many tribes. Of course, the political tactics of ACT UP have involved the disintegration of discrete identities into the many identities united in coalition against the "virus which has no morals." The "ONE TRIBE NATION," Wojnarowicz shows us, is a particularly powerful imagined community, but it is one that cannot withstand the impact of a disease that, in the geography of its transmissions, maps out the limits of identity, the murderous effects of inadequate health care systems, the ideological investments of medical institutions, and the breakdown of even the unity of the Right. This transformation can be capitalized on through imagining a violence that shatters the complacency that prevents people from immediate and spontaneous revolution. "I'm amazed," writes Wojnarowicz, "that we're not running amok in the streets." Here Wojnarowicz echoes June Jordan's poem titled "Poem about My Rights": "We are the wrong people/of the wrong skin on the wrong continent and what/in the hell is everybody being so reasonable about."[29]

Wojnarowicz's answer to his frustration at what he sees as a passive nonresponse to the totalitarianism of the "ONE TRIBE NATION" is to imagine:

I'm beginning to believe that one of the last frontiers left for the radical gesture is the imagination. At least in my ungoverned imagination I can fuck somebody without a rubber, or I can, in the privacy of my own skull, douse Helms with a bucket of gasoline and set his putrid ass on fire.[30]

Hell is a place on earth and heaven is a place in your head and I too believe that "one of the last frontiers left for the radical gesture is the imagination." I too believe that it is by imagining violence that we can harness the force of fantasy and transform it into productive fear. Wojnarowicz's memoir participates in AIDS activism because it confronts the Jesse Helmses of America with the possibility of violent retaliation; it threatens precisely in its potentiality.

Gregg Bordowitz could have been describing *Silverlake Life* or the video scene from *Closer to the Knives* when he quotes Charles Ludlam as saying, "[V]ideo is not an object, but an event, because its production is part of a larger effort to organize increasing numbers of people to take action. Video without the stink of art is TV."[31] Indeed, *Silverlake Life* is precisely an event, an event that we are painfully involved in and that we cannot switch off or tune out; it is video with both the "stink of art" and with the stink of death. It involves us not simply in the work of grieving that occurs as a community event now continually for gay men, but also in the business of disposing of bodies and recognizing the *waste* caused by AIDS—wasting bodies, wasted time, wasted energy, wasted bureaucracy, and finally the actual physical transformation of the sick body into waste or trash to be hauled out.

Silverlake Life intimately, violently, and painfully records the death of the author. Like Joslin's lover Mark, we are left alone and bereft by Tom's death, and the tape offers no succor. Unlike the blockbuster AIDS film, *Philadelphia*, *Silverlake Life* has no feel-good solution to the AIDS crisis. While the mainstreaming of an AIDS narrative demands that the audience be carefully drawn into the AIDS crisis through appeals to a common humanity, the *Silverlake* video spares its audience nothing and in fact attempts to involve the viewer in a spiral of pain, isolation, frustration, and fatigue. When Joslin awakes in the middle of the night, cannot go back to sleep, and turns on the camera to record the live nightmare, there is no place for the viewer to go in order to escape the close and suffocating intimacy of another slow and excruciating death. The voice that confronts us through the gloom of night with its fear and tension, its petty concerns and insurmountable anxieties—this is the voice of AIDS that, as David Wojnarowicz writes, "wakes you up and welcomes you to your bad dream."[32]

On a formal level, *Silverlake Life* engages with the mood of the personal home video, but it also transgresses the "personal" precisely by making AIDS "your" problem. There is no comfortable distance achieved in this tape, the distance of the objective documentary camera; distance collapses as the bodies of the documentary subjects themselves cave in and collapse at the center of the tape. Also, the tape suggests that "Silverlake life" is not confined to its specific geographic location; as Tom Joslin says, "[I]t goes where I go." We travel across country and back in time and around L.A. as well as through an illness. Indeed, the path of the disease is marked by ever-diminishing geographies of mobility. As the disease progresses, the movement of the camera becomes more limited until at the point of Tom's death, the camera is stationary. "Silverlake life" shrinks into itself so that we notice and mourn the loss of something like an "outside." With Tom's decline, the camera's gaze seems to close in upon him so that we no longer leave the neighborhood, then the house, then the room, and finally the bed but ultimately the body. Death, in other words, is a diminishing sphere of influence and the intensification of space until the only space one inhabits is the body and then finally the camera.

The typical mode of recording perspective and exchange in film and video is the shot/reverse shot. Shot/reverse shot literally marks the presence of life—of a view from "here," a view that is responded to from "there." The death of Tom in *Silverlake Life,* however, reduces the scope of the video and flattens out "Silverlake life" to the shot with no reversal of vision. Similarly, the narrative follows the narrative of illness with all of its ups and downs and with its sense of the slow dissolution of life: slowly in the video, the view from here disappears until there is quite simply no view.[33]

Silverlake Life: The View from Here as a whole upends all kinds of documentary expectations by showing scenes that almost seem to violate the subjects. In Joslin's death scene, we watch as his body is placed in a body bag moments after his death. This scene is almost unwatchable because it captures with morbid precision the transition from a persistent spirit of survival to the crushing finality of death. The portrait of the artist as a corpse is chilling: the body of the artist literally shrinks in front of the camera, the skin hangs from the bones, the mouth won't close, the corpse becomes trash to be stuffed into a bag and unceremoniously hauled away. By recording the death of the artist, and by continuing to film after his death, *Silverlake Life* pulls its audience into the grim business of mourning, loss, and recovery. But since we now know that we must face the death of the remaining lover, relief is nowhere in sight.

Silverlake Life, I have been arguing, insists upon an activist response to the AIDS crisis from the viewer by making the viewer intimately a part of Silverlake's lives and deaths. The video has drawn the spectators into the petty details of life and death with AIDS and it passes responsibility for the continuing crisis onto the viewer as a potent legacy. *Silverlake Life* does not need to make grand gestures of outrage and horror in order to spur the viewer onto action; rather, like other art that participates in the construction of an "imagined violence," this tape suggests that if you watch and do not take action, you simply participate in the continuing crisis. Many writers have attempted to chart the use of documentary practices in the AIDS crisis and to suggest the importance of representation to a mobilized response. The relation between representation and response, of course, is hard to judge and harder to manipulate; however, video's mobility, cheapness, and transportability make it into an ideal vehicle for "the view from here."

Wojnarowicz's poetic threat, like the live threat recorded in AIDS documentary video, constitutes postmodern revolt—revolt in the arena of representation. This is the postmodern tactic of ACT UP—the burning of effigies, the carnival protests of art and images that drive the scientists and religious creeps into panic mode. ACT UP chooses symbolic weapons that reconstitute the shape and contours of the real.

Conclusion

It is with the potential for violent response from the so-called "other" that June Jordan ends her poem: "I am not wrong: wrong is not my name / My name is my own my own my own / and I can't tell you who the hell set things up like this / but I can tell you that from now on my resistance / my simple and daily and nightly self-determination / may very well cost you your life." This is the return of the gaze in cinematic terms, the threat of the return of the repressed, an always bloody and violent reentry into the realm of signification. This is the articulation that smashes binarism by refusing the role of peaceful activism and demands to be heard as the voice that will violate—the damage, again, lies in the threat rather than in any specific action. *My* resistance may cost you *your* life; my answer may silence your question; my entry into representation may erase your control over how I am represented. Jordan's "self-determination" takes place within rage, not the rage that explodes mindlessly and carelessly, but a quiet rage, tightly reined, ever so precise and intent upon retribution. "Rights" in the poem signify not simply legal rights but the right to exist, the right to walk at night, the right to write, the right not to be raped, the right to reply, the right to be angry, the right to respond with violence, the right lawfully to inhabit and to populate "a place of rage":

Even tonight and I need to take a walk and clear
my head about this poem about why I can't
go out without changing my clothes my shoes
my body posture my gender identity my age
my status as a woman alone in the evening . . .

"Poem about My Rights" turns legal rights into a fiction of power: rights do not change wrongs and Jordan is "the wrong sex the wrong age the wrong skin," but the poem, her exquisitely tuned anger, threatens to transform wrongs into violent and powerful resistance.

The rage of David Wojnarowicz and June Jordan allows each artist to express fantasies of violence in ways that make queer and black rage palpable and terrifying. Perhaps more than any other recent writers, Wojnarowicz and Jordan use poetic expression as a scare tactic, as the enunciation of a threat. This is the poetics of rage, expression that suggests that retribution in some form is just around the corner. Of course, this sounds like catharsis, a purging of emotion afforded by drama or literary expression. Jordan and Wojnarowicz, however, give no such assurance that their expressions are safely channeled by finding expression in art. Like the activist art of ACT UP demonstrations, Jordan's and Wojnarowicz's writings are more like wake-up calls and active protest than cathartic outlets.

Imagined violence, in this chapter, is the fantasy of unsanctioned eruptions of aggression from the wrong people, of the wrong skin, the wrong sexuality, the wrong gender. We have to be able to imagine violence, and our violence needs to be imaginable because the power of fantasy is not to represent but to destabilize the real. Imagined violence does not necessarily stop men from raping women, but it might make a man think twice about whether a woman is going to blow him away. Imagined violence does not advocate lesbian or female aggression, but it might complicate an assumed relationship between women and passivity or feminism and pacifism. The imagined violence of lesbians against men in *Basic Instinct* also recast the relationship between gay men and lesbians since gay men may well have been threatened by the representation of female violence that empowered lesbians. In this way, imagined violence fractured the fiction of an identity politics.

And in *Silverlake Life: The View from Here* violence became a relation between the eye/I and an imagined "you" who must not be allowed to safely watch but who, like the "you" in Jordan's menacing conclusion to "Poem about My Rights," will be forced to change or be changed. The view from here does not presume to represent the view from there; nor does it depend on or demand a silent witness. This view threatens the viewer with physical and psychic disorientation, threatens to dissolve the bodily integration of the viewer by recording the slow decline of the object of identification. If *Thelma and Louise* calls for imagined solidarity between the women on the screen and the women who watch, and if *Basic Instinct* exposes the disidentifications between different and various queer spectators, *Silverlake Life* confronts the spectator with the stink of his or her own mortality and insists that it is our body as much as the body of filmmaker Tom Joslin that will be carted off in a body bag at the film's conclusion. There is no comfort in the real from the nightmares of imagined violence.

And there is no unity to be found in the imagined community of imagined violence. But unity is not necessarily to be desired, unity is Wojnarowicz's "ONE TRIBE NATION," an imagined consensus that always covers up difference with platitudes. Let politics be postmodern and queer, postidentity and posthuman. Imagined violences create a potentiality, a utopic state in which consequences are imminent rather than actual, the threat is in the anticipation not the act. From Ice-T's controversial rock song "Cop Killer" to the feminist killing spree in *Thelma and Louise*, from the lesbian ice picker in *Basic Instinct* to the AIDS-infected junkie in Wojnarowicz's *Close to the Knives* and the disintegrating self in *Silverlake Life*, and finally in the self-determined black woman who talks back in June Jordan's poem, imagined violences challenge powerful white heterosexual masculinity and create a cultural coalition of postmodern terror.

Notes

1. *Thelma and Louise*, written by Callie Khouri, directed by Ridley Scott, produced by Ridley Scott and Mimi Polk (MGM, 1991).

2. George Lipsitz, *The Possessive Investment in Whiteness: How White People Profit from Identity Politics* (Philadelphia: Temple University Press, 1998).

3. David Wojnarowicz, "Do Not Doubt the Dangerousness of the 12-Inch Politician," in *Close to the Knives: A Memoir of Disintegration* (New York: Vintage Books, 1991), 160.

4. June Jordan, "Poem about Police Violence," in *Naming Our Destiny: New and Selected Poems* (New York: Thunder's Mouth Press, 1989), 84–85.

5. Chuck Philips, "A Q & A with Ice-T about Rock, Race, and the 'Cop Killer' Furor," Calendar, *Los Angeles Times*, 19 July 1992, 7.

6. Ibid.

7. See, for example, *San Diego Union*, 2 May 1992.

8. For an excellent discussion of identity politics that points toward a postidentity politics, see Diana Fuss, *Essentially Speaking: Feminism, Nature, and Difference* (New York: Routledge, 1989), 97–112. Fuss writes: "While I do believe that living as a gay or lesbian person in a post-industrial heterosexist society has certain political effects. . . . I also believe that simply *being* gay or lesbian is not sufficient to constitute political activism" (101). See also Judith Butler, "Imitation and Gender Subordination," in *Inside/Out: Lesbian Theories, Gay Theories*, ed. Diana Fuss (New York: Routledge, 1991): 13–31. For a critique of identity politics in a different context see Chandra Talpade Mohanty,

"Cartographies of Struggle: Third World Women and the Politics of Feminism," in *Third World Women and the Politics of Feminism,* ed. Chandra Talpade Mohanty, Ann Russo, and Lourdes Torres (Bloomington: Indiana University Press, 1991). Mohanty uses the idea of "imagined community" to build feminist political alliances: "The idea of imagined community is useful because it leads us away from essentialist notions of third world feminist struggles, suggesting political rather than biological or cultural bases for alliance. Thus, it is not color or sex which constructs the ground for these struggles. Rather, it is the *way* we think about race, class and gender—the political links we choose to make among and between struggles" (4).

9. Michael Taussig, *The Nervous System* (New York: Routledge, 1992), 2. Taussig asks, how do we "write the Nervous System that passes through us and makes us what we are?" He concludes: "[I]t calls for a mode of writing no less systematically nervous than the Nervous System itself—of which, of course, it cannot but be the latest extension, the penultimate version, the one permanently before last" (10).

10. Douglas Crimp and Adam Rolston, eds., *AIDS Demo Graphics* (Seattle: Bay Press, 1990), 20.

11. Several journals and magazines featured debates for and against the representation of female violence. *Film Quarterly* had a feature called "The Many Faces of Thelma and Louise," which included mostly sympathetic responses to the film from critics like Linda Williams and Carol Clover. *Time* magazine had a more openly hostile forum called "Gender Bender: A White-Hot Debate over *Thelma and Louise*." See *Film Quarterly* 45, no. 1, (1991): 20–31; *Time,* 24 June 1991, 52.

12. See especially John Leo, "Toxic Feminism on the Big Screen," *U.S. News and World Report,* 10 June 1991, 20; see also Laura Shapiro, "Women Who Kill Too Much: Is *Thelma and Louise* Feminism or Fascism?" *Newsweek,* 17 June 1991, 63; Fred Bruning, "A Lousy Deal for Women—and Men," *MacLean's,* 12 August 1991, 9.

13. Judith Butler, "The Force of Fantasy: Feminism, Mapplethorpe, and Discursive Excess," *differences* 2, no. 2 (1990): 106.

14. Benedict Anderson, *Imagined Communities: Reflections on the Origin and Spread of Nationalism* (London: Verso, 1983), 15.

15. Lauren Berlant and Elizabeth Freeman, "Queer Nationality," *boundary 2* (spring 1992): 162.

16. Michel Foucault, *The History of Sexuality,* vol. 1, *An Introduction,* trans. Robert Hurley (New York: Vintage, 1980), 101.

17. *Basic Instinct,* written by Joe Eszterhas, directed by Paul Verhoeven, produced by Allen Marshall (TriStar, 1992).

18. See Christopher Sharrett, "Hollywood Homophobia," *USA Today,* July 1992, 93; Janice C. Simpson, "Out of the Celluloid Closet," *Time,* 6 April 1992, 65; Michaelangelo Signorile, "Hollywood Homophobia," *The Advocate,* 5 April 1992, 37; and David Ehrenstein, "Basic Instinct," *The Advocate,* 21 March 1992, 87. In Ehrenstein's article, his obvious disgust at the infamous Sharon Stone crotch shot revealed that misogyny played a rather large part in gay male journalists' rejection of the film.

19. C. Carr, "Ice Pick Envy: Reclaiming Our Basic Rights," *Village Voice,* 28 April 1992, 35–36.

20. Audre Lorde, "Age, Race, Class, and Sex: Women Redefining Difference," in *Sister Outsider* (Trumansburg, N.Y.: Crossing Press, 1984), 116.

21. Wojnarowicz, *Close to the Knives,* 108.

22. Ibid., 82.

23. Ibid., 35.

24. Ibid., 28–29.

25. *Silverlake Life: The View from Here,* directed by Peter Friedman and Tom Joslin, produced by Doug Block and Jane Weiner (1993).

26. Bill Horrigan, "Notes on AIDS and Its Combatants," in *Theorizing Documentary,* ed. Michael Renov (New York: Routledge, 1994): 171–72.

27. Ibid., 165.

28. Gregg Bordowitz, "The AIDS Crisis Is Ridiculous" in *Queer Looks: Perspectives on Lesbian and Gay Film and Video,* ed. Martha Gever, John Greyson, and Pratibha Parmar (New York: Routledge, 1993), 211.

29. June Jordan, "Poem about My Rights," in *Naming Our Destiny: New and Selected Poems* (New York: Thunder's Mouth Press, 1989), 102–5.

30. Wojnarowicz, *Close to the Knives,* 120.

31. Bordowitz, "The AIDS Crisis Is Ridiculous," 212.

32. Wojnarowicz, *Close to the Knives,* 82.

33. For a brilliant reading of *Silverlake Life* as "thanatography," see Peggy Phelan, "Infected Eyes: Dying Man with a Movie Camera, *Silverlake Life: The View from Here,*" in *Mourning Sex: Performing Public Memories* (New York: Routledge, 1997), 153–73.

About the Contributors

Wendy Arons is an assistant professor in the Department of Film, Television, and Theatre at the University of Notre Dame. She received her Ph.D. in literature from the University of California, San Diego, and is currently working on a book entitled *Sophie Goes to the Theatre: Performances of Gender and Identity in Eighteenth-Century German Women's Writing.* Her publications include a translation of the first vernacular midwives' handbook under the title *When Midwifery Became the Male Physician's Province,* and articles in *Communications from the International Brecht Society* and *Theatre Insight.*

Jeffrey A. Brown is an assistant professor in the Department of Popular Culture at Bowling Green State University. He has published several articles about gender, the body, and action films in such journals as *Screen, Cinema Journal, The Journal of Popular Film and Television,* and *Discourse.* He is the author of the forthcoming book *Black Superheroes: Milestone Comics and Their Fans* (University of Mississippi Press).

Carol M. Dole is an associate professor and chair of the English Department at Ursinus College, where she teaches both literature and film courses. Her research interests include film adaptation, the subject of her essay in *Jane Austen in Hollywood* (University Press of Kentucky, 1999).

Laura Grindstaff is an assistant professor of sociology (and member of the graduate group in cultural studies) at the University of California, Davis. She teaches and does research in the areas of popular culture, media, film, feminist theory, and ethnographic methods. She is the author of *Airing Dirty Laundry: Class and Cultural Hierarchy on Daytime Television Talk Shows* (forthcoming, University of Chicago Press).

Judith Halberstam is an associate professor of Literature at the University of California, San Diego, where she teaches courses in queer studies, cinema, literature, and gender. She is the author of several books including *Female Masculinity* (Duke University Press, 1998) and *The Drag King Book* (Serpent's Tail, 1999).

Neal King is an assistant professor of sociology at Belmont University and studies violence in crime as well as in film. He has written a full-length study of violent cop movies, *Heroes in Hard Times* (Temple University Press, 1999), as well as articles on other genres.

Susan Knobloch received her Ph.D. in film and television critical studies from UCLA in 1998. Her dissertation looks at rock music's effects on forms and feelings in movies. Her essay here is part of her ongoing research into performing women in contemporary Hollywood.

Martha McCaughey is an associate professor of women's studies in the Center for Interdisciplinary Studies at Virginia Tech. Her work examines gender, violence, popular culture, and scientific narratives. She is the author of *Real Knockouts: The Physical Feminism of Women's Self-Defense* (New York University Press, 1997).

Barbara L. Miller has a Ph.D. in visual and cultural studies from the University of Rochester. Before achieving her degree, she worked in the field of data communications. Currently, she is an assistant professor of art history in the Department of Art at Western Washington University. She has published articles on art and new media in such journals as *Afterimage,* and is presently finishing a manuscript entitled *The New Flesh in Art, Photography, and Film.*

Kimberly Springer, Ph.D., is currently the Mellon Fellow in Women's and Gender Studies and African American Studies at Williams College. Her publications include writings on Black feminist organizations, Black women and popular culture, as well as the edited volume *Still Lifting, Still Climbing: African American Women's Contemporary Activism* (New York University Press, 1999). Her current work is in combining activism, research, and public radio journalism/production.

Tiina Vares is currently a doctoral student in the Department of Sociology at the University of Canterbury, Christchurch, New Zealand. Her Ph.D. research investigates women's responses to filmic representations of women as subjects of violence in the 1990s.

Suzanna Danuta Walters is an associate professor of sociology and director of women's studies at Georgetown University. She is the author of numerous books and articles in feminist theory, cultural studies, and lesbian and gay studies, including *Lives Together/Worlds Apart: Mothers and Daughters in Popular Culture* (University of California Press, 1992); *Material Girls: Making Sense of Feminist Cultural Theory* (University of California Press, 1995); "From Here to Queer: Radical Feminism, Postmodernism, and the Lesbian Menace," *Signs* 21, no. 4 (1996): 830–69; and the forthcoming book *All the Rage: The Story of Gay Visibility in America*.

Index

Italic page numbers indicate illustrations

Ice-T: "Cop Killer" (song), 247, 248, 257, 264

identity, politics of, 264–265n8

Imitation of Life, 151

impotency, 32, 35

Impulse, 23n37, 81, 82, 101

incest, 148, 155–158, 166–168

Inness, Sherrie, 18

I Spit on Your Grave, 56, 167, 204

Jagged Edge, 88

James, Darius, 9

Jameson, Fredric, 211–212

Johnny Guitar, 121

Jones, Cleopatra, 179

Jordan, June, 247, 259, 262, 263

journalists: critiques of Sharon Stone, 124–125, 129, 130; responses to *Set It Off,* 181–182; responses to *Thelma and Louise,* 13, 203–207, 220, 265n11; responses to *Waiting to Exhale,* 179–180

Kaminsky, Stuart, 49n9

Kaplan, E. Ann, 29, 152

Katz, Jon, 205

Killing Mind, The, 202

King, Neal, 20n2, 23–24n37, 268

King, Rodney: controversy over beating of, 245, 248–249, 257

King, Stephen, 147, 162

Klein, Kathleen, 84

Knight, Shirley, 107, 111

Knobloch, Susan, 4, 7, 14, 268

Kotker, Joan, 87–88

Kristel, Sylvia, 115

Lacquer, Thomas, 58

La Femme Nikita, 5, 55

Lapdancer, 56

Lap Dancing, 56

Laplanche, Jean, 216, 218n21

Last Dance, 127–130

Latifah, Queen, 180, 189, 196

law enforcement: as homophobic, 253; as oppressive, 113, 148, 158, 167–168, 187, 233, 253; violence by, 193, 227–228, 247–249. *See also* cop action

League of Their Own, A, 89

Lear, Norman, 176

Lee, Leo Ou-Fan, 39, 50n18

Lee, Spike, 175

Lehman, Peter, 23n32, 53, 55, 57–58, 68, 219

Lentz, Kirsten Marthe, 220

lesbians, 31, 35–38, 108, 117, 120, 180, 188, 189, 193, 239, 253

Lethal Weapon, 18

Lethal Weapon series, 86

Lethal Weapon 3, 3

Li, Jet, 45

License to Kill, 201

Li Feifei (The Heroine), 31

Lindemulder, Janine, 71

Lipsitz, George, 246

Logan, Bey, 29

Long Kiss Goodnight, The, 23–24n37, 93–98, *97,* 100–102, 105n56

Lopez, Jennifer, 98, 99, 101

Lorde, Audre, 256

Love Crimes, 202

Ludlam, Charles, 259

Lumet, Sidney, 94, 95–96, 98

Lupino, Ida, 107, 109

Lust for Freedom, 116–117, 119

MacGregor, Brent, 223

Mamet, David, 131

martial arts, 30–31, 127; genre, 27–51

Martin, 176